What Is Taoism?

Courtesy of the Royal Ontario Museum, Toronto, Canada

What Is Taoism?
and Other Studies in
Chinese Cultural History

HERRLEE G. CREEL

The University of Chicago Press

CHICAGO AND LONDON

The University of Chicago Press, Chicago 60637
The University of Chicago Press, Ltd., London

International Standard Book Number: 0-226-12047-3
Library of Congress Catalog Card Number: 77-102905

Contents

Preface

The papers in this volume have appeared, at dates ranging from 1954 to 1968, in a variety of places in Asia and Europe as well as in the United States of America. Because they are not all easily accessible a number of people have suggested to me that they should be brought together in a single volume. One of them made this suggestion to the University of Chicago Press, and this book is the result.

The subject matter of these papers varies greatly, and it may seem that there is no thread that could link Taoism, horses, and bureaucracy. The thread may be tenuous, but all of these papers are products of the study in which I have been engaged, for the past sixteen years, of the origins and the influence of Chinese statecraft. That influence is mentioned in the seventh of these papers. It was considerable, and it moved both by sea and by land. In studying the land communications across Asia I was struck by the fact that the cavalry horse has played a major role, not only in this connection but also in deeply influencing China's history over thousands of years. That role has never, I think, been adequately appreciated or studied; I therefore wrote a paper on it.

The relation between Taoism and government is more obvious. It is well recognized that the rise of Taoism represented, in part, a reaction against the authoritarian government of the Chan-kuo period. Furthermore, what I have called "purposive Taoism" has deeply influenced Chinese administrative thought and practice ever since the third century B. C. A number of these papers are concerned, in one way or another, with the relationships between Taoism and statecraft.

I have made no attempt to revise these papers. Unless one rewrites completely, piecemeal changes may do more harm than good. Inevitably my point of view has changed somewhat over the years, but I do not think that there is anything in these papers with which I should now strongly disagree. The order in which they appear in this volume is topical rather than chronological, but anyone who wishes to read them in the order in which they were written may readily do so.[1]

My indebtedness to many colleagues and friends has been acknowledged in connection with individual papers. My wife has contributed valuable criticism of all of them, and important ideas to some. Miss June Work, my research assistant, has been of the utmost helpfulness with them all.

1. The chronological order of these papers is: 3, 1, 5, 6, 7, 4, 8, 2.

1

What Is Taoism?

If anyone is apprehensive that I am going to give an answer to the question posed by the title of this paper, let me reassure him at once. I shall not be so foolish as to try to propound a single, sovereign definition of what Taoism is. In fact, the more one studies Taoism, the clearer it becomes that this term does not denote a school, but a whole congeries of doctrines.

Nevertheless, if one is to discuss Taoism, he must at least have a reasonably clear conception of what it is. This is made extremely difficult by the nature of the Taoist texts. For every early Taoist book, including the *Chuang Tzŭ* 莊子 and the *Lao Tzŭ* 老子, is in fact an anthology of work by many writers. That the *Chuang Tzŭ* is a compilation has long been generally agreed,[1] but to deny that the *Lao Tzŭ* is homogeneous is still widely decried as heresy. Nevertheless a growing body of scholarship supports, with careful and impressive documentation, the statement of Fung Yu-lan 馮友蘭 that both the *Chuang Tzŭ* and the *Lao Tzŭ* "are

Presidential address delivered before the American Oriental Society meeting at Baltimore, April 10, 1956. Reprinted with permission from the *Journal of the American Oriental Society*, 76 (1956), 139–152. I am greatly indebted to my colleague Professor T. H. Tsien for assistance with many problems of bibliography and of textual interpretation.
1. Opinions on this subject range from the view that the *Chuang Tzŭ* merely contains interpolations, to the conviction that no more than the first seven chapters (if those) can be ascribed to a single author. See: Fung Yu-lan 馮友蘭, *A Short History of Chinese Philosophy* (New York, 1948; reprint of 1953), 65, 104. Marcel Granet, *La Pensée chinoise* (Paris, 1934), p. 503. James R. Hightower, *Topics in Chinese Literature* (rev. ed.; Cambridge, Mass., 1953), 8. Henri Maspero, *La Chine antique* (Paris, 1928), 489–492; and *Le Taoïsme* (Paris, 1950), 230. Sun Tz'ŭ-tan 孫次丹, *Po Ku Shih Pien Ti Ssŭ Ts'ê Ping Lun Lao Tzŭ Chih Yu Wu* 跋古史辨第四冊並論老子之有無 in Lo Kên-tsê 羅根澤, ed., *Ku Shih Pien* 古史辨 VI (Shanghai, 1938), 91. Takeuchi Yoshio 武內義雄 *Rōshi Genshi* 老子原始, translated in Chiang Chia-an 江俠庵, trans., *Hsien Ch'in Ching Chi K'ao* 先秦經籍考 (Shanghai, 1933), II, 306. Arthur Waley, *The Way and Its Power* (1938; reprinted London, 1945), 46, 51.

really collections of Taoist writings and sayings, made by differing persons in differing times, rather than the single work of any one person."[2]

In such composite and sometimes contradictory materials,[3] commonly cryptic at best, it has been possible to find evidence for the most divergent views. This has been going on for a good two thousand years. If two passages in the *Chuang Tzŭ* support a particular view, it has not always been considered necessary to mention the fact that twenty passages may repudiate it, perhaps with derision.

In the kaleidoscopic firmament of Taoism there is one relatively fixed star: the term *tao* 道.[4] But if all that is Taoist has the term *tao*, not every Chinese philosophy that uses the term is Taoist, for in fact they all do. *Tao* at first meant "road" or "path." From this it developed the sense of a method, and of a course of conduct. As a philosophical term it appears first in the Confucian *Analects*. For the Confucians *tao* is the way, the method, of right conduct for the individual and for the state. And the Confucian *tao* was also an entity, since an individual or a state might "possess the *tao*" or "lack the *tao*."[5] But this Confucian *tao* was still only a principle; it was never regarded as a substance, like the *tao* of the Taoists.

Like a number of other scholars I believe that the *Chuang Tzŭ* was written, in large part at least, not far from 300 b. c., and that it contains our finest exposition of Taoist thinking. As the *Chuang Tzŭ* describes the *tao* it is not merely a substance and a thing. It is the only substance and the only thing, for it is the totality of all things whatsoever. It includes, as a persistent questioner was told to. his embarrassment, ordure and urine.[6] While it always seems to be in flux, the balance of its forces is

2. Fung Yu-lan, *A Short History of Chinese Philosophy*, 65. The most voluminous collections of evidence on the composite nature of the *Lao Tzŭ*, known to me, are: Hsü Ti-shan 許地山, *Tao Chiao Shih* 道教史, I (Shanghai, 1934), 23–27. Ku Chieh-kang 顧頡剛, *Ts'ung Lü Shih Ch'un Ch'iu T'ui Ts'ê Lao Tzŭ Chih Ch'êng Shu Nien Tai* 從呂氏春秋推測老子之成書年代, in Lo Kên-tsê, ed., *Ku Shih Pien*, IV (Peiping, 1933), 462–520. Takeuchi Yoshio, *Rōshi Genshi*, translated in Chiang Chia-an, *Hsien Ch'in Ching Chi K'ao*, II, 273–308.

3. Contradictions in the *Chuang Tzŭ* are legion; the point of view of the final chapter, which is a survey of Taoist (and other) philosophies, seems to me quite at variance with the general tone of the work. Hightower (*Topics in Chinese Literature*, 8), comments that the *Chuang Tzŭ* "is not a consistent exposition of Taoist doctrine." Contradictions in the *Lao Tzŭ* are discussed in the works of Hsü Ti-shan and Takeuchi Yoshio, discussed in note 2 above.

4. It seems impossible to find an appropriate rule for capitalizing *tao*. I therefore always write it lower case, which accords with Taoist simplicity.

5. *Lun Yü* 論語, 1. 14, 3. 24, 5. 1, and passim.

6. *Chuang Tzŭ* (*Ssŭ Pu Pei Yao* ed.), 7. 26a. References to the *Chuang Tzŭ* will usually be given both to the text and to James Legge, translator, *The Writings of Kwange-zze*,

forever the same, so that in a larger sense it is unchanging.[7] And it is absolutely indivisible.[8] Since it is indivisible, it follows that it cannot be described in words or even comprehended by thought. It also follows that apparent lesser objects, like you and me, exist only as inseparable parts of the great whole, and we are as old, and as young, as the heavens and the earth.[9] There is no point, then, in feverish attempts to move parts of the *tao* from one place to another. The enlightened man knows that all things are safe "in the one treasury"; he leaves his gold in the fastness of the mountains, his pearls in the depths of the sea.[10] Nor is there any cause for concern as to one's own fate. "In the universe," the *Chuang Tzŭ* tells us, "all things are one. For him who can but realize his indissoluble unity with the whole, the parts of his body mean no more than so much dust and dirt, and death and life, end and beginning, are no more to him than the succession of day and night. They are powerless to disturb his tranquillity."[11]

Sanskrit scholars will have been reminded of the famous statement of the Upanishads, *Tat tvam asi,* "That art Thou."[12] Such resemblances (they were by no means identities) were to play an important role when Buddhism entered China, around the beginning of the Christian Era.

In the *Chuang Tzŭ,* as for the Confucians, *tao* denoted method as well as entity. But a method of doing what? There is not, in this philosophy, a basis for any very positive action. The *tao* is unknowable, in its essence, and the most enlightened sage is ignorant.[13] Morally, Taoist philosophy is completely indifferent. All things are relative. "Right" and "wrong" are just words which we may apply to the same thing, depending upon which partial viewpoint we see it from. "For each individual there is a different 'true' and a different 'false'." From the transcendent standpoint of the *tao* all such things are irrelevant. To advocate such Confucian virtues as benevolence and righteousness is not merely foolish, but likely

"Sacred Books of the East," XXXIX, 125–392, and XL, 1–232 (1891; reprinted London, 1927); these works will be referred to as Legge, *Chuang Tzŭ,* I and II. This reference is Legge, *Chuang Tzŭ,* II, 66.
7. *Chuang Tzŭ,* 1. 15, 6. 11a, 7. 13b–14a, 7. 18a, 7. 29a; Legge, *Chuang Tzŭ,* I, 183, 382–383; II, 37, 47, 71–72. See also Maspero, *La Chine antique,* 499.
8. *Chuang Tzŭ,* 1. 19a, 8. 7a, 10. 17. For translations, see: Fung Yu-lan, trans., *Chuang Tzŭ* (Shanghai, 1933), 57. Richard Wilhelm, trans., *Dschuang Dsi* (Jena, 1923), 177. Legge, *Chuang Tzŭ,* II, 224. See also Maspero, *La Chine antique,* 504.
9. *Chuang Tzŭ,* 1. 18b–19a; Fung Yu-lan, *Chuang Tzŭ,* 56–57.
10. *Chuang Tzŭ,* 5. 2a; Legge, *Chuang Tzŭ,* I, 309–310.
11. *Chuang Tzŭ,* 7. 18b; Wilhelm, *Dschuang Dsi,* 158.
12. See Charles Eliot, *Hinduism and Buddhism* (1921; reprinted London, 1954), I, 81.
13. *Chuang Tzŭ,* 1. 16b, 7.22, 7. 23b–24a; Legge, *Chuang Tzŭ,* I, 185; II, 57–58, 60–61.

to do harm, for the advocate betrays an unwarranted and dangerous assurance.[14]

What, then, should one do? *Wu wei* 无爲, the *Chuang Tzŭ* says, "Do nothing, and everything will be done."[15] And it is very near to really meaning just that. "The small man sacrifices himself in the pursuit of gain, the superior man devotes his whole existence to the struggle for fame. Their reasons for relinquishing the normal feelings of men and warping their natures are quite different, but in that they abandon the proper human course and give over their whole lives to a strange and unnatural endeavor, they are exactly the same. Therefore it is said, 'Do not be a small man, thus to destroy the very essence of your being. And do not try to be a superior man, either. Follow the natural course. No matter whether crooked or straight, look at all things in the light of the great power of nature that resides within you. Look around you! Attune yourself to the rhythm of the seasons. What difference whether it is called "right" or "wrong"? Hold fast to the unfettered wholeness that is yours, carry out your own idea, bend only with the *tao*.'"[16]

But what, one may ask, does this come to in practice? Very little, it must be admitted. The *Chuang Tzŭ* says repeatedly that one should be selfless.[17] But a living being cannot be wholly selfless. At the least one must eat, and this means competition. The *Chuang Tzŭ* itself tells us that some critics said that only a dead man could be a good Taoist, in the sense we have been discussing.[18]

This is not the place to expatiate upon the merits of this particular aspect of Taoism. It may be noted, however, that while it is quite lacking in any practical program, it has provided a haven of inner strength, a refuge from vicissitude, for great numbers of Chinese from antiquity to the present day. Four years ago I read before this Society a paper

14. *Chuang Tzŭ*, 1. 13b–15a, 3. 13a–14a, 4. 1b, 5. 16; Legge, *Chuang Tzŭ*, I, 181–183, 255–257, 268, 338–340.
15. *Chuang Tzŭ*, 7. 22b; Legge, *Chuang Tzŭ*, II, 59. The expression *wu wei* is extremely common in the *Chuang Tzŭ*.
16. *Chuang Tzŭ*, 9. 23a. In my opinion this passage is not satisfactorily rendered either in Legge, *Chuang Tzŭ*, II, 179, or in Herbert A. Giles, trans., *Chuang Tzŭ* (rev. ed.; London, 1926), 400–401. Certainly the passage is difficult. My own translation is based in part on Yüan Yü-sung 阮毓崧, *Chuang Tzŭ Chi Chu* 莊子集註 (rev. ed.; Shanghai, 1936), *hsia* 2. 14b–15a.
17. *Chuang Tzŭ*, 1.5a, 5. 6a, 7. 10b; Legge, *Chuang Tzŭ*, I, 169, 317–318, II, 31.
18. *Chuang Tzŭ*, 10. 18a; Legge, *Chuang Tzŭ*, II, 225. This *T'ien Hsia* 天下 chapter is itself critical of the point of view that has been described in this paper as typical of the *Chuang Tzŭ*. It was mentioned earlier that in my opinion the tone of the *T'ien Hsia* chapter is at variance with that of the rest of the work.

in which I proposed calling this aspect of Taoism "contemplative Taoism."[19]

There is another aspect of philosophical Taoism, which I proposed to call "purposive." For reasons I suggested in the earlier paper, I believe that "contemplative" Taoism represents the philosophy in its original purity, while "purposive" Taoism was a secondary development. It is clear enough, for instance, that the poise and inner calm that may be derived from the attitude of contemplative Taoism elevates him who holds it above the struggling mass of harried men, and may even give a psychological advantage in dealing with them. Very well, says the "purposive" Taoist; cultivate this attitude as a means to power! Be without desire in order to gain the things that you desire.[20] It is by not venturing to put himself forward that one is able to gain the first place.[21] Thus a sage is able, by means of the *tao,* to become chief of all the ministers.[22] "He who wishes to be above the people must speak as though he were below them. . . . It is just because he does not contend that no one in the world is able to contend with him."[23]

This tendency to treat the *tao* as a method of control, of acquiring power, occurs sporadically in the *Chuang Tzŭ,* but it is far more prominent in the text that is known both as the *Lao Tzŭ* and as the *Tao Tê Ching* 道德經.[24] Traditionally the *Lao Tzŭ* was held to have been written by an older contemporary of Confucius. Most critical scholars now believe that it was composed much later. And a considerable number, of whom I am one, believe that the *Lao Tzŭ* was probably put together somewhat later than the earliest parts of the *Chuang Tzŭ* were written.[25]

There was a great tendency, from at least the third century B. C. on,

---

19. At Boston on April 3, 1952. See pp. 37–47.
20. *Lao Tzŭ,* chap. 7.
21. Ibid., chap. 67.
22. Ibid., chap. 28. There is no doubt, I think, that *p'u* 樸 here is another name for the *tao.*
23. Ibid., chap. 66.
24. For a somewhat similar opinion, see Fung Yu-lan, *A History of Chinese Philosophy,* trans. Derk Bodde (rev. ed.; Princeton, 1952), I, 174–175, 334.
25. See: Ch'ien Mu 錢穆, *Kuan Yü Lao Tzŭ Ch'êng Shu Nien Tai Chih I Chung K'ao Ch'a* 關於老子成書年代之一種考察, in Lo Kên-tsê, ed., *Ku Shih Pien,* IV, 411. Fung Yu-lan, *A Short History of Chinese Philosophy,* 83, 87, 93–94, 104, 172. Hightower, *Topics in Chinese Literature,* 8. Ku Chieh-kang, *Lun Shih Ching Ching Li Chi Lao Tzŭ Yü Tao Chia Shu* 論詩經經歷及老子與道家書, in Ku Chieh-kang, ed., *Ku Shih Pien,* I (fourth ed.; Peking, 1927), 57. Sun Tz'ŭ-tan, *Po Ku Shih Pien Ti Ssŭ Ts'ê Ping Lun Lao Tzŭ Chih Yu Wu,* in Lo Kên-tsê, ed., *Ku Shih Pien,* VI, 91. Takeuchi Yoshio, *Rōshi Genshi,* in Chiang Chia-an, *Hsien Ch'in Ching Chi K'ao,* II, 304–306. Arthur Waley, *Three Ways of Thought in Ancient China* (1939; reprinted London, 1946), 11, and *The Way and Its Power,* 86.

to attribute many sayings to the vague character known as Lao Tzŭ, "the Old Master." We even find good Confucian sayings that occur in the *Analects* repeated almost verbatim, prefaced by the words, "Lao Tzŭ said."[26] At some point someone brought together many of the best of these sayings, and may have collected and written other materials to go with them, and made the book called the *Lao Tzŭ*.[27] The fact that it is an anthology accounts for the large number of repetitions in the text.

The editing was excellent and gives, on the whole, a remarkable appearance of homogeneity. This is partly because the materials selected are always terse and aphoristic, commonly cryptic, and often rhymed. The *Lao Tzŭ* includes some of our finest expressions of Taoist philosophy, as well as some trivia. It has much of the "contemplative," but more of the "purposive" aspect. Thus whereas the *Chuang Tzŭ* is in the main politically indifferent or even anarchistic, the *Lao Tzŭ* gives a great deal of advice to kings and feudal lords and ministers on how to get and hold power.[28] It is less concerned with the vision of the *tao* as the great whole, and more with the *tao* as a technique of control.[29]

The terse and cryptic nature of the sayings in the *Lao Tzŭ* had consequences not foreseen by their authors. They could be, and were, interpreted in various and even opposite ways. The recently published

26. In the work known as *Wên Tzŭ* 文子, virtually every paragraph is headed "Lao Tzŭ said." This, plus the fact that it contains many passages identical with material in other books and was said to have been written by "a disciple of Lao Tzŭ," has caused the *Wên Tzŭ* to be denounced as a late forgery. It is almost never quoted by writers on Taoism, although it contains material important for the history of Taoist thought. Liang Ch'i-ch'ao 梁啓超 condemned the *Wên Tzŭ* on the basis, it seems to me, of inadequate evidence; see Liang Ch'i-ch'ao, *Han Shu I Wên Chih Chu Tzŭ Lüeh K'ao Shih* 漢書藝文志諸子略考釋, 21, in *Yin Ping Shih Hê Chi* 飲冰室合集, vol. 18 (Shanghai, 1936). A work by this name was listed in the *Han Shu I Wên Chih* 漢書藝文志 and apparently in the *Ch'i Lüeh* 七略 of Liu Hsin 劉歆. More than one hundred thirty passages in the *T'ai P'ing Yü Lan* 太平御覽 are attributed to the *Wên Tzŭ*; I have checked a certain number of these with the current text and found them to correspond. Kê Hung 葛洪, in his *Pao P'u Tzŭ* 抱朴子 (*Ssŭ Pu Pei Yao* ed., 8. 3b), refers to the *Wên Tzŭ* together with the *Lao Tzŭ* and the *Chuang Tzŭ*; this work dates from around A. D. 300. For these and other reasons I believe it is probable that at least a considerable portion of the present *Wên Tzŭ* dates from the Han period. For Confucian statements attributed to *Lao Tzŭ*, compare: *Wên Tzŭ* (*Ssŭ Pu Pei Yao* ed.), *hsia* 2a with *Lun Yü*, 12. 22.1. *Wên Tzŭ*, *hsia* 27b with *Lun Yü*, 7. 2.

27. There is general agreement, even among scholars who do not consider the *Lao Tzŭ* to be an anthology, that it contains materials which also occur in other works; see: J. J. L. Duyvendak, translator, *Tao Tê Ching* (London, 1954), 6–7. Waley, *The Way and Its Power*, 128, 149, n. 1.

28. *Lao Tzŭ*, chaps. 22, 25, 29, 30, 39, 57, 60, 65, 80.

29. Cf. Duyvendak, *Tao Tê Ching*, 12; Fung Yu-lan, *A History of Chinese Philosophy*, I, 175; Waley, *The Way and Its Power*, 92.

translation by the late Professor J. J. L. Duyvendak aroused wide interest by its rendering of the first six characters of the *Lao Tzŭ*, which gave them a meaning quite opposed to the usual interpretation and new, in so far as I am aware, among translations.[30] Yet Duyvendak's interpretation is quite old in Chinese literature; it was evidently made by a wing of Taoist thought that leaned heavily toward Legalism.[31]

The convenient ambiguity of the *Lao Tzŭ* (which Granet said with some truth is impossible to translate)[32] was exploited to the full in what is sometimes called Neo-Taoism and sometimes called religious Taoism. This movement—one hesitates to call it a school—was in itself complex and various, including both ignorant religious fanatics and highly cultivated scholars. It appears to have arisen close to the beginning of the Christian Era, and taken form during the first several centuries A. D.

A distinctive name for this kind of Taoism is badly needed. Both "Neo-Taoism" and "religious Taoism" are somewhat ambiguous.[33] This kind of Taoism, in its varying manifestations, is marked by one constant aim: the achievement of immortality. The goal is to become a *hsien* 仙, a Taoist immortal. In Chinese works written as early as the first century B. C. we find its practices called *hsien tao* 仙道, "the way of the *hsien*."[34] I propose to call this doctrine "Hsien Taoism," to distinguish it from philosophical Taoism.

The immortality in question was a perpetuation of the physical body. It might be possible, by special means, for one already in the tomb to

30. Duyvendak, *Tao Tê Ching*, 17.
31. *Wên Tzŭ, hsia* 35b–36a. There is one other passage in the *Wên Tzŭ (shang* 3b–4a) which in its opening section espouses the interpretation favored by Duyvendak, but then changes direction completely. This curious passage is in part based on one which appears both in the *Huai Nan Tzŭ* 淮南子 and in the *Han Fei Tzŭ* 韓非子, adds statements found in the *Lao Tzŭ,* and confuses the whole almost hopelessly. A number of other passages in early literature seem to show that the interpretation made by Duyvendak was espoused only by distinctly minority opinion among early Taoists. I have written but not yet published a monograph on the meaning of the first twelve characters of the *Lao Tzŭ.*
32. Granet, *La Pensée chinoise*, 502–503. See also Derk Bodde, "Two New Translations of Lao Tzŭ," in *Journal of the American Oriental Society*, LIV (1954), 216–217.
33. Pelliot, like many others, used "Neo-Taoism" to denote the quest for immortality; Paul Pelliot, "Meou-tseu ou les doutes levés," in *T'oung Pao*, XIX (Leyden, 1920), 414–415, n. 385. Fung Yu-lan, however, calls this "religious Taoism" while using "Neo-Taoism" to denote a "revived Taoist philosophy"; Fung Yu-lan, *A Short History of Chinese Philosophy*, 211.
34. Takigawa Kametaro 瀧川龜太郎, *Shih Chi Hui Chu K'ao Chêng* 史記會注考證 (Tokyo, 1932–1934; referred to hereafter as *Shih Chi*), 117. 79. (The form 僊 which occurs here seems to be regarded universally as interchangeable with 仙.) *Pao P'u Tzŭ, Nei* 8. 5a. *Wei Shu* 魏書 (*T'ung Wên* ed., 1884), 114. 26a.

be resurrected,[35] but best of all was during life to become a *hsien,* forever deathless and ageless. Many ways, *tao,* were believed to conduce to that happy state. One of the most important was to take drugs, sometimes herbal but more frequently, it seems, the products of alchemical manipulations.[36] Complex techniques involving breath control and gymnastics, which have been compared to the Hindu yoga, are prominent.[37] One should not eat any of the five grains.[38] He must repent his sins, practice virtue (including such Confucian virtues as filial piety and *jên* 仁, "benevolence"), and give to the poor.[39] A single bad action will wipe out an accumulation of 1,199 good ones.[40] Varying emphasis was given to sexual practices which curiously combined license with austerity.[41] Feats of magic and charms played a prominent part in Hsien Taoism;[42] mirrors were potent talismans, and many of the bronze mirrors that have come down to us were no doubt considered magical.[43] In a series of heavenly palaces deities (in many cases identified with stars) function as *T'ien kuan* 天官, "Heavenly officers," in a graded hierarchy.[44] A *hsien* who goes to heaven must take a lower place, since he has no seniority;

35. Wang Ch'ung 王充, *Lun Hêng* 論衡 (*Ssǔ Pu Pei Yao* ed.), 7. 8. Kê Hung, *Pao P'u Tzǔ, Nei* 2. 6a. Maspero, *Le Taoïsme,* 50, 68, 83–85.

36. Wang Ch'ung, *Lun Hêng,* 7. 2b, 5a, 11a. Kê Hung, *Pao P'u Tzǔ, Nei* 4. 2, 6. 2b, 8. 1b, 16. 3a. Maspero, *Le Taoïsme,* 89–90.

37. Wang Ch'ung, *Lun Hêng,* 7. 10a. Kê Hung, *Pao P'u Tzǔ, Nei* 3. 1a, 5. 2b, 6. 2b, 8. 1b-2a, 15. 6b. *Chêng T'ung Tao Tsang* 正統道藏 (photolithographic reprint of 1447 ed.; Shanghai, 1923), *Ts'ê* 569, *T'ai Shang Lao Chün Yang Shêng Chüeh* 太上老君養生訣. Henri Maspero, "Les Procédés de 'Nourrir le principe vital,'" in *Journal Asiatique,* CCXXIX (Paris, 1937), 414, 424. Waley, *The Way and Its Power,* 116–120.

38. Wang Ch'ung, *Lun Hêng,* 7. 9b, 25. 15. Kê Hung, *Pao P'u Tzǔ, Nei* 2. 5a, 5. 3b-4b, 6. 1, 11. 10a, 12. 1a, 12. 5a, 15. 1a–3a. Henri Maspero, "Le Songe et l'ambassade de l'Empereur Ming," in *Bulletin de l'École Française d'Extrême-Orient,* X (Hanoi, 1910), 100, n. 1.

39. Kê Hung, *Pao P'u Tzǔ, Nei* 2. 4b–5a, 3. 5b–6a, 6. 4a. *Chêng T'ung Tao Tsang, Ts'ê* 38, *T'ai Shang Tung Hsüan Ling Pao Wu Liang Tu Jên Shang P'in Miao Ching* 太上洞玄靈寶无量度人上品妙經, 24b. Maspero, *Le Taoïsme,* 22, 85–89.

40. Kê Hung, *Pao P'u Tzǔ, Nei* 3. 6a.

41. The best description of these practices I know is in Maspero, "Les Procédés de 'Nourrir le principe vital,'" 401–413; see also Maspero, *Le Taoïsme,* 166–167. They seem to be referred to somewhat cryptically in Wang Ch'ung, *Lun Hêng,* 2. 6b. See also Kê Hung, *Pao P'u Tzǔ, Nei* 6. 2b, 6. 5b, 8. 2b–3a, 13. 3a.

42. Wang Ch'ung, *Lun Hêng,* 7. 2a, 7. 6b. Kê Hung, *Pao P'u Tzǔ, Nei* 3. 4b, 4. 8a, 15. 4, 17. 7a–18b, 18. 2a. Maspero, *Le Taoïsme,* 158.

43. Kê Hung, *Pao P'u Tzǔ, Nei* 17. 1b. Many Han dynasty mirrors mention *hsien* in their inscriptions; see Liu T'i-chih 劉體智, *Hsiao Chiao Ching Kê Chin Shih Wên Tzǔ* 小校經閣金石文字 (1935), 15. 10, 15. 13a, 15. 23–27, etc.

44. Wang Ch'ung, *Lun Hêng,* 2. 4b–5a, 6. 16b, 22. 4b. Kê Hung, *Pao P'u Tzǔ, Nei* 3. 5, 4. 5a. Maspero, *Le Taoïsme,* 30–31.

this is why some prefer to stay on earth.[45] Furthermore, this whole spiritual hierarchy has its exact counterpart in spirits living inside the body of every human being.[46] There were periodic collective ceremonies designed to achieve various ends.[47] One important objective, in Hsien Taoism, was to avoid or abbreviate the tortures of hell.[48]

The differences between Hsien Taoism and philosophic Taoism are striking, to say the least. The mere idea of all this toiling for immortality is repugnant to that of *wu wei*, not striving. The Confucian moral tone, and concern for rank in a heavenly hierarchy, conflict with the moral indifference and robust anarchism of Taoist philosophy. As for the idea of hell, it is doubtful that the authors of the *Chuang Tzŭ* ever heard of it, but if they had it would undoubtedly have struck them as exceedingly funny. Yet both doctrines are called Taoism, and the distinction between them is sometimes made poorly if at all. How did this situation come about?

There are many views, but most explanations are variations on a single theme. It is generally believed that in some manner Taoist philosophy gradually took into itself indigenous practices and "superstitions," absorbed much from Buddhism, and was transformed into Hsien Taoism. Maspero calls this view "superficial";[49] certainly it leaves a vast amount unexplained.

The brilliant scholar Kuo Mo-jo 郭沫若 propounded a solution ten years ago which has been influential in both China and Japan.[50] In Han 漢 times Taoism was sometimes known as the doctrine of Huang-Lao 黃老, a combination of the names of Huang Ti 黃帝, the "Yellow Emperor," and Lao Tzŭ. "Huang-Lao" is a confusing term. By the second century A. D. it was being used to mean Hsien Taoism, but as late as the second century B. C. it appears to have still denoted philosophical

45. Kê Hung, *Pao P'u Tzŭ, Nei* 3. 5b.
46. *Chêng T'ung Tao Tsang, Ts'ê* 46, *Yüan Shih Wu Liang Tu Jên Shang P'in Miao Ching Chu Chieh* 元始无量度人上品妙經註解, *chung* 30b–31b. Fu Ch'in-chia 傅勤家, *Chung Kuo Tao Chiao Shih* 中國道教史 (Shanghai, 1937), 104–110. Maspero, *Le Taoïsme*, 33–34, 123, 137–138.
47. *Wei Shu*, 114. 25a. Maspero, *Le Taoïsme*, 156–173.
48. *Chêng T'ung Tao Tsang, Ts'ê* 38, *Yüan Shih Wu Liang Tu Jên Shang P'in Miao Ching Ssŭ Chu* 元始无量度人上品妙經四注, 1. 24a. Henri Maspero, *Les Religions chinoises* (Paris, 1950), 60, 82–83.
49. Maspero, *Le Taoïsme*, 201–202.
50. Kuo Mo-jo, *Chi Hsia Huang Lao Hsüeh P'ai Ti P'i P'an* 稷下黃老學派的批判, in *Shih P'i P'an Shu* 十批判書 (1946), 133–161. Tu Shou-su 杜守素, *Hsien Ch'in Chu Tzŭ P'i P'an* 先秦諸子批判 (Shanghai, 1948), 104. Akitsuki Kan-ei 秋月觀映, *Kōrō kannen no keifu* 黃老觀念の系譜, in *Tōhōgaku* 東方學, X (1955), 69–81.

Taoism.[51] Kuo says that the Huang-Lao doctrine arose at the capital of the state of Ch'i 齊 around 300 B. C. Other scholars have asserted, however, that the term "Huang-Lao" appears first in the *Historical Records,* written around 100 B. C.;[52] I know no evidence to the contrary, and Kuo offers none. Certainly the *Historical Records* does say that the Huang-Lao doctrines were studied in Ch'i around 300 B. C.,[53] but this does not even prove that the term "Huang-Lao" was actually employed at that time. And it is certainly not evidence that the practices of Hsien Taoism, later associated with the term "Huang Lao," were then in use. In fact, the reverse seems to be true. Kuo, however, notes that Ch'i is also said to be the place of origin of magical practices later used in the search for immortality, and concludes that they were somehow associated with Taoist philosophy. This bothers him, for he sees clearly that the philosophy of the *Chuang Tzŭ* would regard the pursuit of immortality with lofty contempt.[54] Nevertheless, he says, that philosophy appears to have degenerated—so much so that, he suggests, the very magicians who hoodwinked Ch'in Shih Huang Ti 秦始黃帝, shortly before 200 B. C., into undertaking the search for immortality, may have been disciples in the direct line of transmission from Chuang Tzŭ.[55]

This conclusion is, in my opinion, untenable. Yet Kuo Mo-jo is a most able scholar, and his understanding of the *Chuang Tzŭ* is excellent. It is only his failure to scrutinize his sources rigorously that misled him away from the truth.

Henri Maspero says that we err in thinking that Lao Tzŭ, Chuang Tzŭ, and Lieh Tzŭ 列子 picture all of the Taoism of their times. They represent, he says, only a branch, "un petit cercle à tendances mystiques et philosophiques; c'étaient des lettrés instruits qui transformaient en philosophie les enseignements souvent grossiers de la secte . . ." But in fact, he says, even from their times "la recherche de l'immortalité tient une place capitale dans la religion taoïste . . ." To speak of a "corruption" of Taoist philosophy is therefore, he holds, quite erroneous. Maspero says that the quest for immortality held only a secondary place for Chuang Tzŭ, but he quotes, from chapter 12 of the *Chuang Tzŭ,* a passage stating that after a thousand years on earth the Taoist sage mounts to heaven as a

51. None of the occurrences of "Huang-Lao" in the *Shih Chi* seems to show any clear linkage with the immortality cult.
52. Akitsuki, op. cit., 70.
53. *Shih Chi,* 74. 12.
54. Kuo Mo-jo, *Shih P'i P'an Shu,* 167.
55. Ibid., 183.

hsien.[56] Please bear that passage in mind. We shall consider it again.

Henri Maspero spent several decades in the study of what I call Hsien Taoism. His articles on the subject, and his posthumous works edited by Paul Demiéville, form an indispensable introduction to this formidable study which will long command the gratitude of all who undertake it.[57] In full recognition of this fact, I also believe that his preoccupation with Hsien Taoism caused him to overemphasize its apparent resemblances to philosophical Taoism, and to ignore the gulf that separates the two.

My own solution of this problem is one that has at least been hinted at by many scholars. Fung Yu-lan, for instance, has pointed out the great difference between "Taoism as a philosophy . . . and the Taoist religion. . . . Their teachings," he says, "are not only different; they are even contradictory."[58] Fung seeks to explain the rise of what he calls the Taoist religion in terms of influence from the "Yin-Yang school" and from Buddhism.[59] This is certainly an important part of the story, but not the whole.

In my opinion, philosophic Taoism (including both the "contemplative" and the "purposive" aspects) and Hsien Taoism not only were never identical; their associations, even, have been minimal. At an undetermined date, perhaps around 300 B. C., there arose what we might call a cult of immortality. Also around 300 B. C., and perhaps in the same areas, Taoist philosophy arose. The cult and the philosophy seem to have been almost entirely distinct until perhaps as late as the middle of Former Han times. During the Han dynasty those seeking immortality gradually took over the name of Taoism (perhaps for the respectability it afforded) and much of the jargon of "purposive" Taoism, but they did not take over Taoist Philosophy. In Latter Han times Hsien Taoists took over Buddhist practices to develop a popular Taoist religion. Although there was some miscegenation, Taoist philosophers have commonly considered the quest for immortality to be fatuous or worse, and some Hsien Taoists have reciprocated the lack of cordiality. The evidence for this hypothesis is voluminous. Here it can only be summarized.

From the Shang 商 oracle bones we know that already in the second millennium B. C. it was believed that spirits of the dead might harm the

---

56. Maspero, *Le Taoïsme*, 203. See also ibid., 201–222.
57. The three posthumous volumes, of which *Le Taoïsme* is the second, are: Maspero, *Mélanges posthumes sur les religions et l'histoire de la Chine* (Paris, 1950).
58. Fung Yu-lan, *A Short History of Chinese Philosophy*, 3.
59. Fung Yu-lan, *The Spirit of Chinese Philosophy*, trans. E. R. Hughes (London, 1947), 128.

living, and apparently influence their health.[60] From an early day there were individuals known as *wu* 巫, often called "shamans," who held seances with spirits and were believed able to heal the sick.[61] The invention of medicine is attributed to a certain *wu*.[62] From healing the sick and forestalling death temporarily, it is only a jump to the idea of forestalling death permanently. *Wu* are said to have been especially numerous in the southern state of Ch'u 楚, and also in Ch'i which occupied roughly the area of the modern Shantung Province.

Wu are important in the background of Hsien Taoism, and so are magicians, who also flourished in Ch'i. The *Historical Records* says that magicians of the states of Ch'i and Yen 燕, claiming command of the art of immortality, "transmitted but could not understand" the methods of the philosopher Tsou Yen 鄒衍, whose name is associated with the rise of the doctrine of *wu hsing* 五行 or "five forces," and (perhaps erroneously) with the *yin yang* 陰陽 theory.[63] It seems also to be in Ch'i, and again not far from 300 B. C., that the first mention occurs of the Yellow Emperor.[64] Although he appeared so late, his fame spread with great rapidity. His name, also, is linked with medicine. He was early, though by no means universally, associated with longevity and immortality. He came to be regarded as the earliest ruler of China, and a patriarch of Hsien Taoism.[65]

Since Chuang Tzŭ is believed to have lived in the latter half of the fourth century B. C., and at least two important philosophical Taoists are said to have lived and written at the capital of Ch'i at this time, this has been pointed out as a striking association between the origins of what I call Hsien Taoism, and philosophical Taoism.[66] But it should not be forgotten

60. Yen I-p'ing 嚴一萍, *Yin Ch'i Chêng I* 殷契徵鑿 (Taipei, 1951).

61. For much interesting information on the *wu* see Arthur Waley, *The Nine Songs, a Study of Shamanism in Ancient China* (London, 1955). I am doubtful, however, about the occurrence of the character *wu* on the Shang oracle bones, which Waley speaks of as "fairly certain" (p. 18). I have examined a number of inscriptions in which it is alleged to occur, and believe the identification to be erroneous.

62. *Lü Shih Ch'un Ch'iu* 呂氏春秋 (*Ssŭ Pu Pei Yao* ed.), 17. 9a. See also: Ibid., 3. 5a. *Shan Hai Ching Chien Su* 山海經箋疏 (*Ssŭ Pu Pei Yao* ed.), 11. 5a.

63. *Shih Chi*, 6. 23–24; Édouard Chavannes, translator, *Les Mémoires historiques de Se-ma Ts'ien* (Paris, 1895–1905; referred to hereafter as *Mem. Hist.*), III, 435–436. See also Fung Yu-lan, *A History of Chinese Philosophy*, I, 383.

64. Kuo Mo-jo, *Shih P'i P'an Shu*, 133. *Ku Shih Pien*, IV, 501–502; VII (Lü Ssŭ-mien 呂思勉, ed.; Shanghai, 1941), *shang*, 189–209.

65. *Shih Chi*, 28. 64–66; *Mem. Hist.*, III, 486–489. *Huai Nan Tzŭ* 淮南子 (*Ssŭ Pu Pei Yao* ed.), 6. 6b, 19. 11b. Wang Ch'ung, *Lun Hêng*, 3.22a.

66. Cf. *Shih Chi*, 74. 10 and *Chuang Tzŭ*, 10. 17a–18b. Kuo Mo-jo, *Shih P'i P'an Shu*, 133–183.

that the great Confucian Mencius 孟子, and later on Hsün Tzŭ 荀子 also spent time at this same capital. Ch'i was a center for many kinds of intellectual activity, and not entirely by accident. King Hsüan 宣, who reigned from 332 to 314, spent large sums to attract hundreds of scholars to his capital, and give them very comfortable livings. This method succeeded quite well, as it often does.[67] Scholars like to eat.

As early as the fourth century B. C. there was already, in embryo at least, what we might call an immortality cult. There was talk of men who lived for centuries, of sorcerers who soared through the heavens on distant journeys, and of some of the techniques for attaining immortality that were later espoused by Hsien Taoism. Such things are mentioned in philosophical Taoist books, but not there alone by any means. We find them referred to in the history called the *Chan Kuo Ts'ê* 戰國策, in the Legalist work *Han Fei Tzŭ* 韓非子, and even in the one bearing the name of that tough-minded Confucian rationalist, Hsün Tzŭ.[68] Such references are no more proof that the authors of these books espoused the immortality cult than the mention of Methusaleh in *Genesis* proves that Judaism is a religion devoted to longevity.

As a prime proof that there was already a Taoist religion devoted to the search for immortality in the fourth century B. C., Maspero cites the poet Ch'ü Yüan 屈原. He says, "Sur cette montée au pays du Seigneur d'En Haut, cet ancêtre du Paradis des Immortels du Taoïsme moderne, nous sommes renseignés par deux poèmes mystiques de K'iu Yuan, grand seigneur du pays de Tch'ou au IVe siècle, devenu taoïste, le *Li-sao* et le *Yuan-yeou*."[69] James R. Hightower has recently published a preliminary report of his extensive studies on poems attributed to Ch'ü Yüan.[70] I am entirely of his opinion that there is little evidence to show that any poem in the *Ch'u Tz'ŭ* 楚辭 but the *Li Sao* 離騷 was written by Ch'ü Yüan. I also agree with Hightower that the *Yüan Yu* 遠遊 and the *Li Sao* are not by the same hand, and can offer additional evidence. Maspero and some other scholars insist that the *Li Sao* is a Taoist work. Yet its entire tone of uncompromising self-righteousness, its setting up of fame as a goal, and its praise of Confucian heroes and Confucian virtues, is almost the reverse of the tone of the *Chuang Tzŭ*. I see nothing specifically

67. *Shih Chi*, 46. 31, 74. 10–12.
68. *Chan Kuo Ts'ê* (*Ssŭ Pu Pei Yao* ed.), 5. 13a, 17. 3b–4a. Wang Hsien-shên 王先愼, *Han Fei Tzŭ Chi Chieh* 韓非子集解 (1896), 7. 15b, 11. 7. Liang Ch'i-hsiung 梁啓雄, *Hsün Tzŭ Chien Shih* 荀子柬釋 (Shanghai, 1936), 13.
69. Maspero, *Le Taoïsme*, 202–204.
70. James R. Hightower, "Ch'ü Yüan Studies," in *Silver Jubilee Volume of the Zinbun-Kagaku-Kenkyusyo*, 192–223.

Taoist in the *Li Sao*. It employs the character *tao* as a philosophical concept exactly twice, and both times in the Confucian manner. In so far as the *Li Sao* may be said to have a philosophy, it appears Confucian; certainly it is not Taoist in any sense.[71] The *Yüan Yu*, on the other hand, uses *tao* in the Taoist sense, employs various technical Taoist terms, and refers to breath control, immortality, and *hsien*, "immortals."[72] It appears probable to me that the *Yüan Yu* was written much later than the *Li Sao*. It may not properly, I think, be cited (as it commonly is) as evidence that the immortality cult was already linked with Taoist philosophy in the fourth century B. C.

The critical testing ground is the *Chuang Tzŭ*, which a number of scholars have believed to be shot through with the search for immortality. This is largely because there is a good deal of the Taoist insistence that most men, by their unnaturally hectic way of life, not only destroy their peace of mind but shorten their lives. It is of interest to note that the medical profession is saying the same thing today. There is some emphasis on longevity in the *Chuang Tzŭ*, but every student of bronze inscriptions knows that this is one of the most ancient and universal Chinese desires. Yet even this is also ridiculed, in the *Chuang Tzŭ*, as stupid preoccupation with the vicissitudes of one's body.[73]

The prevailing attitude in the *Chuang Tzŭ* is that "no one is so long-lived as a child who dies in infancy, and P'êng Tsu 彭祖 [supposed to have lived for many centuries] died young; heaven and earth were born together with me, and all things with me are one."[74] Time after time we are told that for the enlightened Taoist both death and life are matters of indifference, and in some passages death is even called desirable.[75] Despite the fact that Hsien Taoists later took the Yellow Emperor and Lao Tzŭ as their patriarchs, in the *Chuang Tzŭ* both of these sages are quoted as advising that no importance be attached to either life or death.[76] A number of scholars, including Fung Yu-lan, Kuo Mo-jo, and Arthur Waley, have pointed out that this is the dominant position concerning death in the *Chuang Tzŭ*.[77]

71. *Ch'u Tz'ŭ Pu Chu* 楚辭補注 (*Ssŭ Pu Pei Yao* ed.), 1. 6b–7a, 1. 9b, 1. 12b–13b, 1. 14b, 1. 18b–19a, 1. 25a.
72. Ibid., 5. 2, 5. 4a–5a.
73. *Chuang Tzŭ*, 6. 15b–16a; Legge, *Chuang Tzŭ*, II, 1–2.
74. *Chuang Tzŭ*, 1. 18; Fung Yu-lan, *Chuang Tzŭ*, 56.
75. *Chuang Tzŭ*, 1. 21b, 1. 23a, 2. 3, 2. 19b, 2. 21, 3. 2, 3. 4b, 3. 5b, 3. 7a–13a, 5. 2a, 6. 15b–19b, etc.
76. *Chuang Tzŭ*, 2. 19b, 7. 18. 7. 22a–23a; Legge, *Chuang Tzŭ*, I, 229, II, 48, 58–59.
77. Kuo Mo-jo, *Shih P'i P'an Shu*, 163–183. Fung Yu-lan, *A Short History of Chinese Philosophy*, 114–115. Arthur Waley, *The Way and Its Power*, 53–55.

This is not to say that there is no reflection, in the *Chuang Tzŭ*, of the immortality cult that was so prevalent when it was written. There is mention of men who lived for centuries and other comparable prodigies.[78] Various elements later found in Hsien Taoism are referred to—often derogatorily. A sorcerer, *wu*, is elaborately derided.[79] One passage which describes the practice of breath control and gymnastics has often been cited as showing that the *Chuang Tzŭ* advocates such exercises. But in fact, this passage says that these are the pursuits of those who are merely "avid for longevity"; the enlightened man, it avers, does not bother with such practices, but regards death calmly, as a natural event.[80] Already in the *Chuang Tzŭ* we see the conflict between the immortality cult and Taoist philosophy.

A few of the passages that have been collected into the *Chuang Tzŭ* probably show direct influence from the immortality cult. But most of the evidence on which the *Chuang Tzŭ* has been alleged to espouse the search for immortality depends upon rather elaborate interpretation. Broad latitude for interpretation has been claimed on the ground that Taoism is a mystical philosophy. Certainly Taoism involves mysticism according to some definitions of that term. But when it is said that Taoist philosophy is based upon ecstatic mystical experience, and that "Taoist mystics hardly differ from Christian and Muslim mystics except by the explanations which they give of identical experiences,"[81] the data will not support the conclusion. A number of scholars have generalized about mysticism in the *Chuang Tzŭ*, giving undue weight to isolated passages and terms, and inadequate attention to the work as a whole.[82] The Taoist conception of man's relation to the universe is quite different from that of the West, and this profoundly modifies Taoist mysticism. Marcel Granet was certainly correct in calling the *Chuang Tzŭ* "more intellectual than mystical."[83] This entire subject needs further study.

There is one passage in the *Chuang Tzŭ*, and only one, which refers to a *hsien*, an "immortal," and advocates that one should rise to the heavens

78. *Chuang Tzŭ*, 1. 6b–7b, 3. 6a, 4. 18a–19b; Legge, *Chuang Tzŭ*, I, 170–171, 245, 298–300.
79. *Chuang Tzŭ*, 3. 17a–18b; Legge, *Chuang Tzŭ*, I, 262–265.
80. *Chuang Tzŭ*, 6. 1a–2a; Legge, *Chuang Tzŭ*, I, 363–365.
81. Maspero, *Le Taoïsme*, 217–218. See also ibid., 210–212, and Maspero, *La Chine antique*, 492–497.
82. Much is made, for instance, of the expression *tso wang* 坐忘. It occurs, however, only in a single passage in the *Chuang Tzŭ* (3. 14b), not at all in the *Lao Tzŭ*, and once in the *Huai Nan Tzŭ* (12. 14a); the latter is a version of the same incident reported in the *Chuang Tzŭ*.
83. Granet, *La Pensée chinoise*, 571, n. 1.

as a *hsien*.[84] It is played as a trump card by all those who would find the immortality cult in the *Chuang Tzŭ*. Yet the paragraph in which it occurs is not only out of harmony with the work as a whole, but specifically contradicts other parts of the chapter in which it occurs on several points.[85] Legge, Giles, Kuo Mo-jo, and other scholars have pointed out its dubious character.[86] It not only conflicts with the philosophy of the *Chuang Tzŭ*, but in several details coincides exactly with later Hsien Taoist tenets.[87] There would seem to be no doubt that this passage is an interpolation.

It is surprising, in view of subsequent history, that in the *Lao Tzŭ* there are even fewer unmistakable reflections of the immortality cult than in the *Chuang Tzŭ*. But few things in the *Lao Tzŭ* are stated so plainly as to leave no room for varying interpretation. That is what has made the work so attractive to those who have wished to read their own ideas into it.

The immortality cult as a clear historic phenomenon seems to appear first in the activities of Ch'in Shih Huang Ti, who reigned 221-210 B. C. The *Historical Records* tells of his efforts to search out *hsien*, "immortals," and his patronage of certain magicians who used arts later associated with Hsien Taoism. But although such magicians were "too numerous to count" the emperor's efforts to obtain the drug of immortality failed and he died.[88] Despite the fact that Ch'ih Shih Huang has been execrated in the orthodox Chinese tradition, accounts of the history of Hsien Taoism accord him an important place, and a Taoist scripture written around A. D. 500 identifies him among the heavenly divinities.[89] Against this background it is interesting to note that what appears to be the earliest account of these activities of Ch'in Shih Huang, in the *Historical Records,* does not associate him with Taoism. He is merely described as a seeker after immortality.

We are fortunate in having something of cross-section of the thought of the time in the *Lü Shih Ch'un Ch'iu* 呂氏春秋, an eclectic work compiled

84. *Chuang Tzŭ*, 5. 3b–4b; Legge, *Chuang Tzŭ*, I, 313–314.
85. Cf. *Chuang Tzŭ*, 5. 2a; Legge, *Chuang Tzŭ*, I, 309–310.
86. Legge, *Chuang Tzŭ*, I, 313, n. 2. Giles, *Chuang Tzŭ*, 142. Kuo Mo-jo, *Shih P'i P'an Shu*, 182. Ch'ien Mu 錢穆, *Chuang Tzŭ Tsuan Chien* 莊子箋纂 (Hongkong, 1951), 93. Chang Hsin-Ch'êng 張心澂, *Wei Shu T'ung K'ao* 偽書通考 (Changsha, 1939), 719.
87. Cf. Kê Hung, *Pao P'u Tzŭ, Nei* 3. 5b, 8. 3b.
88. *Shih Chi*, 28. 23–26; *Mem. Hist.*, III, 429–438.
89. Kê Hung, *Pao P'u Tzŭ, Nei* 2. 4, 13. 3, 20. 2–3. *Wei Shu*, 114. 24a. Maspero, *Le Taoïsme*, 130–131. *Chêng T'ung Tao Tsang, Ts'ê* 73, *Tung Hsüan Ling Pao Chên Ling Wei Yeh T'u* 洞玄靈寶眞靈位業圖, 24b.

under the patronage of Lü Pu-wei 呂不韋.[90] Lü, who was reputed to be the actual father of Ch'in Shih Huang, ruled the state during the emperor's minority. Many parts of this work are Taoist, and if the immortality cult had been fused with Taoist philosophy at this time, the fact should appear here. On the contrary this book asserts repeatedly that death is inevitable. It says that the Yellow Emperor died and that *wu*, magicians, cannot prolong life. It ridicules attempts to revive the dead by means of drugs, and to prolong life by abstaining from eating grain.[91] In the *Lü Shih Ch'un Ch'iu* Taoist philosophy seems to be in full tilt against the burgeoning immortality cult.

There are many indications that the immortality cult became increasingly the vogue in the early Han period. A companion-in-arms of the founder, Chang Liang 張良 by name, is described as seeking immortality by means of gymnastics and abstention from grain. This famous hero was later claimed by Hsien Taoism, but his detailed biography in the *Historical Records* does not link him with Taoism in any way.[92] As late as the first century A. D. Wang Ch'ung 王充 recounted his history without connecting him with Taoism.[93]

The sixth Han ruler, Emperor Wu 武 (140-87 B. C.), sought immortality in a manner reminiscent of Ch'in Shih Huang Ti. Abstention from grain, alchemy, and drugs were exploited by magicians whom the emperor favored highly and later, in some cases, put to death for cheating him.[94] One of these magicians was later honored as a Taoist "immortal," and two works in the sacred canon of Hsien Taoism are devoted to the exploits of Emperor Wu.[95] Yet the contemporary account, in the *Historical Records,* does not suggest that his striving for immortality had anything to do with Taoism.[96]

Both of the remarkable historians who produced the *Historical Records* served as officials under Emperor Wu. Ssǔ-Ma T'an 司馬談 was strongly partial to Taoism, and his son Ssǔ-Ma Ch'ien 司馬遷 certainly had in-

90. This work is accepted with very little question by the critics, though a few interpolations are suspected; see Chang Hsin-ch'êng, *Wei Shu T'ung K'ao*, 838–839. The work is carefully translated, with valuable annotations, in Richard Wilhelm, *Frühling und Herbst des Lü Bu We* (Jena, 1928).
91. *Lü Shih Ch'un Ch'iu* (*Ssǔ Pu Pei Yao* ed.), 3. 5a, 10. 3, 10. 5b, 14. 21a, 22. 3a, 25. 3a; Wilhelm, *Frühling und Herbst des Lü Bu We*, 31, 120, 123, 203, 389–390, 435.
92. *Shih Chi*, 55. Kê Hung, *Pao P'u Tzu, Nei* 5. 3.
93. Wang Ch'ung, *Lun Hêng*, 22. 8b–9b.
94. *Shih Chi*, 28. 45–89; *Mem. Hist.*, III, 461–519.
95. Wang Ch'ung, *Lun Hêng*, 7. 8a. Kê Hung, *Pao P'u Tzǔ, Nei* 2. 6. *Chêng T'ung Tao Tsang, Ts'ê* 137, *Han Wu Ti Nei Chuan* 漢武帝內傳, *Han Wu Ti Wai Chuan* 漢武帝外傳.
96. See note 94, above.

clinations in that direction.[97] Their history has confused our picture of
Taoism somewhat by the frequent practice of referring to it as the doctrines of "Huang-Lao," "the Yellow Emperor and Lao Tzŭ,"[98] even
with reference to a time when the Yellow Emperor had not yet been fully
accepted as an adherent of Taoism, much less its patriarch.[99] It is significant that the expression "Huang-Lao," though made much of by some
scholars, does not occur in the *Chuang Tzŭ*, the *Lao Tzŭ*, the *Lü Shih
Ch'un Ch'iu*, the *Huai Nan Tzŭ* 淮南子, or the *Lieh Tzŭ*.[100] The *Historical
Records* includes biographies of Lao Tzŭ and Chuang Tzŭ, and a description of Taoism; in none of these accounts is it suggested that Taoism has
anything to do with the quest for immortality.[101]

A relative and vassal of Emperor Wu, the Prince of Huai Nan, is said
by Hsien Taoist tradition to have soared to the heavens as an immortal,
along with his dogs and cocks who accidentally drank some of the elixir

97. *Mem. Hist.*, I, XLIX–LII, CCXLI. H. G. Creel, *Confucius, the Man and the Myth*
(New York, 1949), 244–248 and 325, n. 26; (London, 1951), 266–270.
98. Commonly, but not always, abbreviated; see *Shih Chi*, 28. 45, 49. 14, 54. 13, 56. 23,
63. 13, 63. 14, 74. 12, 80. 17, 101. 21, 102. 10, 104. 2, 107. 8, 120. 3, 121. 7, 126. 15,
127. 13, 130. 59. In Hsien Taoism Huang Lao Chün 黃老君 came to be the name of a
single deity, at a date that is not clear to me. Maspero says (*Le Taoïsme*, 219–220) that
Huang-Lao was a single divinity as early as the second century B. C. As evidence he
cites the first, third, and eleventh of the passages just cited in the *Shih Chi*, plus the stricture
of Pan Piao 班彪 (see *Mem. Hist.*, I, CCXLI). This is completely unconvincing. Comparison of the passages cited above will show that (as all scholars Chinese and Western
known to me, except Maspero, seem to agree), the *Shih Chi* simply used "Huang-Lao"
as an abbreviation for "Huang Ti and Lao Tzŭ." The passage in *Shih Chi*, 28. 45, which
Maspero cites as evidence, is repeated almost verbatim in *Shih Chi*, 49. 14, with the
significant difference that it reads "Huang Ti Lao Tzŭ." Wang Ch'ung (*Lun Hêng*, 18. 4)
in the first century A. D., and the Hsien Taoist Kê Hung (*Pao P'u Tzŭ, Nei* 10. 4a) in
the fourth, understood Huang Lao to refer to two persons. This does not mean that they
may not have denoted a single person earlier, but I know no clear evidence that
they did.
99. *Shih Chi*, 74. 12 says that four scholars studied the doctrines of "Huang-Lao." Three
of them are mentioned in the *Chuang Tzŭ*, and all four are dated by Ch'ien Mu at about
the time of the writing of the earliest part of that work; see Ch'ien Mu, *Hsien Ch'in
Chu Tzŭ Hsi Nien* 先秦諸子繫年 (2d ed.; Shanghai, 1936), 102. But while Huang Ti
is often mentioned with respect in the *Chuang Tzŭ*, there are also passages in which he is
severely criticized for action contrary to Taoist principle; see *Chuang Tzŭ*, 4. 16b, 9. 20b;
Legge, *Chuang Tzŭ*, I, 295, II, 172–173. And chapter 33 of the *Chuang Tzŭ*, which under-
takes to give a history of Taoism, makes only one purely incidental reference to Huang
Ti, and does not even indicate that he was a Taoist, much less a "founding father" of
the doctrine.
100. Perhaps even more significant, there is no special association of Huang Ti with Lao
Tzŭ in any of these works.
101. *Shih Chi*, 63. 2–12, 130. 9. It is stated that according to some accounts Lao Tzŭ
lived for centuries, but this is not immortality.

of immortality.[102] A book written under his patronage by various scholars, called the *Huai Nan Tzŭ*, is eclectic but predominantly Taoist in tone. It contains a good deal of mention of techniques for seeking immortality but never, I believe, recommends them. On the contrary, it insists repeatedly that death and life are just the same, and neither should be sought or feared.[103] It ridicules breath control and gymnastics, which are designed to perpetuate the body but in fact confuse the mind.[104] It speaks derisively of the man who claimed he could raise the dead and who, when asked how, replied that he had a drug which had proved quite successful in treating the half-paralyzed, so that to raise the dead he would need only to double the dose.[105] The *Huai Nan Tzŭ* seems to attack the immortality cult with special insistence, perhaps because it had become so much the fashion.[106]

In short, there seems to be very little evidence that the immortality cult was associated with Taoist philosophy up to roughly 100 B. C. But Wang Ch'ung, writing his *Lun Hêng* 論衡 in the second half of the first century A. D., repeatedly associates the pursuit of immortality with the cultivation of *tao*, and attributes the avoidance of grain, the use of drugs, gymnastics, and breath control aiming at immortality to the *tao chia* 道家, "Taoist school." He calls the magicians patronized by the Han Emperor Wu *tao shih* 道士, "practitioners of *tao*." And he says that there are those who believe that by means of the doctrine of Lao Tzŭ immortality may be achieved.[107] Wang Ch'ung is not, to be sure, a disinterested reporter; despite his exaggerated reputation as a rationalist, he tried the regimen of drugs and gymnastics to forestall old age, but alas! he tells us, unsuccessfully.[108] Nevertheless it is quite clear, from a variety of evidence, that during the first several centuries of the Christian Era the quest for immortality came commonly to be associated in men's minds with Taoism. With substantial borrowings from Buddhism, Hsien Taoism developed public and semipublic ceremonies having broad popular appeal.[109]

102. Kê Hung, *Shên Hsien Chuan* 神仙傳, *Lung Wei Mi Shu I Chi* 龍威秘書一集 (*Ta Yu Shan Fang* ed., 1794), *Ts'ê* 4, 4. 1a–5a. Wang Ch'ung, *Lun Hêng*, 7. 2b.
103. *Huai Nan Tzŭ* (*Ssŭ Pu Pei Yao* ed.), 2. 2, 2. 4a, 7. 3b–4a, 7. 5a–6b, 7. 7, 7. 8b, 7. 10b–11a, 10. 13b, 11.9b, 12. 17b–18a, 16. 12b, 17. 2a, 17. 3a, 17. 11, 21. 1b.
104. Ibid., 7. 6b.
105. *Huai Nan Tzŭ*, 6. 4a; more detail is given in *Lü Shih Ch'un Ch'iu*, 25. 3a.
106. *Huai Nan Tzŭ*, 7. 9b, 11. 9b, 12. 15, 18. 18b, 19. 2b, 19. 11b.
107. Wang Ch'ung, *Lun Hêng*, 6. 16b, 7. 2, 7. 5a, 7. 8a, 7. 9a–11a, 16. 4a, 25. 15.
108. Ibid., 30. 10a.
109. Maspero recognizes Buddhist influence, but in my opinion there is clear evidence that its importance was much greater than he suggests.

A priori it seems almost incredible that Taoist philosophy, which rejected both the possibility and the desirability of immortality, could have become linked in any way with the immortality cult. A few of the reasons for this curious phenomenon stand out clearly. One is a simple pun. Taoist philosophy got its name from the fact that it used the term *tao* to denote the whole of reality. And from an early date the term *tao* was also used to denote the "methods" by which magicians sought immortality.[110]

Of salient importance is the fact that practitioners of the immortality cult were looked down upon as charlatans, even by some who believed immortality possible.[111] Such practices as the sexual technique, which at the extreme seems to have proposed that one man should have intercourse with twelve hundred girls sixteen or seventeen years of age, called forth social condemnation.[112] The immortality cult needed the shelter of a respected philosophy.

Taoism was highly respected in Han times, and many of the sayings attributed to Lao Tzŭ were so ambiguous that they could be interpreted to mean almost anything. Practitioners of the immortality cult took full advantage of this,[113] while making relatively little use of the *Chuang Tzŭ*, which was a forbidding work from their point of view.

Yet even Taoism as set forth in the *Chuang Tzŭ* had grist for their mill. Confusing paradoxes, dazzling figures of speech, talk of soaring through the heavens beyond the ends of the earth—if taken literally, these are much like the mystifying patter of the magician. A story in the philosophical Taoist work *Lieh Tzŭ* at once demonstrates the gulf between philosophic Taoism and Hsien Taoism, and the reasons why they could be confused. A magician of marvelous powers was entertained by the Chou king Mu 穆 with every luxury that royalty could command, and yet he seemed unsatisfied. The magician then invited the king to visit his home. Hand in hand they soared into the heavens, to an exquisite palace such as the world has never seen. After the king had enjoyed himself there for,

---

110. *Shih Chi*, 28. 24, 28. 46, 28. 65; *Mem. Hist.*, III, 436, 463, 488. Wang Ch'ung, *Lun Hêng*, 2. 7b, 7. 8a–9a.
111. *Shih Chi*, 28. 52–53, 28. 57–69, 28. 88; *Mem. Hist.*, III, 470–471, 477–493, 518–519. Wang Ch'ung, *Lun Hêng*, 7. 1a–11b. Kê Hung, *Pao P'u Tzŭ*, *Nei* 14. 1, 20. *Wei Shu*, 114. 32b. *Sui Shu* 隋書 (T'ung Wên ed.), 35. 31a. The latter two references are translated in James R. Ware, "The *Wei Shu* and the *Sui Shu* on Taoism," in *Journal of the American Oriental Society*, LIII, 242, 249–250.
112. Maspero, "Les Procédés de 'Nourrir le principe vital,'" 381, 396, 409–412.
113. For far-fetched interpretations of the *Lao Tzŭ* by Hsien Taoists, see: Kê Hung, *Pao P'u Tzŭ*, *Nei* 18. 3a. Maspero, *Le Taoïsme*, 154. Hsü Ti-shan, *Tao Chiao Shih*, 182. *Mou Tzŭ* 牟子 (Ch'ung Wên Shu Chü ed., 1875), 13b; Paul Pelliot, "Meou-tseu ou les Doutes Levés," in *T'oung Pao*, XIX (Leyden, 1920), 319–320.

it seemed to him, decades, they one day soared still higher, until the king became dizzy and asked to return. At once he found himself sitting on his throne, where, his courtiers told him, he had dozed for only a moment. When the king asked the magician for an explanation he was told, "We just made a mental journey. Why should our bodies have moved? And what difference could there be between those regions we visited and your own palace?"[114]

The *Lieh Tzŭ*, in which this incident occurs, is the only one of the major Taoist philosophical books that we have not yet considered. Its date has been hotly debated. While some Western scholars would assign it to a time as early as the third century B. C.,[115] the prevailing opinion of current Chinese scholarship, while granting that it incorporates early materials, considers the work to have reached its present form perhaps as late as the third century A. D.[116] Internal evidence seems clearly to indicate that this text, as we now have it, was produced early in the Christian Era, at a time when Buddhist philosophy and Taoist philosophy were influencing and enriching each other. The philosophy of the *Lieh Tzŭ* is very much like that of the *Chuang Tzŭ*, with a certain added scope similar to that of Buddhism and some admixture of Buddhist ideas and even Buddhist terminology.[117] But in the *Lieh Tzŭ* Confucius is almost always mentioned with great respect, as a figure of established and

114. *Lieh Tzŭ* 列子 (*Ssŭ Pu Pei Yao* ed.), 3. 1a–3a; Lionel Giles, *Taoist Teachings from the Book of Lieh Tzŭ* (1912; reprinted London, 1947), 58–61.
115. Maspero, who is of this opinion, states that the argument of Ma Hsü-lun 馬叙倫 against assigning an early date to the *Lieh Tzŭ* "a été facilement réfuté par M. Takenouchi" (*La Chine antique*, 491–492). This is true, but it is also true that much of Ma's argument was of the most feeble character. Its refutation has little bearing upon the important, valid case that other scholars have made for placing the editing of our present text within the Christian Era.
116. Fung Yu-lan, *A Short History of Chinese Philosophy*, 232. Chang Hsin-ch'êng, *Wei Shu T'ung K'ao*, pp. 699–712.
117. A number of ideas in the *Lieh Tzŭ* are at least strongly suggestive of Buddhist influence. These include: the dissolution of the individual at death (cf. *skandhas*), the doctrine that heaven and earth will come to an end, the giving of alms to acquire merit, and the ceremonial release of living creatures to show benevolence; *Lieh Tzŭ*, 1. 9b 1. 15a, 8. 10a, 8. 14b; Giles, *Taoist Teachings from the Book of Lieh Tzŭ*, 24–25, 31, 118–119. The doctrine that all is illusion (*Lieh Tzŭ*, 3. 4b–5a) sounds Indian, and the character used here, *huan* 幻, is said to be used in Chinese Buddhist texts to translate the Sanskrit *māyā*; see W. E. Soothill and Lewis Hodous, *A Dictionary of Chinese Buddhist Terms* (London, 1937), 149, and Fung Yu-lan, *A History of Chinese Philosophy*, II, 257, 342. In fact, this passage in the *Lieh Tzŭ* seems to have some resemblance to one found in a Buddhist text; see Ting Fu-pao 丁福保, *Fo Hsüeh Ta Tz'ŭ Tien* 佛學大辭典 (3d ed.; Shanghai, 1929), 741. For further data on Buddhist influence on the *Lieh Tzŭ*, see the discussion in Sung Lien 宋濂, *Chu Tzŭ Pien* 諸子辨, in *Ku Shu Pien Wei Ssŭ Chung* 古書辨 偽四種 (Shanghai, 1935), 9–10.

commanding prestige.[118] The struggle of Taoist ideas against Confucianism, a vital matter in the *Chuang Tzŭ*, has become almost a dead issue.

The struggle now is against the immortality cult, which is attacked with redoubled insistence.[119] This is quite natural if the *Lieh Tzŭ* as we have it was compiled in a period when the name of "Taoist" had been taken over by the immortality cult, so that Taoist philosophers felt obliged to dissociate themselves from the cult. The quest for immortality is now branded as not merely foolish and futile, but even immoral.[120] The practice of *yang shêng* 養生, "preserving life," mentioned repeatedly in the *Chuang Tzŭ*, has been alleged to indicate that Taoist philosophy embraced the immortality cult. One passage in the *Lieh Tzŭ* is an outright refutation of this proposition. *Yang shêng*, it declares, should be understood to mean to give free rein to one's desires, regardless of whether this shortens one's life or not. But to submit to a repressive regimen, merely to prolong one's life, is not worth while even if it permits one to live "a thousand years, or ten thousand years!"[121]

Vigorous rebuttal, from the camp of the Hsien Taoists, was not lacking. Kê Hung 葛洪, who flourished around A. D. 300, is perhaps the ablest theoretician of Hsien Taoism; he is quoted frequently by Maspero and others who write on the subject. He speaks slightingly of the *ch'ing t'an* 清談 or "pure conversation" in which his philosophical Taoist contemporaries engaged.[122] Kê Hung attacks the *Chuang Tzŭ* bitterly and repeatedly, declaring that it "says that life and death are just the same, brands the effort to preserve life as laborious servitude, and praises death as a rest; this doctrine is separated by millions of miles from that of *shên hsien* 神仙 (spirits and immortals)."[123] Lao Tzŭ, as a patriarch of Hsien Taoism, is commonly though not always treated more respectfully.

---

118. *Lieh Tzŭ*, 1. 10a–12a, 2. 14a, 2. 23b–24b, 3. 9b, 4. 1a–6b, 6. 1a, 8. 4b; Giles, *Taoist Teachings from the Book of Lieh Tzŭ*, 26–27, 51, 55–57, 68, 73–75, 97–98, 111. In the *Chuang Tzŭ*, while Confucius is in some passages honored as a Taoist sage, in others he is sharply criticized.

119. *Lieh Tzŭ*, 1. 6a, 1. 9b, 1. 11a–13a, 2. 2a, 6. 1, 6. 7a, 6. 8a, 6. 9a, 6. 11a–12, 7. 3a, 7. 4a–5a, 7. 7b–8a, 7. 11b, 8. 14; Giles, *Taoist Teachings from the Book of Lieh Tzŭ*, 22–25, 27–28, 38, 97–99, 101–102. In two passages, in this composite and heterogeneous work, *hsien* are described as inhabiting distant and fanciful lands, but it is not suggested that men in general may become *hsien*: *Lieh Tzŭ*, 2. 2b–3b, 5. 4a–5b. One passage (*Lieh Tzŭ*, 8. 14) discusses with Taoist impartiality the possibility that a man who claimed to know the technique of immortality, but died, might not have been a charlatan.

120. *Lieh Tzŭ*, 1. 12b–13a; Giles, *Taoist Teachings from the Book of Lieh Tzŭ*, 28.

121. *Lieh Tzŭ*, 7. 4.

122. Kê Hung, *Pao P'u Tzŭ*, *Wai* 25. 5a, 46. 3a.

123. Ibid., *Nei* 8. 3b. See also *Wai* 4. 3a, 14. 3b–4a, 33. 1b, 42. 1, 43. 2a, 48. 1a. Kê Hung is not always of the same mind about Chuang Tzŭ; see also ibid., *Nei* 14. 2a.

But the book attributed to Lao Tzŭ, the *Tao Tê Ching*, is entirely too vague and general, according to Kê Hung. He warns that anyone who hopes to learn from it the method of attaining immortality will be disappointed.[124]

The contrast between philosophic Taoism and Hsien Taoism may be seen in the two earliest commentaries on the *Lao Tzŭ* that have come down to us. One, of uncertain date,[125] is attributed to Hê Shang Kung 河上公, "the old man of the river bank," an unknown character who is alleged to have himself become a *hsien*.[126] In this commentary the *Lao Tzŭ* is found constantly to emphasize the cultivation of longevity, to state that immortality may be attained, to recommend breath control, and to speak of guardian spirits and spirits dwelling in the organs of the body.[127] All of these are characteristic of Hsien Taoism. Let us look now at the commentary of the philosophical scholar Wang Pi 王弼, who lived from 226 to 249. In the same text he finds none of these things, save for a single rather obscure reference to longevity.[128]

It would probably be possible to find representatives of these two kinds of Taoism at any subsequent period. In this connection it should not be forgotten that the philosophy of Ch'an (or Zen) 禪 Buddhism is remarkably similar to philosophic Taoism, and that at least some of its founders were quite familiar with the *Chuang Tzŭ*.[129]

What, then, is "Taoism"? Clearly, the term has been used to embrace

---

124. Ibid., *Nei* 8. 3.
125. Traditionally dating from the second century B. C.; see *Lao Tzŭ Tao Tê Ching, Hê Shang Kung Chang Chü* 老子道德經, 河上公章句 (*Ssŭ Pu Ts'ung K'an* ed.), preface. Eduard Erkes dates it at "about A. D. 200"; see Eduard Erkes, "Ho-shang-kung's Commentary on Lao-tse," in *Artibus Asiae*, VIII (Basel, 1940), 124–127. It is evidently to this work that Waley refers (in *The Way and Its Power*, 129) when he says that "some time about the fourth century A. D. an unknown Taoist produced what purported to be an independent text, together with what pretended to be a lost Han commentary." Waley adds that it was "a commentary designed to bring the *Tao Tê Ching* into line with contemporary Taoism, which was a very different thing from the Taoism of six hundred years before." Paul Pelliott assigned it to a time not later than the end of the sixth century; see Pelliot, "Meou-tseu ou les Doutes Levés," 334, n. 22. For the opinions of Chinese scholars, see Chang Hsin-ch'êng, *Wei Shu T'ung K'ao*, 743–745.
126. Kê Hung, *Shên Hsien Chuan*, 3. 1a–2a.
127. *Lao Tzŭ Tao Tê Ching, Hê Shang Kung Chang Chü, shang* 1a, 2b–3b, 4b–5b, 8, 14b, 17a–18a; *hsia* 7a, 8b, 11b, 17a.
128. *Lao Tzŭ, shang* 19.
129. Eliot, *Hinduism and Buddhism*, III, 305–306. Fung Yu-lan, *A Short History of Chinese Philosophy*, 246–247, 257. Hu Shih, "Development of Zen Buddhism in China," in *The Chinese Social and Political Science Review*, XV (Peiping, 1931–1932), 475–505. Hu Shih "Ch'an (Zen) Buddhism in China," in *Philosophy East and West*, III (Honolulu, 1953), 3–24. Granet, *La Pensée chinoise*, 581. Waley, *The Way and Its Power*, 120.

the most diverse doctrines. They may be grouped, in the most general way, under two headings. On the one hand we have philosophic Taoism, a philosophy saying much that is still pertinent even in this day of great sophistication and scientific complexity. This philosophy has not always been studied with the seriousness it deserves, in part because it has often been regarded as a system of mystical incomprehensibilities. Another part of the reason is that it has sometimes been confused with the other kind of Taoism, which I suggest should be known as Hsien Taoism. The doctrines that fall under this heading, aiming at the achievement of immortality by a variety of means, have their roots in ancient Chinese magical practices and an immortality cult. Hsien Taoism also incorporates elements from Confucianism, Moism, and Buddhism. But there is one element that we might expect to find which is completely absent from Hsien Taoism. That is the central insight of philosophical Taoism.

2

The Great Clod

In the Western intellectual tradition it has commonly been taken for granted that man's mind, or his essential nature, enjoys a special and rather intimate relationship with the essential nature of the universe. For Judaism and Christianity the basis for this is laid in the first chapter of Genesis, which says both that God created man in his own image and that God created the heaven and the earth. In Greek thought, at least as it is represented by Plato, while the basis may be different the conviction that man stands in a special position with regard to the universe is no less strong.

In philosophic Taoism,[1] on the other hand, as we see it especially in the *Chuang-tzu*, there is no special relationship between man, or man's mind, and the nature of the universe. This difference of view has important consequences for such matters as the theory of knowledge.

Plato draws a sharp distinction between knowledge and opinion. He speaks of "the very being with which true knowledge is concerned; the colourless, formless, intangible essence, visible only to mind, the pilot of

Reprinted with permission from *Wen-lin*, ed., Chow Tse-tsung (Madison: The University of Wisconsin Press; ©1968 by the Regents of the University of Wisconsin), 257–268.
1. The term "Taoism" is used to denote a wide variety of doctrines. The most obvious difference is between philosophical Taoism and what is sometimes called "religious Taoism." The latter gives relatively little attention to such problems as that of the nature of the universe, and is largely concerned with the problem of gaining immortality. I have proposed calling it "Hsien Taoism"; see pp. 1–24. Within philosophical Taoism, I further distinguish two aspects, "contemplative" and "purposive"; see pp. 37–47. Purposive Taoism seems to me to be a slightly posterior development, found predominantly (but not exclusively) in the *Lao-tzu*; it is chiefly concerned with the control of phenomena, and relatively little with the nature of the universe. The latter is, however, a major concern of contemplative Taoism, which in my opinion represents the earliest and most authentic form of Taoist philosophy; it is found predominantly (but again not exclusively) in the *Chuang-tzu*.

the soul."[2] And, he says, "the soul is like the eye: when resting upon that on which truth and being shine, the soul perceives and understands and is radiant with intelligence; but when turned towards the twilight of becoming and perishing, then she has opinion only."[3]

If "becoming and perishing" do not characterize reality, then it must be that the truly real is unchanging. Thus Plato writes in the *Cratylus*:

> *Socrates.* I myself do not deny that the givers of names did really give them under the idea that all things were in motion and flux; which was their sincere but, I think, mistaken opinion. . . . And can we rightly speak of a beauty which is always passing away, and is first this and then that; must not the same thing be born and retire and vanish while the word is in our mouths?
>
> *Cratylus.* Undoubtedly.
>
> *Soc.* Then how can that be a real thing which is never in the same state? For obviously things which are the same cannot change while they remain the same; and if they are always the same and in the same state, and never depart from their original form, they can never change or be moved.
>
> *Crat.* Certainly they cannot.
>
> *Soc.* Nor can they yet be known by anyone. . . . But if the very nature of knowledge changes, at the time when the change occurs there will be no knowledge; and if the transition is always going on, there will always be no knowledge, and, according to this view, there will be no one to know and nothing to be known: but if that which knows and that which is known exist ever, and the beautiful and the good and every other thing also exist, then I do not think that they can resemble a process or flux, as we were just now supposing.[4]

The position of Plato is clear and consistent. Thought operates in terms of concepts, but concepts (names) cannot be forever changing to correspond to the phenomena of a universe in constant flux. Thus if the universe were constantly changing, accurate or "absolute" knowledge would be impossible; for this reason, Plato concludes, reality is not in flux. The *Chuang-tzu*, written at the other end of Eurasia perhaps half a century after the death of Plato,[5] made a remarkably similar analysis

---

2. Plato, *Phaedrus* [Stephanus 247], in *The Dialogues of Plato*, trans. Benjamin Jowett (New York, 1937), I, 252.

3. Plato, *Republic* [Stephanus 508]; Jowett, I, 770.

4. Plato, *Cratylus* [Stephanus 439–440]; Jowett, I, 228–229.

5. I speak of "the *Chuang-tzu*" rather than of the putative author, Chuang-tzu, because it is quite clear that this work was composite. While the man called Chuang-tzu doubtless

of the same problem, but arrived at an opposite result; the *Chuang-tzu* concluded that knowledge, in any absolute sense, is impossible.

Concerning the universal flux, the *Chuang-tzu* says:

> The *Tao* has no beginning or end. Things die and are born, never resting in their culmination. . . Decay is followed by growth, and fullness by emptiness; when there is an end, there is also a beginning. . . . The existence of all creatures is like the galloping of a horse. With every movement there is alteration; at every moment they are undergoing change.[6]
>
> 道無終始物有死生不恃其成 · · · 消息盈虛終則有始 · · · 物之生也若驟若馳無動而不變無時而不移

And again:

> All the various species of things transform into one another by the process of variation in form. Their beginning and ending is like an unbroken ring, of which it is impossible to discover the principle.[7]
>
> 萬物皆種也以不同形相禪始卒若環莫得其倫

The meaning of this latter passage is, I think, fairly clear. There is, for instance, a progression that begins with an acorn and ends with dust or soil, when the process begins all over again. But no one can say at what moment the acorn becomes a tree, the tree wood, the wood dust, and so on. These transformations compose a circle in which there is no break into which we can insert our intelligence, so as to form an immutable concept. The sense is quite similar to that of Plato's statement in the *Cratylus,* quoted earlier.

To Plato's propositions the author of our passage in the *Chuang-tzu* would reply, "Precisely!" There is no knowledge, in any absolute sense. And there are no discrete things, which exist in and of themselves without regard to their changing environment; within this total environment, what we call "things" are merely inseparable and constantly changing aspects. Therefore, in any absolute sense it is perfectly true that there is "no one to know and nothing to be known." Thus the *Chuang-tzu* tells us:

---

existed, and wrote some part of this book, our knowledge of him is slight, and perhaps no scholar today would suppose that all of this work was from a single hand. Contemporary scholarship tends to date this work, or at least its earliest portions, as having been written somewhere in the neighborhood of 300 B. C.

6. *Chuang-tzu* (*SPPY* ed.), 6.11a; cf. also Richard Wilhelm, trans., *Dschuang Dsi* (Düsseldorf/Köln, 1951), 129; James Legge, trans., *The Writings of Kwang-zze,* I (*Sacred Books of the East,* vol. 39; Oxford, 1927), 382–383.

7. *Chuang-tzu,* 9.7b; cf. also Wilhelm, *Dschuang Dsi,* 207; Legge, *The Writings of Kwang-zze,* II (*Sacred Books of the East,* vol. 40; Oxford, 1927), 144.

There is one respect in which the understanding of the men of
antiquity reached the highest point. Wherein did they excel? They
believed that things did not exist.[8] This is the highest point,
the culmination; nothing can be added to it. Next below this is the
state of believing that things exist, but that there are no distinctions
between them.[9]

古之人其知有所至矣惡乎至有以爲未始有物者至矣盡矣不可以加矣其次以爲
有物矣而未始有封也

The Taoists call the totality of existence the *Tao,* but in fact it cannot
be known and this is not even really its name. The *Chuang-tzu* says:

> The *Tao* cannot be heard; what is heard is not it. The *Tao* cannot be
> seen; what is seen is not it. The *Tao* cannot be talked about; what is
> talked about is not it. . . . There is no name that truly corresponds to
> the *Tao.*[10]

道不可聞聞而非也道不可見見而非也道不可言言而非也···道不當名

Certainly one cannot generalize to the extent of calling the Platonic
"the Western," and the Taoist "the Chinese," view of reality. Exceptions
can be found both in China and in the West. It is undoubtedly true, as
Joseph Needham and others have pointed out,[11] that the recent developments of modern science conduce to a view that has some remarkable
similarities to that of early Taoism. Yet, however much we may intel-
lectually reject the concept of absolutes, many of us still feel a strong
emotional pull toward such abstract ideas as "truth." The main stream

8. In my opinion most of the translators of this passage — including Fung Yu-lan, Wilhelm, and Legge, whose translations are cited in the following note — have been misled
by their interpretation of the expression *wei shih* 未始, which they take in some such sense
as "not yet begun." Certainly this is the usual sense of the characters. But *wei shih* is a
very common expression in the *Chuang-tzu,* and at some points it quite unmistakably
functions as a simple negative, which I think it very clearly is here. James R. Ware,
trans., *The Sayings of Chuang Chou* (New York, 1963), 23, here renders *wei shih* as a simple
negative, but I do not find his translation of the whole passage satisfactory. For other
passages in which *wei shih* must be taken as a simple negative, see *Chuang-tzu,* 2.7b
and 8.15b. Fung's partial translation of the *Chuang-tzu* includes only the first of these two
passages, but in each occurrence of these passages Fung, Legge, and Wilhelm render
wei shih as a simple negative. See Fung Yu-lan, trans., *Chuang Tzŭ, a New Selected Translation* (Shanghai, 1933), 80; Legge, *The Writings of Kwang-zze,* I, 209, II, 100; Wilhelm,
Dschuang Dsi, 29, 185.
9. *Chuang-tzu,* 1.16b; cf. also Fung, *Chuang Tzŭ,* 53; Wilhelm, *Dschuang Dsi,* 15; Legge,
The Writings of Kwang-zze, I, 185.
10. *Chuang-tzu,* 7. 28a; cf. also Legge, *The Writings of Kwang-zze,* I, 185.
11. Joseph Needham, *Science and Civilisation in China,* II (Cambridge, 1956), 496–505.

of Western thinking has followed a course that has not paralleled that of the Taoist conception of reality.

This fact has made it difficult for many Western students effectively to understand the Taoist conception. This becomes apparent when we examine the manner in which most of them translate the term *Tao*, as it appears in the *Chuang-tzu* and the *Lao-tzu*. Insofar as one can judge from these translations, most of them appear to have understood the Taoist conception of the universe as being quite similar to that which is dominant in Western thought: a conception that establishes a special relationship between the essential nature of man and the essential nature of reality. Arthur Waley writes that

> in a particular school of philosophy whose followers ultimately came to be called Taoists, *tao* meant "the way the universe works"; and ultimately, something very like God, in the more abstract and philosophical sense of that term. Now it so happens that all the meaning-extensions of this word *tao* (even including the last: "I am the Way") also exist in European languages, so that Western scholars have had no difficulty in understanding it.[12]

And a number of scholars have rendered the term *Tao* as "God."[13]

It was almost inevitable that the term *logos* should be used to render *Tao*. The Gospel of John opens with the words, "In the beginning there was the *logos*." This, and the kindred sense of "reason," have been favored as translations of *Tao* by many.[14] Abel-Rémusat, who was the

---

12. Arthur Waley, *The Way and Its Power* (London, 1934; reprint of 1949), 30–31.

13. C. G. Alexander, *Lao-tsze the Great Thinker* (London, 1895), 55; Victor von Strauss, *Laò-tsè's Taò Tĕ Kïng* (Leipzig, 1924), xxxiv–xxxv. Ware, *The Sayings of Chuang Chou*, passim. Ware writes (pp. 7–8): "From Chuang Chou (300 B. C.), one of China's great minds, we get the world's most intelligible and diverting discussion of God. In the book translated here, Chuang Chou describes for his contemporaries the almighty, all-embracing, everlasting God comparable to the One defined in the Judaeo-Christian tradition by the equation God=Life. . . . The term usually employed by Chuang Chou is the sobriquet Tao (see 11. 70). In addition, he uses about twenty epithets. All of these I am translating 'God' . . ."

14. Abel-Rémusat, "Mémoire sur la vie et les opinions de Lao Tseu," in *Mémoires de l'Institut Royal de France, Académie des Inscriptions et Belles-Lettres*, VII (Paris, 1824), 23; G. Pauthier, *Premier Livre du TAO-TE-KING de Lao-TSEU* (1838), 7; John Chalmers, *The Speculations . . . of "The Old Philosopher," Lau-tsze* (London, 1868), vol. I; Paul Carus, *The Canon of Reason and Virtue* (Chicago and London, 1913; reprint of 1945), 73; Wilhelm, *Dschuang Dsi*, 3. James Legge, in the Introduction to his work *The Texts of Taoism* (*Sacred Books of the East*, XXXIX, 12–33) discusses the meaning of *Tao*, and says, "The first translation of the Tào Teh King into a Western language was executed in Latin by some of the Roman Catholic missionaries, and a copy of it was brought to England by a Mr. Matthew Raper, F.R.S., and presented by him to the Society on the 10th of January, 1788 . . . .

first Professor of Chinese in the Collège de France, wrote in 1824: "It seems impossible to translate this word *Tao* otherwise than by the word *logos* and its derivatives, in the triple sense of *supreme being, reason,* and *word.*"[15]

Stanislas Julien, who was a student of Abel-Rémusat and his successor at the Collège de France, objected strongly to the rendering of *Tao* as *logos.* The best way to see what the term means, Julien said, was to see what the *Lao-tzu* and other early Taoist works had to say about it. After quoting a number of passages he concluded:

> It follows from the preceding passages, and from a great many others that I could cite, that in *Lao-tzu* and the oldest philosophers of his school before the Christian Era, the use and the definition of the word *Tao* excludes any idea of *intelligent cause* . . . . *Lao-tzu* represents the Tao as a being devoid of action, thoughts, or desires and he wishes man, in order to arrive at the highest degree of perfection, to remain like the Tao in a state of absolute quiet, divesting himself of thoughts, desires, and even of the light of intelligence, which according to him is a cause of disorder.[16]

Although it is a century and a quarter since Julien wrote, at a time when those in the Western world who could even read Chinese with real comprehension were few indeed, his understanding of this aspect of Taoism was in my opinion superior to that of most of the scholars who have studied it since his day.[17] It is interesting to note, however, that a somewhat similar view is stated by one of the most recent translators of the *Lao-tzu,* J. J. L. Duyvendak. He writes: "The Way, *Tao,* here remains a formal notion. It is not a First Cause, it is not a Logos. It is nothing but the process of change, of growth. The world is no longer viewed in static, but in dynamic terms."[18]

In this version Tâo is taken in the sense of Ratio, or the Supreme Reason of the Divine Being, the Creator and Governor." Herbert A. Giles, trans., *Chuang Tzŭ: Mystic, Moralist, and Social Reformer* (London, 1926), XXIV–XXV, indicates that, while he does not translate *Tao,* he finds it to be used very much as Heraclitus uses *logos.*

15. Abel-Rémusat, "Mémoire sur la vie et les opinions de Lao Tseu," 24.

16. Stanislas Julien, trans. *Le Livre de la voie et de la vertu* (Paris, 1842), XIII–XIV.

17. This does not mean that Julien did not share certain mistaken ideas, on such matters as the dating of certain Taoist texts, that were general in his day. He did; it could scarcely have been otherwise.

18. J. J. L. Duyvendak, trans., *Tao Te Ching* (London, 1954), 9. While there is much that is good in this work, on a number of points I do not find Duyvendak's translation and interpretation satisfactory. In particular, it seems to me that his rearrangement and editing of the text is based upon a mistaken conception of its character.

Tao is not only, however, "the process of change." It is also that which changes. It is, as the *Lao-tzu* (chapters 21 and 25) tells us, a "thing," *wu* 物. Indeed, since individual things do not really exist as such, it would perhaps be correct to say that the *Tao* is the only thing there is. It may be called, the *Chuang-tzu* tells us, "'complete,' 'all-embracing,' 'the whole'; these are different names for the same reality, denoting the One."[19] "周，徧，咸，三者異名同實，其指一也。" It is simply—if this is simple—the totality of all that is. It is indeed *mind,* since men have minds. It is also a great many other things.

> Tung-kuo Tzu asked Chuang-tzu, "Where is that which you call *Tao*?" Chuang-tzu said, "Everywhere." Tung-kuo Tzu said, "You must be more specific." Chuang-tzu said, "It is in this ant." "In what lower?" "In this grass." "In anything still lower?" "It is in tiles." "Is it in anything lower still?" Chuang-tzu said, "It is in ordure and urine." Tung-kuo Tzu had nothing more to say.[20]
> 東郭子問於莊子曰所爲道惡乎在莊子曰無所不在東郭子曰期而後可莊子曰在螻蟻曰何其下邪曰在稊稗曰何其愈下邪曰在瓦甓曰何其愈甚邪曰在屎溺東郭子不應．

This is indeed, in William James's phrase, a "tough-minded" conception of the universe. It makes not the least concession to human vanity or sentiment. The ultimate nature of the universe has just as much, and just as little, relation to my mind as it has to the smallest pebble lying in the road. Certainly other men, besides Chinese Taoists, have been able to accept a view so unflattering to the human race. If most of them have flinched from it, surely one reason is the dark specter of death, which makes men long to believe that elsewhere in the universe, beyond the tiny span of human life, there is something that vibrates in special sympathy to human aspirations. Yet there have been countless mortals who have faced death bravely without this consolation, from philosophers of antiquity to the New England poet, William Cullen Bryant, who wrote in "Thanatopsis":

> Earth, that nourished thee, shall claim
> Thy growth, to be resolved to earth again,
> And, lost each human trace, surrendering up
> Thine individual being, thou shalt go

19. *Chuang-tzu,* 7.26b; Legge, *The Writings of Kwang-zze,* II, 66–67; Wilhelm, *Dschuang Dsi,* 165.
20. *Chuang-tzu,* 7.26a; Legge, *The Writings of Kwang-zze,* II, 66; Wilhelm, *Dschuang Dsi,* 164.

> To mix forever with the elements,
> To be a brother to the insensible rock
> And to the sluggish clod, which the rude swain
> Turns with his share, and treads upon. The oak
> Shall send his roots abroad, and pierce thy mould.

And the conclusion:

> So live, that when thy summons comes to join
> The innumerable caravan, which moves
> To that mysterious realm, where each shall take
> His chamber in the silent halls of death,
> Thou go not, like the quarry-slave at night,
> Scourged to his dungeon, but, sustained and soothed
> By an unfaltering trust, approach thy grave,
> Like one who wraps the drapery of his couch
> About him, and lies down to pleasant dreams.[21]

Noble words, and brave. But they are brave because death remains, in spite of everything, a prospect in the face of which bravery is needed. The best that we are offered is eternal sleep, with the dubious prospect of "pleasant dreams." To the author of "Thanatopsis" it is clearly a melancholy fate that, after having attained to humanity, one must become "a brother to the insensible rock, and to the sluggish clod."

Not so the Taoist. "When there is an end," the *Chuang-tzu* tells us, "there is also a beginning" (see n. 6, above). Regarding death there seems to be a human tendency to go to one of two extremes: either what happens to the body is said to be of no importance whatever, or attention may be centered upon the rather unpleasant process of its immediate dissolution. But if man's life is short, the time required for the decay of his flesh is shorter. What then? If "the oak shall send his roots abroad," and pierce the mould of what was once a man, that same mould becomes a part of the oak. And why merely an oak? One of the most memorable passages in the *Chuang-tzu*, as translated by Fung Yu-lan, says:

> The universe carries us in our bodies, toils us through our life, gives us repose with our old age, and rests us in our death. That which makes our life a good makes our death a good also.... No matter how well you hide things, smaller ones in larger ones, there is always [a] chance for them to be lost. But if you hide the universe in the universe, there will be no room for it to be lost. This is a great truth.

21. Quoted from Tremaine McDowell, *William Cullen Bryant* (New York, 1935), 3–5.

To have attained to the human form is a source of joy. But, in the infinite evolution, there are thousands of other forms that are equally good. What an incomparable bliss it is to undergo these countless transitions![22]

夫大塊載我以形勞我以生佚我以老息我以死故善吾生者乃所以善吾死也 . . . 藏小大有宜猶有所遯若夫藏天下於天下而不得所遯是恆物之大情也特犯人之形而猶喜之若人之形者萬化而未始有極也其為樂可勝計邪

The expression with which this passage begins, which Fung renders as "the universe," is *ta k'uai* 大塊. James Legge translates it as "the great Mass (of nature)," Léon Wieger as "la grande masse (du cosmos, de la nature, du tout)," and Richard Wilhelm as "das grosse All."[23] Herbert A. Giles renders it as "nature," James R. Ware as "God (The Mass of Greatness)," and Evan Morgan as "Heaven."[24] Literally it means "the Great Clod."[25]

The expression *ta k'uai* occurs several times in the *Chuang-tzu*, and from the way in which it is used it seems clearly to be a synonym for *Tao*.[26] While the renderings of translators, and the explanations of some commentators, tend to suggest this, none that I know of says explicitly that *ta k'uai* is used as a designation for the *Tao*.[27] This is perhaps scarcely remarkable.

---

22. *Chuang-tzu*, 3.4b–5b; Fung, *Chuang Tzŭ*, 116–117.

23. Legge, *The Writings of Kwang-zze*, I, 242; Léon Wieger, trans., *Les Pères du système taoïste: Lao-tzeu, Lie-tzeu, Tchoang-tzeu* (Paris, 1950), 253; Wilhelm, *Dschuang Dsi*, 48.

24. Giles, *Chuang Tzŭ*, 75; Ware, *The Sayings of Chuang Chou*, 48; Evan Morgan, *Tao, The Great Luminant: Essays from Huai Nan Tzŭ* (Shanghai, 1933), 33. In the latter work, the expression *ta k'uai* occurs in the quotation of this same passage, with minor textual variations; see *Huai-nan-tzu* (SPPY ed.), 2.2a.

25. That *k'uai* early had the sense of "a clod of earth" is clear from a passage in the *Tso-chuan*; see James Legge, trans., *The Chinese Classics*, V: *The Ch'un Ts'ew [Ch'un-ch'iu], with the Tso Chuen* (London, 1872), 184 (text), 186 (translation). This is part of the story of the wanderings of Chung-er, the future Duke Wen of Chin. Legge translates: "Travelling through Wei, Duke Wăn treated him discourteously; and as he was leaving it by Woo-luh, he was reduced to beg food of a countryman, who gave him a clod of earth [*k'uai*]. The prince was angry, and wished to scourge him with his whip, but Tsze-fan [Hoo Yen] said, 'It is Heaven's gift [a gift of the soil; a happy omen].' On this he bowed his head to the earth, received the clod, and took it with him in his carriage."

26. *Chuang-tzu*, 1.10b, 3.4b–5a, 3.9b; Legge, *The Writings of Kwang-zze*, I, 177, 242, 249; Wilhelm, *Dschuang Dsi*, 11, 48; Fung, *Chuang Tzŭ*, 43, 116, 122. I believe that there are three more instances of this expression in the *Chuang-tzu* but with *k'uai* changed to another character; see the following note.

27. For the opinions of various commentators on the meaning of this expression see Liu Wen-tien, *Chuang-tzu Pu-cheng* (Shanghai, 1947), 1B.2b. The explanation that *ta k'uai* means "Earth" is clearly not adequate to the contexts; most of the others could be taken as equating it with *Tao*, though none says so definitely.

Of all the many terms that have been used to designate the sum total of reality, "the Great Clod" is perhaps the most surprising. At first sight it seems so incongruous that one supposes that of course the characters cannot mean what they seem to, so that some go so far as to interpret them as "God" or "Heaven." I believe, nevertheless, that these characters mean exactly what they say, and that if we do not understand them in their literal sense we miss something that is very important indeed.

We find the term *k'uai*, "clod," elsewhere in the *Chuang-tzu*. One passage appears to quote Shen Tao as saying, "A clod of earth (*k'uai*) does not err with regard to the *Tao*."[28] "夫塊不失道." Another relates the manner in which Lieh-tzu attained to Taoist enlightenment. "He had nothing to do with what went on in the world. He discarded everything artificial and reverted to primitivity. Like a clod (*k'uai*) he stood alone, self-contained amid the confusion of the world, holding fast to the One to the end."[29]

If an early Taoist could have read "Thanatopsis," one can well imagine that he would have demurred at the reference to "the sluggish clod." Is not the earth composed of clods, and are they not the ultimate source from which comes life, both vegetable and animal? Sluggish, indeed! It is the very quicksilver stuff of which all things are made. What is the *Tao* itself but a clod of unimaginable proportions?

By choosing this striking name for the universe, the Taoists threw into strong relief their view of the nature of reality—a conception that stands in sharp contrast to the Platonic view. For Plato, true reality does not lie

---

I strongly suspect that *ta k'uai* in an altered form also occurs three times in *Chuang-tzu*, 8.13b. Here the expression is *ta wei* 大隗. The alteration of the character would involve changing the *t'u* 土, which means "earth," of *k'uai*, to the *fou* 阜, meaning "earthen mound," of *wei*. The T'ang dynasty commentator Ch'eng Hsüan-ying explained *ta wei* as an epithet of "the great *Tao*," and Lu Te-ming of the same dynasty gave "great *Tao*" as one of the meanings assigned to it (Liu, *Chuang-tzu Pu-cheng*, 8B.6b). Some translators have considered *ta wei* to be the name of an individual, but several interpret it as standing for *Tao*. Legge (*The Writings of Kwang-zze*, II, 96, n. 1) transliterates the characters as "Tâ-kwei" and writes: "The whole paragraph is parabolic or allegorical; and Tâ-kwei is probably a personification of the Great Tâo itself, though no meaning of the character kwei can be adduced to justify this interpretation." Giles, *Chuang Tzŭ*, 316, simply translates *ta wei* as "Tao." Wilhelm, *Dschuang Dsi*, 242, n. 5, says that it is an "allegorische Bezeichnung für den SINN"; SINN is Wilhelm's standard translation for *Tao*. This whole problem can best be resolved, I believe, by the hypothesis that *ta wei* is an altered form of *ta k'uai*.

28. *Chuang-tzu*, 10.18a; Legge, *The Writings of Kwang-zze*, II, 225. I do not agree with Legge's translation of this passage.

29. *Chuang-tzu*, 3.19a; Fung, *Chuang Tzŭ*, 140–141; Legge, *The Writings of Kwang-zze*, I, 265–266.

in the world of things—of clods. This is very clear in *The Republic,* when he describes the proper way to study astronomy:

> And will not a true astronomer . . . think that heaven and the things in heaven are framed by the Creator of them in the most perfect manner? But he will never imagine that the proportions of night and day, or of both to the month, or of the month to the year, or of the stars to these and to one another, and any other things that are material and visible can also be eternal and subject to no deviation—that would be absurd; and it is equally absurd to take so much pains in investigating their exact truth.
>
> I quite agree, though I never thought of this before.
>
> Then, I said, in astronomy, as in geometry, we should employ problems, and let the heavens alone if we would approach the subject in the right way and so make the natural gift of reason to be of any real use.[30]

This is one view of reality, a view that has held sway over a large part of mankind. It holds that the apparent, gross, visible, tangible things of the world are inferior if not contemptible. However beautiful the cup of a flower may seem, it is only an inadequate attempt to imitate a perfect circle. This attitude harmonizes with the view that "beyond this vale of tears, there is a life above," in which the flaws and limitations of this imperfect world will be transcended. It forbids acceptance of nature, and enjoins the struggle against nature. It brands contentment as sin, and lays upon men the never-ending obligation to *know,* to scorn mere opinion, to seek at the center of the universe that final solution to all mysteries that must be there if we could only find it.

The Taoist view is very different. If one could win through to the very center of the universe, and enter the holy of holies, he would find there only a simple clod: utterly simple, because it is essentially like the clod that lies here at my feet; and utterly mysterious because, like everything else, it can never be understood in an absolute sense at all. Nothing can be understood absolutely. Man's mind is not a machine constructed for the purpose of understanding everything; neither is it a bit of the special essence of the universe implanted by special grace in human beings. What we call man's mind is rather a complex of functions, akin to the complex we call "man's digestion." All digestion is good, because insofar as there is digestion at all it solves a human problem. Some digestion is better than other digestion, but there is no perfect digestion and no

30. Plato, *The Republic* [Stephanus 530]; Jowett, I, 789–790.

absolute standard by which to measure it. Similarly, all thought is good insofar as it solves a human problem. Some thought may be better than other thought, but there is no perfect thought and no standard of absolute truth. Thus the opinion of every man is worthy of consideration, and no one is entitled to suppose that his own view must be accepted without question.

This curious Taoist term for the universe has naturally caught the fancy of poets, and been much used by them.[31] A similar attitude is perhaps found in the West most often among poets, who more than the rest of us find excitement in the seemingly trivial, and scorn the pompous. But in China something of this attitude has been found in all who have been touched by Taoism.

Let others be awed by the lofty remoteness of absolute knowledge, and spend their lives in pursuit of it like quixotic knights seeking the Grail; the Taoist does not believe in it. Let others honor the universe by endowing it with human qualities, calling it "infinite mind" or "absolute reason." The Taoist, with an apparent simplicity that is wholly deceptive, with the approach to the ridiculous that always characterizes the sublime, calls it The Great Clod.

31. See quotations from T'ao Ch'ien, Li Po, Po Chu-i, and others in *P'ei-wen Yün-fu* (1711), 70.169a. In the works of Li Po, my colleague Professor T. H. Tsien has kindly furnished me with the following references: *Fen-lei Pu-chu Li T'ai-po Shih* 分類補注李太白詩 (*SPTK* ed.), 3.32a, 11.26a, 15.11a, 28.9a.

3

On Two Aspects in Early Taoism

The Taoists are well known to be fond of paradoxes, but the greatest paradox to be found in their doctrines was probably unintentional. It is well known to every student of Taoism.

A great deal of Taoist doctrine advocates complete liberty of action for the individual, and decries all governmental restraints. "I have heard of letting the world alone," the *Chuang Tzŭ* says, "but not of governing the world."[1] The libertarian tendency of Taoism has been so persistent that only a few years ago Ch'ên Tu-hsiu, then head of the Chinese Communist Party, complained that the anarchistic influence of the Taoist tradition made it difficult to recruit young Chinese to Communism.[2]

Expressions of quite another tenor, however, can also be found in early Taoist works. The same book of the *Chuang Tzŭ* that was quoted above later says, "Although the law is harsh, it is impossible to dispense with setting it forth."[3] And the *Lao Tzŭ* tells us that "the sage, in governing, empties the people's minds and fills their bellies, weakens their wills and strengthens their bones."[4] Taoism became so much identified with the art of government that the *I Wên Chih* of the *Han Shu* described Taoism as "the method by which a ruler governs."[5] Various Legalist philosophers

Reprinted with permission from the *Silver Jubilee Volume of the Zinbun-Kagaku-Kenkyusyo, Kyoto University,* 1954, pp. 43–53.
1. *The Writings of Kwang-zze,* trans. James Legge, "Sacred Books of the East," XXXIX, 125–392, and XL, 1–232 (1891; reprinted London, 1927), I, 291. Hereafter references to this work will be given under the title *Chuang Tzŭ,* I and II. My translations, however, will often differ considerably from those of Legge.
2. Benjamin I. Schwartz, *Chinese Communism and the Rise of Mao* (Cambridge, Mass., 1951), 33.
3. *Chuang Tzŭ,* I, 305.
4. *Lao Tzŭ,* chap. 3.
5. Pan Ku, *Ch'ien Han Shu* (Chin Ling Shu Chü ed., 1869), 30.16a.

took Taoism as the metaphysical background against which to construct their system of complete totalitarian despotism.

Many students of Taoism attribute this paradox to the differing tendencies, or emphases, of different individuals or schools within Taoism. It is the thesis of this paper, however, that we have to deal here with something more than just two phases of the same doctrine. It would appear, in fact, that there were two quite different aspects within early Taoist thought. And of these the second, or "purposive," aspect, was in some respects a contradiction of the very essence of the first, or "contemplative," aspect.

The Taoist texts with which this paper will principally deal are the *Lao Tzŭ* and the *Chuang Tzŭ*. Reference will be made only to the books, and not to men called by these names. This has nothing to do with the question of when, or whether, a man by the name of Lao Tzŭ ever lived. I frankly do not know, and for the present purpose this is not vitally important. Many scholars have long since agreed that the *Chuang Tzŭ* is a compilation of Taoist documents from various hands,[6] and the same is probably true of the *Lao Tzŭ*. Takeuchi Yoshio has pointed out many differences of style, usage, and ideology in various parts of the work,[7] and Fung Yu-lan, while not going as far, has stated that the *Lao Tzŭ* as we have it "cannot really be said to be the work of one man."[8] Ku Chieh-kang has expressed the opinion that the *Lao Tzŭ* is composed of materials that were written over a period of three centuries.[9]

It is generally agreed that the doctrines of Yang Chu are somehow related to Taoism, though scholars differ widely as to what the relationship was. It is very difficult to know what his doctrines were, since our knowledge comes almost entirely from a few very brief statements about them in early works. Chapter seven of the *Lieh Tzŭ* is entitled *Yang Chu,* and Maspero considered this to be "a fragment of his works."[10] Other scholars such as Fung Yu-lan believe, however, that this chapter was

6. See Chiang Chia-an 江俠庵, ed., *Hsien Ch'in Ching Chi K'ao* 先秦經籍考 (Shanghai, 1933), II, 306; Henri Maspero, *La Chine antique* (Paris, 1927), 489–490; Fung Yu-lan, *A Short History of Chinese Philosophy* (New York, 1948), 104. Arthur Waley says the *Chuang Tzŭ* may "contain teachings of several different schools"; *The Way and Its Power* (1934; reprinted London, 1949), 46.

7. Unfortunately I do not have available the original work, Takeuchi Yoshio 武內義雄, *Rōshi Genshi* 老子原始 and must therefore refer to a Chinese translation; see Chiang Chia-an, *Hsien Ch'in Ching Chi K'ao*, II, 273–308.

8. Fung Yu-lan, *A History of Chinese Philosophy,* trans. Derk Bodde (Princeton, 1952 and 1953), I, 172.

9. Lo Kên-tsê 羅根澤, ed., *Ku Shih Pien* 古史辨, IV (Peiping, 1933), 516.

10. Maspero, *La Chine antique,* 508.

written much later, and does not properly represent the ideas of Yang Chu.[11]

All students seem to be agreed that Yang Chu was an individualist who felt that life as it is ordinarily lived is not worthwhile, and that he therefore advocated and practiced withdrawal from the usual pursuits of men. Maspero wrote that his system was "a pessimistic fatalism pushed to the extreme, which considered life as one evil and death as another, both of which should be borne with indifference, since they have been allotted to us by destiny . . ." Perhaps this goes a little farther than our sure evidence will warrant, but there seems no doubt that Maspero was right when he said that the thought of Yang Chu lacked the quality of mystical joy that characterizes Taoist thought in general.[12]

Examples of pessimism similar to that attributed by the *Lieh Tzŭ* to Yang Chu can be found in the *Chuang Tzu*. We read: "To labor away one's whole lifetime, but never see the result, and be utterly worn out with toil and have no idea where it is leading—is this not lamentable? Men may say, 'It is not death,' but what good does that do? When the body decomposes, the mind goes with it—is this not deplorable?"[13]

Such passages are not common in Taoist literature, however. The dominant note is quite different. Maspero insisted that the belief in and the search for immortality were central from the very beginning. The prevalent idea that this search was a symptom of the degeneration of Taoism, from its original philosophic purity, was dismissed by Maspero as "superficial."[14]

He wrote:

From the fourth and third centuries B. C. the Taoists were seekers of immortality; from its origin, Taoism has been a doctrine of individual salvation which claimed to conduct the adept to immortality. . . . The methods must have varied: each master had his own, which he kept secret and transmitted only to certain chosen disciples; from this time on we see practiced most of those which were to be current at the time of the Six Dynasties and T'ang.[15]

Maspero argues his case eloquently, and with a great deal of citation of evidence. But the difficulty is that even if what is said in these passages

11. Fung Yu-lan, *A History of Chinese Philosophy*, I, 133.
12. Maspero, *La Chine antique*, 514–515.
13. *Chuang Tzŭ*, I, 180.
14. Henri Maspero, *Le Taoïsme* (Paris, 1950), 201–202.
15. Ibid., 205.

he quotes from the *Chuang Tzŭ* and the *Lao Tzŭ* is properly understood (and this is not always easy), one still has no way of being certain when these particular statements were made, or by whom.

Despite his insistence upon the importance of the search for immortality, Maspero himself points the way to another interpretation. Basically, he demonstrates, the early Taoists were mystics, intent like all mystics upon union with the Absolute, which in their case was called the *Tao*. And for them, Maspero says, "basically, immortality was only a secondary consequence of the mystic union. For the Taoists, as for the mystics of all religions, the mystic experience, because of its acute and vivid character and the impression of transcendent reality which it produces, is all that counts; the rest is only interpretation. They simply interpreted their experience in Taoist terms, that is to say, in the terms of a religion devoted to the search for immortality."[16]

To say this is to assume, however, that before there was the mystic experience there was a Taoist "religion devoted to the search for immortality," as a result of which the former was interpreted in terms of the latter. This leaves us, as Maspero would apparently wish, with the impression that Taoism originated as, and sprang from, the quest for immortality. This seems most improbable.

It is hard to see how the simple quest for personal—and even bodily—survival, which led to an increasing welter of magical and alchemical procedures often practiced by charlatans, could have been the efficient cause of the magnificent cosmic philosophy we know as Taoism. On the other hand, it is quite easy to understand how the mystical imagery of the greatest Taoist philosophers, dimly comprehended by lesser minds and combined with current superstitions, might eventuate in practices designed to banish the fear of death—a fear of which the great Taoists were utterly contemptuous.

There are two celebrated passages in the *Chuang Tzŭ* which make light of death. At the end of the third book we read:

> When Lao Tan died Ch'in Shih, having gone to condole, uttered three cries and then went out. A disciple asked, "Were you not the Master's friend?" "I was," Ch'in Shih replied. "Then is it fitting that you should do no more than this in condoling?" "It is," Ch'in Shih told the disciple. "At first I thought he was the man of men, but now I know differently. When I went in just now to condole, there were elders wailing as if for their own sons, and young men weeping as if

16. Ibid., 211.

for their mothers. Thus he must have, in gaining their adherence to himself, done that which caused them involuntarily to speak and wail as they were doing. This was to flee from nature, to exaggerate human emotion, and to forget that which was in accord with his circumstances. Anciently this was called 'the punishment of fleeing from nature.' The Master came into the world when it was time for him to be born. When he died, it was the natural sequence of events. He who accepts with tranquillity all things that happen in the fullness of their time, and abides in peace with the natural sequence of events, is beyond the reach of either sorrow or joy."[17]

After his wife had died, Chuang Tzŭ was reproached for beating on a bowl and singing. But he replied:

> When she had just died, even I could not remain unaffected. But then I reflected that in the beginning she had been without life. In fact, she had not only lacked life, she had no form. Indeed, she had not only lacked form but also lacked breath. In the mingling of the waste and chaos, with one change there came breath, with another form, and with yet another life. Now with still another change she goes in death. This is like the movement of the four seasons, from spring to autumn, from winter to summer. Now, when she lies sleeping in the great dwelling, if I were to start bawling and bewailing her, I would merely show that I did not understand destiny.[18]

These do not sound in the least like pronouncements of a "religion devoted to the search for immortality." Their authors would, one feels sure, have felt only pity for deluded mortals who busied themselves with the manifold petty procedures for nursing the human frame into enduring a few—or a thousand—more years, which Maspero quotes from the *Chuang Tzŭ*. This is not to say that Maspero is mistaken in finding these procedures there (though there are problems of interpretation in connection with some passages), but only that the *Chuang Tzŭ* is by no means a homogeneous work. And the search for immortality was not, in my opinion, the central theme or even any theme at all of the great philosophers who were the fathers of Taoism.

What was their central theme?

It was a mad intoxication with the wonder and the power of Nature. "Do the heavens revolve?" the *Chuang Tzŭ* asks. "Does the earth stand

17. *Chuang Tzŭ*, I, 201.
18. Ibid., II, 4–5.

still? Do the sun and the moon contend for their positions? Who directs these things? . . . Do the clouds make rain? Or does the rain make the clouds? . . . Who is it that has the leisure to devote himself, with such abandoned glee, to making these things happen? . . . The winds rise in the north. One blows east, another west, others whirl upwards erratically. Who does this mighty puffing? Who is it that has the leisure to toss things about in this way?"[19]

These great Taoists were so thrilled by the fact that they were inalienably a part of this mighty cosmos that the incident of personal death seemed quite insignificant. As the *Chuang Tzŭ* says: "The universe is the unity of all things. If one once recognizes his identity with this unity, then the parts of his body mean no more to him than so much dirt, and death and life, end and beginning, disturb his tranquillity no more than the succession of day and night."[20] Elsewhere the *Chuang Tzŭ* states: "When life comes, it is because it is time for it to do so. When life goes, this is the natural sequence of events. To accept with tranquillity all things that happen in the fullness of their time, and to abide in peace with the natural sequence of events, is to be beyond the reach of either sorrow or joy. This is the state of those whom the ancients called 'released from bondage.'"[21] The *Lao Tzŭ* tells us that true longevity consists in the realization that "when one dies, he is not lost" from the universe.[22]

For the great Taoist philosophers, then, the death of the individual was simply of no importance at all. It was an integral part of the vast cosmic process, which they delighted to contemplate. The *Chuang Tzŭ* says:

> The Great Mass [the Tao] gives me the support of my bodily form, my toil in life, my ease in old age, my rest in death. Thus what makes my life good also makes my death good. You may hide away a boat in the ravine of a hill, and hide the hill in the midst of a lake, and call it safe; nevertheless, in the middle of the night a strong man may carry it away without your knowledge. No matter in how suitable a place things, whether small or large, may be concealed, there is still the danger of loss. But if you hide the whole universe in the whole universe, there is no place left for it to go. This is the great truth of the Enduring Thing.

19. Ibid., I, 345.
20. Ibid., II, 48.
21. Ibid., I, 248. This passage repeats some of the language of the passage referred to in note 17, above.
22. *Lao Tzŭ*, chap. 33.

We rejoice at merely attaining the human form, but there are ten thousand other transformations that are equally good, and these still do not exhaust the possibilities. How can one calculate the joys [which this promises]? Therefore the sage man roams with light heart through the universe, in which nothing can ever be lost because all is preserved. And he finds early death good, old age good, his beginning good, and his end good.[23]

This is, as Maspero has so well demonstrated, a mystical doctrine.[24] It is a pantheistic mysticism. Like other mystics, the great Taoists found their satisfaction in the mystical experience itself; they felt no need of the activities, and the rewards, sought by ordinary men. Thus we are informed that when Chuang Tzǔ was invited to become prime minister of Ch'u he declined with a smile.[25] In the *Chuang Tzǔ* we read that after Lieh Tzu was enlightened he "went home and for three years did not go out. . . . He took no interest in what went on. . . . He stood like a clod, sealed up within himself despite all distractions, and continued thus to the end of his life."[26]

The order of nature, in this Taoist view, is so beautifully regulated that there is no need for man to do anything, and indeed if he does do anything he is likely only to interfere with it. Thus the *Chuang Tzǔ* states, "The perfect man does nothing, and the great sage originates nothing; that is to say, they merely contemplate the universe."[27]

This is the first aspect of early Taoism that I wish to distinguish. I have proposed calling it the "contemplative" aspect.

This contemplative Taoism is mystical, and it is a mysticism of a rarefied philosophical order. True mystics are seldom very numerous, and it was hardly to be expected that there would be found, in late Chou China, a very large number of men capable of understanding or practicing a rarefied philosophical mysticism.

Yet while few could appreciate the essence of Taoist philosophy, there was much about Taoism that could not fail to attract men of the Chan Kuo period. The Taoist mystic, intoxicated with the vastness of the cosmos and identifying himself with it, felt himself to be infused with all the power of the universe itself. And while others might not be prepared to accept this opinion at face value, there is no doubt that the

23. *Chuang Tzǔ*, I, 242–243.
24. Maspero, *Le Taoïsme*, 227–242.
25. *Chuang Tzǔ*, I, 390.
26. Ibid., I, 265–266.
27. Ibid., II, 60–61.

Taoist withdrawal from ordinary life, and the practice of meditation and exercises resembling those of the Indian yogi,[28] had two very practical values. On the one hand they gave to the Taoist a calm and poise that contrasted sharply with the hurly-burly of the times. And they set the Taoist apart as a man reputedly endowed with power, a man unique, and a man who did not want to take any part in the government.

These qualities would inevitably have caused rulers of states in the Chan Kuo world to want to get the Taoists into their service. One may doubt the story that the ruler of Ch'u asked Chuang Tzǔ to become his prime minister,[29] but it is improbable that all of the stories of this character, in the Taoist literature, are completely false. Yet it is rarely if ever, in the Chuang Tzǔ or the Lao Tzǔ, that a specifically named Taoist consents to take part in government. They prefer to continue their contemplation of the universe.

We know, however, that in Chan Kuo China any doctrine that could make its adherents sought after was sure to attract adherents. But the adherents who would be attracted to Taoism for this reason would not be Taoists of the pure mystical type, desirous only of contemplating the universe and achieving inner peace, but men whose ultimate purpose was to *exercise* the power that Taoist practices were supposed to confer.

It is undoubtedly to such Taoists that we owe the many statements in the Lao Tzǔ and the Chuang Tzǔ to the effect that "he who wishes to be above the people must speak as though he were below them," stating that the Tao "outwardly forms the king," and relating the manner in which the Taoist sage practices government.[30] In the most extreme form of these statements we find the Lao Tzǔ declaring that the sage, in governing, "empties the people's minds and fills their bellies, weakens their wills and strengthens their bones,"[31] while the Chuang Tzǔ tells us that "the true men of old . . . considering punishments to be the substance of government, were liberal in their infliction of the death penalty."[32]

This is far from the first, or "contemplative," aspect of Taoism. I have proposed calling it the "purposive" aspect. It would appear to have arisen from the attempt to utilize an essentially mystical doctrine for

28. This is not to say that the Taoists either were, or were not, subject to influence from India. This subject requires and deserves much more study.
29. Chuang Tzǔ, I., 390.
30. See for example Lao Tzǔ, chap. 66, and Chuang Tzǔ, II, 214 and 217.
31. Lao Tzǔ, chap. 3.
32. Chuang Tzǔ, I, 240. The word "liberal" in my translation is ambiguous, but this stems from what seems an irreducible ambiguity in the text.

the furtherment of personal ambitions and political purposes. Waley seems to suggest something of the sort when he writes: "What strikes us at first sight as inconsistent with Quietism [under which term Waley includes Taoism] is the idea of founding an empire at all. By the middle of the third century, however, it had been generally recognized that the peace for which everyone longed could only come through the unification of China under one strong state."[33]

"Contemplative" Taoism and "purposive" Taoism are not merely different. Logically and essentially they are incompatible. For the calm and poise and inner power that come from complete detachment from human affairs are necessarily lost the moment one seeks to intervene in human affairs. "It is just because the sage does not contend," the *Lao Tzŭ* tells us, "that no one in the world can contend with him."[34] But such detachment cannot be maintained when one, as the *Lao Tzŭ* says, "wishes to be above the people"[35] and "weakens their wills and strengthens their bones,"[36] nor when, as the *Chuang Tzŭ* tells of "the true men of old," one is "liberal in the infliction of the death penalty."[37] The Taoist works are ingenious in informing us that these activities are not in fact meddling with things, but only designed to return the people to their natural state, but this does not really alter the case.

Less obviously yet quite as certainly, the search for personal immortality, which Maspero believed to have been a part of Taoism from its beginning, is a part of the "purposive" aspect and flatly contradicts the "contemplative" position. A number of passages from the *Chuang Tzŭ*, some of which were quoted above, emphasize the folly of placing any value on the individual as distinguished from the universe, and the ridiculous futility of regarding death as an evil and trying to forestall it. Yet the quest for immortality, which also figures repeatedly in the *Chuang Tzŭ*, implies that death is the greatest of evils, and requires that the individual shall dedicate his every effort to its circumvention.

It is seldom, however, that men are wholly governed by logic. And the fact that two views are logically incompatible seldom prevents people from holding them simultaneously. It is for this reason, I believe, that we find "contemplative" Taoism and "purposive" Taoism lying cheek by jowl, and sometimes scrambled in a grand mixture, in the *Lao Tzŭ*

33. Waley, *The Way and Its Power*, 93.
34. *Lao Tzŭ*, chap. 22.
35. Ibid., chap. 66.
36. Ibid., chap. 3.
37. *Chuang Tzŭ*, I, 240.

and the *Chuang Tzŭ*. At one extreme there were undoubtedly some "pure" contemplative Taoists, and at the other some "pure" purposive Taoists (some of the latter were Legalists in embryo). But in between there were the many Taoists who were sometimes one, sometimes the other, and usually a mixture of both. And they gave its general character to early Taoism.

To all this it might be objected that what I have done is simply to select fragments arbitrarily from the *Lao Tzŭ* and the *Chuang Tzŭ*, and rearrange them into two arbitrary patterns. Furthermore, it might be pointed out, I speak of the contemplative as the first, and the purposive as the second, aspect of early Taoism, yet I have given no evidence that the one preceded the other chronologically.

If these objections were made, I should have to admit that they seemed to have some justification. As for the two aspects of Taoism that I have distinguished, I can only say that to me they seem logical and reasonable, rather than merely arbitrary. As to the sequence of development of the two aspects, it seems to me that if one grants that the two did exist, it then follows logically, for reasons I have already stated, that the "contemplative" must have preceded the "purposive," rather than the reverse.

As to the chronology of this development, there may be some evidence. For while both aspects are present in both the *Lao Tzŭ* and the *Chuang Tzŭ*, the *Chuang Tzŭ* seems to show primarily the contemplative aspect, while the *Lao Tzŭ* is dominantly purposive. Fung Yu-lan has observed that "the philosophy of the *Lao-tzŭ* . . . is concerned with how one should respond to the world," while "that of Chuang Tzŭ . . . rises to a plane above human affairs."[38] This would seem to have some correspondence to my purposive and contemplative aspects, respectively. Similarly Arthur Waley has stated that the *Lao Tzŭ* "is a description of how the Sage (*shêng*) through the practice of Tao acquires the power of ruling without being known to rule," while in the *Chuang Tzŭ* "Taoism is in certain passages treated as a way of life for individual adepts."[39]

This might seem to demolish my argument, since my hypothetically first aspect is predominantly in the *Chuang Tzŭ* and the second aspect chiefly in the *Lao Tzŭ*, which reverses the traditional belief as to the chronological order of these books. Of course if, as I like a number of other scholars believe, both the *Lao Tzŭ* and the *Chuang Tzŭ* are

38. Fung Yu-lan, *A History of Chinese Philosophy*, I, 175.
39. Waley, *The Way and Its Power*, 92.

anthologies of Taoist literature, the problem of dating them becomes enormously complex. However, there is a rather general tendency among scholars to regard the first seven chapters of the *Chuang Tzǔ* (the *Nei P'ien*) as being earlier than the rest of the book, and some regard them as the work of the man called Chuang Tzǔ.[40] In this first portion of the *Chuang Tzǔ* we find chiefly (though not quite unmixed) "contemplative" Taoism. A formidable number of scholars have gone on record as doubting the traditional sequence, and believing that the book of *Lao Tzǔ* was compiled at a date later than that of the man called Chuang Tzǔ; among these may be mentioned Takeuchi Yoshio, Ku Chieh-kang, Arthur Waley, and Fung Yu-lan.[41]

It is possible that these two aspects of Taoism are referred to in the Taoist works themselves. The final book of the *Chuang Tzǔ* includes a critique on the practices of various Taoists. Near its beginning it says: "Whence does the spiritual descend? From where does the intelligent come forth? There is that which gives birth to the sage, and that which forms the king—both have their origin in the One."[42] The opening chapter of the *Lao Tzǔ* says: "He that is constantly without desire can see the essence [of the Tao], while he that is constantly desiring sees its results. These two come from the same source, but are called by different names. Together, we call them the Mystery."

These passages may have something to do with the two aspects of Taoism that I have sought to distinguish, but I should not care to be insistent on this point. Dogmatic certainty is never appropriate when one is dealing with Taoism.

40. Chang Hsin-ch'êng 張心澂, ed., *Wei Shu T'ung K'ao* 僞書通考 (1939), 712–734.
41. Chiang Chia-an, *Hsien Ch'in Ching Chi K'ao*, II, 304–306; Lo Kên-tsê, *Ku Shih Pien*, IV, 518–519; Arthur Waley, *Three Ways of Thought in Ancient China* (London, 1939), 11, and *The Way and Its Power*, 86.
    This opinion of Fung Yu-lan's emerges clearly only if we compare four passages in his *Short History of Chinese Philosophy*: Pp. 93–94: "I now believe it [the *Lao Tzǔ*] was written or composed after Hui Shih and Kung-sun Lung, and not before. . . ." P. 83: "Hui Shih (fl. 350–260). . . ." P. 87: "Kung-sun Lung (fl. 284–259). . . ." P. 104: "Chuang Chou, better known as Chuang Tzǔ (c. 396–c. 286). . . ."
42. *Chuang Tzǔ*, II, 214.

4

On the Origin of *Wu-wei* 無爲

For two thousand years it has been supposed that the concept of *wu-wei* 無爲, as we find it in Taoist works, was essentially Taoist in origin, and that when we find *wu-wei* used similarly in works of the *Fa-chia* 法家 it has been borrowed from the Taoist context. This opinion was formed, however, when the *Lao-tzu* 老子 was supposed to have been written at least two centuries earlier than the date that is now assigned to it. The problem of the origin of *wu-wei* demands reexamination in the light of current scholarly opinion.

Few critical scholars still believe that, as tradition holds, the *Lao-tzu* was written by a contemporary of Confucius. Opinions as to its nature and authorship vary, but there is now a general tendency to date its composition in the third century B. C.[1] The other one of the early Taoist works, the

Reprinted with permission from *Symposium in Honor of Dr. Li Chi on his Seventieth Birthday* Pt. I (Taipei, Taiwan, China, 1965), 105–137. My colleague Professor T. H. Tsien has been of material assistance in connection with a number of problems involved in this paper. Its preparation has been greatly facilitated by two manuscript concordances prepared by my research assistant, Miss June Work. One is a concordance to the *Ssu-pu Pei-yao* 四部備要 edition of the *Lao-tzu* 老子. The other is a concordance to my reconstructed and collated text of fragments of the *Shen-tzu* 申子, the lost book attributed to Shen Pu-hai 申不害, together with my collection of quotations attributed to Shen Pu-hai in various books. Miss Work has also independently checked all concordances referred to in this paper, thus verifying the results of my own examination of them.

1. Ch'ien Mu 錢穆 believes that the most probable author of the *Lao-tzu* is Chan He 詹何, whose life he dates approximately between the years 350 and 270 B. C.; see Ch'ien, *Hsien-Ch'in Chu-tzu Hsi-nien* 先秦諸子繫年, rev. ed. (Hongkong, 1956), 223–226, 448–449, 619. Ku Chieh-kang 顧頡剛 deduced that the *Lao-tzu* was compiled during the latter half of the third century B. C. but not widely disseminated until the second century B. C.: see Ku, *Ts'ung Lü-shih Ch'un-ch'iu T'ui-tse Lao-tzu chih Ch'eng-shu Nien-tai* 從呂氏春秋推測老子之成書年代 in *Ku-shih Pien* 史古辨, IV (Peiping, 1933), 516–518. Fung Yu-lan 馮友蘭 has written, "I now believe that it [the *Lao-tzu*] was written or composed after Hui Shih and Kung-sun Lung," and he dates the latter as "fl. 284–259"; see Fung, *A Short History of Chinese Philosophy* (New York, 1948; reprint of 1953), 87, 93–94. J. J. L.

Chuang-tzu 莊子,[2] is commonly dated (as regards the earliest parts of this composite book) from the latter half of the fourth century B. C. or the beginning of the third, that is, from around 300 B. C.[3] This means that our earliest datable Taoist work is now moved down from around 500 B. C. to around 300 B. C. And this in turn requires that we reconsider some propositions that have long been taken for granted concerning the relationships between various schools of thought in ancient China.

The many similarities between Taoism and the doctrines of the *Fa-chia* (in English commonly, but in my opinion erroneously, called the "Legalist School")[4] have been noticed since Han times. Ssu-Ma Ch'ien 司馬遷, in his biographies of two of the most important members of the *Fa-chia*, Shen Pu-hai and Han Fei-tzu, said of both of them that their doctrines were "based on Huang Lao 黃老,"[5] presumably referring to the doctrines of

Duyvendak, *Tao Te Ching* (London, 1954), 7, puts its composition not earlier than "about 300 B. C." Arthur Waley, *The Way and Its Power* (London, 1934; reprint of 1949), 86, 127–128, said that it was produced "about 240 B. C." Henri Maspero considered the *Lao-tzu* to date "probably from the beginning or the middle of the fourth century [B. C.]"; Maspero, *Le Taoïsme* (Paris, 1950), 229—see also Henri Maspero, *La Chine antique*, rev. ed. (Paris, 1955), 402. Maspero was a great authority on the Taoism of Han and later periods, but in my opinion was less sound on pre-Han Taoism; see pp. 10–11.

2. A third book, the *Lieh-tzu* 列子, has long been held by a number of Western scholars to be a Taoist text of the third century B. C., while Chinese scholars have tended to date this work to a time as late as the third century A. D. In 1956 I published the evidence which led me to conclude that "this text, as we now have it, was produced early in the Christian Era, at a time when Buddhist philosophy and Taoist philosophy were influencing and enriching each other" (pp. 21–22). In 1961 A. C. Graham published a very searching study of this text, from which he concluded that a book called *Lieh-tzu* disappeared early, to be replaced by a forgery (incorporating some earlier materials) produced "not long after . . . [A. D.] 281": Graham, "The Date and Composition of Liehtzyy 列子," in *Asia Major*, new series, VIII (1961), 139–198. This admirable paper would seem to settle the matter.

3. Ch'ien Mu dates Chuang Chou 莊周 as having lived not earlier than 365 and not later than 290 B. C. (Ch'ien, *Hsien-Ch'in Chu-tzu Hsi-nien*, 618). Fung Yu-lan, *A Short History of Chinese Philosophy*, 104, gives his dates as "c. 369–c. 286" B. C. Arthur Waley says that the *Chuang-tzu* was "written mainly at the beginning . . . of the 3rd century B. C."; Waley, *Three Ways of Thought in Ancient China* (London, 1939; reprint of 1946), 11. Maspero, *La Chine antique*, 405, says that Chuang Chou lived during the second half of the fourth century.

4. In my opinion the *Fa-chia* was a combination of two schools. One of these, based on the doctrines of Shang Yang 商鞅, stressed rewards and punishments, and penal law, and may properly be called "Legalist." The other, stemming from the ideas of Shen Pu-hai, emphasized administrative methods and was not "Legalist" at all. They were combined, very imperfectly, by Han Fei-tzu 韓非子. I suspect that when Ssu-Ma T'an 司馬談 called this combined school the *Fa-chia*, he may have been making a deliberate pun, utilizing the fact that *fa* 法 means both "law" and "method." For a full exposition of this view see pp. 92–120.

5. Takigawa Kametaro 瀧川龜太郎, *Shih-chi Hui-chu K'ao-cheng* 史記會注考證 (Tokyo, 1932–1934) (referred to hereafter as *Shih-chi*), 63.13–14.

Huang Ti 黃帝 and Lao-tzu.[6] And modern scholars have, with something close to unanimity, regarded Taoist ideology as the basis upon which much of the doctrine of the *Fa-chia* was built. Thus Waley says of the *Fa-chia*: "It is not surprising that all surviving expositions,[7] despite their repudiation of abstract principles and ideals, do in fact seek a foundation in Taoist mysticism."[8] Fung Yu-lan says that "the Legalist school has been greatly influenced by the Taoists."[9] Duyvendak writes that "the ideas developed in the *Tao-tê-ching*" (including that of *wu-wei*) "were further elaborated in the School of Law."[10] I myself wrote, as recently as 1954, that "various Legalist philosophers took Taoism as the metaphysical background against which to construct their system of complete totalitarian despotism."[11] In a book published in 1963, Chin Chien-te 金建德 devotes six pages to an investigation of the statement of Ssu-Ma Ch'ien that the doctrines of Shen Pu-hai were "based on Huang Lao." He compares various statements about Shen's doctrines, and quotations attributed to him, with passages in the *Lao-tzu,* and concludes that "this observation by Ssu-Ma Ch'ien corresponds to the actual facts."[12]

If the proposition is stated in the broadest terms, it is certainly true that many *Fa-chia* scholars were influenced by Taoism. So, also, were many Confucian scholars. But it is evident that Confucianism, in its earliest form, could not have been based on Taoism, for the simple chronological reason that all our evidence indicates that Taoism as a recognizable philosophy did not exist until long after Confucianism was well established. And a similar chronological problem exists with regard to the *Fa-chia* and Taoism—a problem not nearly so clear and sharp, but nevertheless a problem.

The chronological difficulty is clearest when we examine the statement of the *Shih-chi* that the doctrines of Shen Pu-hai were based upon those

6. At a date that I have been unable to determine, the term Huang-lao Chün 黃老君 came to be used as the name of a single deity, in what I have called "Hsien Taoism." But two individuals seem clearly to be denoted here. See pp. 9–10, 18.

7. Except, he says in a note, that of the *Shang-chün Shu* 商君書; Waley, *The Way and Its Power,* 83.

8. Waley, *The Way and Its Power,* 83. Waley calls the *Fa-chia* "the Realists"; ibid., 68, n. 1.

9. Fung Yu-lan, *A History of Chinese Philosophy,* trans. Derk Bodde, I, 2d ed. (Princeton, 1952), 334.

10. Duyvendak, *Tao Te Ching,* 12.

11. See pp. 37–38. During the past decade I have given much study to the origins and nature of the *Fa-chia*; I no longer call it "Legalist," nor do I think that all *Fa-chia* adherents espoused "complete totalitarian despotism."

12. Chin Chien-te, *Ssu-Ma Ch'ien So-chien Shu K'ao* 司馬遷所見書考 (Shanghai, 1963), 241–246. I am indebted to Professor T. H. Tsien for bringing this work to my attention.

of Huang Ti, the "Yellow Emperor," and of Lao Tzu. Shen Pu-hai died in 337 B. C.[13] while, as I have pointed out elsewhere, Huang Ti was not even fully accepted as having been a Taoist, much less as a patriarch of Taoism, as late as 300 B. C.[14] And we have seen that almost all critical opinion dates the composition of the *Lao-tzu* from a time so late that it could not have provided the basis of the philosophy of Shen Pu-hai, who died in 337 B. C.[15]

This does not, of course, make it impossible that Taoist ideas, developing before they were written down in the *Chuang-tzu* and the *Lao-tzu*, could have influenced early *Fa-chia* thinkers including Shen Pu-hai. But it must be noted that while the earliest development of Taoist thought undoubtedly antedated the earliest Taoist books, *Fa-chia* thought had a very long history before Shen Pu-hai. The concepts of governmental organization and administrative technique with which the names of Shen Pu-hai and other *Fa-chia* thinkers are linked were clearly in the process of evolution as early as the seventh century B. C.[16]

There has long been an assumption, partly unconscious, that Taoist thought predated *Fa-chia* thought. Even scholars who did not make this assumption have tended (I myself certainly no less than others) to take it for granted that if identical or very similar ideas are found both in Taoist and in *Fa-chia* thought, the *Fa-chia* must have taken them over from Taoism. This can no longer, in the light of the present dating of our earliest Taoist works, be taken for granted. Neither, of course, can we reverse the formula and assume that such ideas must ipso facto have been borrowed by Taoism from the *Fa-chia*. In each case, we must make a careful examination of the evidence before passing judgment. This paper proposes to examine the evidence concerning the concept of *wu-wei*.

Wu-wei is clearly one of the central concepts of Taoism. In his essay on the philosophical schools, Ssu-Ma T'an has two passages on Taoism. The second begins: 道家無爲又曰無不爲其實易行其辭難知 "The Taoists [advocate] not acting, [but they] also say [that, by virtue of this non-action], nothing is left undone. The content [of these words] is easy to put into practice, but the words [themselves] are difficult to

13. *Shih-chi*, 15.72. While there is some problem about some aspects of the chronology of the life of Shen Pu-hai, 337 B. C. is insofar as I know universally accepted as the date of his death. See Ch'ien, *Hsien-Ch'in Chu-tzu Hsi-nien*, 202, 238.
14. Pp. 9–10, 18.
15. See note 1, page 48.
16. Pp. 121–159.

understand."[17] Fung Yu-lan remarks that "when it is said of the early Han Emperors . . . that they ruled through quiescence (*ching* 靜) and non-activity (*wu wei* 無爲), this simply means that they were following the tenets of Lao Tzu."[18] Duyvendak, in the introduction to his translation of the *Lao-tzu,* discusses *wu-wei* at length as one of its "principal ideas." The *Lao-tzu,* he writes, "always has exercised a great influence in China and its doctrine of *Wu-wei* has become a recognized principle of government. Above the imperial throne these two words were written on a beautiful lacquered tablet, as an eloquent testimony of the political ideal: to govern without active interference."[19]

Wu-wei is also a typically Taoist concept because the statements that are made about it are paradoxical. Both the *Lao-tzu* and the *Chuang-tzu* say: 無爲而無不爲 "By doing nothing there is nothing that is not done."[20] This is excellent rhetoric, but superficially it does not seem to agree with common sense. Common sense tells us that one who does nothing accomplishes nothing.

Since the concept of *wu-wei* is at first sight so strange, commentators and translators have made various attempts to explain it. Wang Pi 王弼 wrote: 自然已足爲則敗也 "The natural is sufficient. If one strives then he fails."[21] Duyvendak explains that "the Taoist Saint . . . keeps to the weak and lowly, and refrains from any conscious effort, any striving after a set purpose. In a sense therefore he may be said to have a purpose. His *Wu-wei* is practiced with a conscious design; he chooses this attitude in the conviction that only by so doing the 'natural' development of things will favour him."[22] Maspero says that the Taoist "Saint, in order to bring himself into conformity with the Tao, must practice Non-action, *wu-wei.* . . . To act is wrong, because this differentiates one from the Tao, which is immutable."[23] And Fung Yu-lan tells us that "*wu-wei* can be translated literally as 'having-no-activity' or 'non-action.' . . . According to the theory of 'having-no-activity', a man should restrict his activities to what is necessary and what is natural. 'Necessary' means necessary to the achievement of a certain purpose, and never over-doing. 'Natural' means following one's *Te* with no arbitrary effort."[24]

17. *Shih-chi,* 130.12.
18. Fung, *A History of Chinese Philosophy,* I, 175.
19. Duyvendak, *Tao Te Ching,* 9–14.
20. *Lao-tzu* 老子 (*Ssu-pu Pei-yao* ed.), *hsia,* 7b (chap. 48). *Chuang-tzu* 莊子 (*Ssu-Pu Pei-yao* ed.), 7.22b.
21. *Lao-tzu, shang.* 2a (chap. 2).
22. Duyvendak, *Tao Te Ching,* 10–11.
23. Maspero, *Le Taoïsme,* 238.
24. Fung, *A Short History of Chinese Philosophy,* 100–101.

None of this is very helpful, from the point of view of common sense. Wang Pi says that one should do only what is "natural," but how, exactly, can one distinguish "natural" from "unnatural" activity? Duyvendak explains that the Taoist Saint "refrains from any conscious effort," but that nevertheless "he may be said to have a purpose" so that "his *Wu-wei* is practiced with a conscious design." Maspero tells us that the Taoist Saint "must practice Non-action, *wu-wei*," because to act "differentiates one from the Tao, which is immutable." That the *tao*, the totality of all things, is essentially immutable is not hard to conceive. But individual things, including people, are, as the *Chuang-tzu* repeatedly insists, always undergoing transformation.[25] And even if it were possible for an individual to emulate the *tao* and avoid all change, it is anything but clear how such practice of "non-action" would cause "everything to be done."

Most baffling of all, perhaps, is Fung Yu-lan's explanation that "according to the theory of 'having-no-activity,' a man should restrict his activities to what is necessary and what is natural." This means, then, that some activities must be branded as "unnecessary" and "unnatural." Not only are the criteria for such judgments unclear; the very passing of such judgments is condemned in Taoist literature. This is indeed the subject of chapter 2 of the *Chuang-tzu*, called *Ch'i Wu-lun* 齊物論, which Fung Yu-lan translates as "The Equality of Things and Opinions." Here is a pertinent passage from that chapter, as Fung himself translates it:

> If men are to be guided by opinions, who will not have such a guide? Not only those who know the alternations of right and wrong and choose between them have opinions; the fools have theirs too. The case in which there are no opinions, while yet a distinction is made between right and wrong, is as inconceivable as that one goes to Yüeh (越) today, but arrived there yesterday. . . . How is *Tao* obscured that there should be a distinction between true and false? How is speech obscured that there should be a distinction between right and wrong?[26]

Yet if no distinction is made between right and wrong, and no opinion formed as to what is "necessary" and what "unnecessary," it is hard to see how anyone can practice *wu-wei* as Fung has described it.

Wu-wei as a Taoist concept has never been considered easy to comprehend. We have seen that two thousand years ago Ssu-Ma T'an, who

25. *Chuang-tzu*, 3.2a–5b; 7.13b–14b, 18ab, 24b–26a.
26. *Chuang-tzu*, 1.13b–14a. Fung Yu-lan, *Chuang Tzŭ: A New Selected Translation with an Exposition of the Philosophy of Kuo Hsiang* (Shanghai, 1933), 48.

was strongly inclined toward Taoism,[27] called it "hard to understand." Fung Yu-lan quotes the commentary on the *Chuang-tzu* attributed to Kuo Hsiang 郭象 (died c. A. D. 312) as saying: "Hearing the theory of non-action [*wu-wei*], some people think that lying down is better than walking. These people are far wrong in understanding the ideas of Chuang Tzu." Nevertheless, Fung adds, "despite this criticism, it would seem that in their understanding of Chuang Tzu such people were not far wrong."[28]

Another circumstance makes the concept of *wu-wei*, as it occurs in the *Lao-tzu* and the *Chuang-tzu*, still more baffling. We have seen that both Fung Yu-lan and Duyvendak consider *wu-wei*, as a principle of Chinese government, to be derived from the *Lao-tzu*.[29] Duyvendak also says that "the *Tao-tê-ching* addresses its message in the first place to the Saint as ruler. . . . The consequence of *Wu-wei* in ruling a State is the abstention from all government interference."[30] The last sentence of chapter 3 of the *Lao-tzu* reads: 為無為則無不治. Waley translates this, "Yet through his actionless activity all things are duly regulated," and in a note explains: "*Wu-wei*, 'non-activity,' i.e. rule through *tê* ('virtue,' 'power') acquired in trance."[31]

Examination of the texts of the *Lao-tzu* and the *Chuang-tzu* shows that *wu-wei* does indeed figure, in a considerable proportion of its occurrences, as a technique of government. In the *Lao-tzu*, there are twelve instances of *wu-wei*;[32] of these, at least six are clearly concerned with government.[33] In the *Chuang-tzu*, *wu-wei* occurs some fifty-six times.[34] In at least eighteen

27. This appears clearly in his essay on six philosophical schools, where he gives most space to the Taoists and speaks of them with much the greatest favor: *Shih-chi*, 130.7–14.
28. Fung, *A Short History of Chinese Philosophy*, 225. Fung thinks that this commentary incorporates the work not only of Kuo Hsiang, but also of Hsiang Hsiu 向秀: see ibid., 220.
29. Fung, *A History of Chinese Philosophy*, I, 175. Duyvendak, *Tao Te Ching*, 14.
30. Duyvendak, *Tao Te Ching*, 12.
31. Waley, *The Way and Its Power*, 145.
32. *Lao-tzu, shang.* 2a (chap. 2), 2b (chap. 3), 5b (chap. 10), 21a (chap. 37); *hsia.* 1a (chap. 38), 6a (chap. 43) (twice), 7b (chap. 48) (twice), 13a (chap. 57), 16b (chap. 63), 17b (chap. 64). This statement is based upon the manuscript concordance to the *Lao-tzu* prepared by Miss June Work.
33. *Lao-tzu, shang.* 2b (chap. 3), 5b (chap. 10), 21a (chap. 37); *hsia.* 7b (chap, 48) (twice), 13a (chap. 57).
34. I say "some" fifty-six times because complete accuracy is difficult in dealing with a text of this magnitude. Here I have depended upon *A Concordance to Chuang Tzu,* Harvard-Yenching Institute Sinological Index Series, Supplement No. 20 (Peiping, 1947). Under *wu-wei* 無為 it lists fifty-four passages (ibid., 212–213); I have examined each of these in the text. I have also examined each entry under *wu* 无 and *wu* 無 (ibid., 206–212, 532–533). There are eight cases in which the characters *wu wei* 无為 occur together

cases the context associates *wu-wei* with government.[35] Thus *wu-wei* is treated as a technique of government in fifty per cent of its occurrences in the *Lao-tzu,* and in thirty-two per cent of its occurrences in the *Chuangtzu.* (The higher percentage in the *Lao-tzu* is significant; we shall return to it.)

The Sage, in governing, the *Lao-tzu* tells us, "practices inaction (*wu-wei*), and as a consequence there is nothing that is not properly governed."[36] The *Chuang-tzu* says that "for the *chün-tzu* 君子 who cannot avoid governing the world, nothing is so good as doing nothing (*wu-wei*)."[37]

In terms of common sense, this advice may well seem absurd. No government, in any time or place, has been able to follow a policy of doing nothing for very long and stay in power. If this were possible, the last place in which it would have been possible was the China of the Chan-kuo period, in which Taoism developed. Beyond the borders of every state there were others eager to exploit any weakness and to invade if not annex its territory. Within the state, rivals were watchful for any opportunity to topple the ruler and seize his throne. To protect his state and himself, the ruler had to collect revenues, and the people of Chan-kuo China were no more ready to give up wealth to the state, without at least the tacit threat of force, than people have usually been to pay taxes elsewhere. If a Chan-kuo ruler were to maintain himself, many things had to be done, constantly. A policy of inaction, in any simple sense, would have been literally suicidal.

Shall we conclude, then, that those who wrote the *Lao-tzu* and the *Chuang-tzu* were stupid? This is impossible. The *Lao-tzu,* a collection of materials from many sources,[38] includes many splendid passages. The *Chuang-tzu* is in my estimation the finest philosophical work known to me, in any language. Its authors included some of the keenest minds that the world has known. Why, then, do many of its statements on *wu-wei* war with common sense? I do not think that we can take the way out that Waley offers, and say that *wu-wei* is "rule through *tê* ('virtue,' 'power')

---

fortuitously, but do not constitute the expression *wu-wei*: *Chuang-tzu,* 2.21a, 3.8a, 3.19a (four times), 9.23a (twice). There are also two cases of the expression which *A Concordance to Chuang Tzu* omits from its listings under *wu-wei*; those occur in ibid., 28 (line 54) and 56 (line 36), and in *Chuang-tzu,* 4.20b, 7.18b. There are also six occurrences of *wu wei wei* 無為謂, all in the same chapter; see *Chuang-tzu,* 7.22a–23a. It seems quite clear that this is one of the fanciful proper names that abound in the *Chuang-tzu,* and does not involve the expression *wu-wei.*

35. *Chuang-tzu,* 4.15b (twice), 4.16a, 4.22b, 5.1a, 5.1b, 5.12a (thrice), 5.12b (twice), 5.13b (six times), 5.14a.

36. *Lao-tzu, shang.* 2b (chap. 3).

37. *Chuang-tzu,* 4.15b.

38. See pp. 1–2, 5–6.

acquired in trance."[39] This would not, I think, have stopped the powerful armies or coped with the scheming courtiers of Chan-kuo China. Nor, I believe, would the authors of the *Chuang-tzu* have supposed it would.

Wu-wei, as we find it in the *Lao-tzu* and the *Chuang-tzu*, is not a simple concept. Such abstruse ideas do not usually spring full-blown from the foreheads of their creators; they have simpler beginnings. What is said about *wu-wei* as a method of government, in the *Lao-tzu* and the *Chuang-tzu*, does not seem adequate to permit us fully to understand it. It looks as if perhaps there were some further explanation, some key, that was in the minds of those who wrote, and as if they wrote under the assumption that this key would be available to their readers. In order to look for a simpler beginning of the concept of *wu-wei*, and a key to understanding it as a technique of government, let us see how *wu-wei* is used in earlier Chinese literature.

If we are to look for *wu-wei* in the literature, we must first be sure what we are looking for. The mere fact that the two characters occur in that sequence does not mean that the expression *wu-wei* is necessarily present. For instance, the *Chuang-tzu* has the clause 孰能以無爲首, which Fung Yu-lan translates: "Whosoever can make nothing the head of his existence. . . ."[40] It is evident that the expression *wu-wei* does not occur here. Neither does it occur in the admonition, also found in the *Chuang-tzu*, 無爲君子, "Do not be a *chün-tzu*."[41]

The expression *wu-wei*, as it is being discussed in this paper, may occur in two forms. (1) It may be a substantive, having the sense of "non-action." (2) *Wu* may function as a verb, having a subject, as in 道常無爲, "The *tao* constantly lacks action."[42] But: *Wei* can never have an object. It is not a question of the lack of doing, being, or acting upon a particular thing or in a particular way, but of the absence of all *wei*.

Wu-wei does not occur in the original text of the *I-ching* 易經,[43] nor

39. Waley, *The Way and Its Power*, 145.   40. *Chuang-tzu*, 3.8a. Fung, *Chuang Tzŭ*, 120.
41. *Chuang-tzu*, 9.23a.   42. *Lao-tzu, shang.* 21a (chap. 37).
43. This statement is based upon my own examination of the text. I have also consulted *A Concordance to Yi Ching*, Harvard-Yenching Institute Sinological Index Series, Supplement No. 10 (Peiping, 1935), 35–37, 127. It lists a single occurrence of *wu-wei*, in the appendix entitled *Hsi-tz'u* 繫辭; see *Chou-i Chien-i* 周易兼義, in *Shih-san Ching Chu-su* 十三經注疏 (Nanchang, 1815), 7.24b. The passage reads: 易无思也无爲也. Legge translates it: "In (all these operations forming) the Yì, there is no thought and no action"; see James Legge, trans., *The Yì King*, in *Sacred Books of the East*, XVI, 2d ed. (Oxford, 1899), 370. Wilhelm renders it: "Die Wandlungen haben kein Bewusstsein, keine Handlung"; see Richard Wilhelm, trans., *I Ging: Das Buch der Wandlungen* (Düsseldorf-Köln, 1960), 291. It would be very difficult to date this appendix as certainly having been written before the *Lao-tzu* and the *Chuang-tzu*, and this passage does not in any case seem important in the history of *wu-wei*; it will therefore not be considered further.

in the *Shu-ching* 書經.[44] In the *Shih-ching* it occurs once in one poem, and three times in another.[45] The latter is a love poem, in which the lover[46] says *wu-wei* in each of the three stanzas.[47] Legge translates it, "I do nothing;"[48] Waley, "I can do nothing;"[49] and Karlgren, "I know not what to do."[50] This would seem to have little significance for the later history of the expression.

Somewhat more important, perhaps, is the one remaining instance of *wu-wei* in the *Shih*.[51] The poem begins by speaking of a hare that moves slowly and cautiously, while a rash pheasant falls into the net. It then says: 我生之初尙無爲我生之後逢此百罹. Karlgren translates this: "In the early part of my life would that I had not acted. In the latter part of my life I have met with these hundred sorrows."[52] Here, then, we have *wu-wei* in the sense of "not acting," praised as a preferred course that may keep one out of trouble.

I have found no instance of the expression *wu-wei* in the *Ch'un-ch'iu* 春秋, the *Tso-chuan* 左傳,[53] or the *Kuo-yü* 國語.[54]

44. Not even, interestingly enough, in the *ku-wen* 古文 sections. This statement is based upon examination of all entries under *wu* 無 and *wei* 爲 in the *Shang-shu T'ung-chien* 尙書通檢, compiled by Ku Chieh-kang 顧頡剛 (Harvard-Yenching Institute, 1936), 197–199.

45. This statement is based upon my own examination of the text, the results of which I have confirmed by consulting *A Concordance to Shih Ching*, Harvard-Yanching Institute Sinological Index Series, Supplement No. 9 (Peiping, 1934), 153–155. There is one occurrence of the characters *wu wei* that does not involve the expression; see *Mao-shih Chu-su* 毛詩注疏, in *Shih-san Ching Chu-su*, 17 *chih* 4.18a

46. Legge makes the beloved in this poem a woman, Waley a man, and Karlgren leaves the question open.

47. *Mao-shih Chu-su*, 7 *chih* 1.16b–17b.

48. James Legge, trans., *The She King, The Chinese Classics*, IV (London, 1871), 213–214.

49. Arthur Waley, trans., *The Book of Songs* (Boston and New York, 1937), 44.

50. Bernhard Karlgren, trans., *The Book of Odes* (Stockholm, 1950), 92.

51. *Mao-shih Chu-su*, 4 *chih* 1.12b–13b.

52. Karlgren, *The Book of Odes*, 47; see also his note, 47–48. Both Legge, *The She King*, 117–118, and Waley, *The Book of Songs*, 307, translate *shang wu wei* somewhat differently, but I believe that Karlgren's rendering is clearly preferable.

53. I have searched the texts of the *Ch'un-ch'iu* and *Tso-chuan* for *wu-wei*, but it is of course difficult to be certain that no case has been overlooked in such a large work as the latter. *Wu-wei* as an expression is not listed in the *Combined Concordances to Ch'un-ch'iu, Kung-yang, Ku-liang, and Tso-chuan*, Harvard-Yenching Institute Sinological Index Series, Supplement No. 11 (Peiping, 1937). I have also searched this work, as has my research assistant Miss June Work (in the case of all concordances cited in this paper), under both the character *wu* 无 and *wu* 無. The characters *wu wei* occur, but not as the expression, in four cases: *Ch'un-ch'iu Tso-chuan Chu-su* 春秋左傳注疏, in *Shih-san Ching Chu-su*, 25.21a, 46.20b, 50.11b (see also *Chiao-k'an Chi* 校勘記, 4b), 60.24b.

54. I have searched this text for *wu-wei*. Insofar as I am aware, no complete concordance listing each occurrence of every character in this work has been published, but there is

What seems to be the earliest important clue to the development of the concept of *wu-wei* occurs, interestingly enough, in the single occurrence of that expression in the *Lun-yü* 論語,[55] in a speech that is attributed (correctly, I believe) to Confucius. It reads: 子曰無爲而治者其舜也與夫何爲哉恭己正南面而已矣.[56] I would translate it: "The Master said, 'Was it not Shun who did nothing and yet ruled well? What did he do? He merely corrected his person and took his proper position as ruler.'"

Arthur Waley translates this: "The Master said, Among those who 'ruled by inactivity' surely Shun may be counted. For what action did he take? He merely placed himself gravely and reverently with his face due south; that was all." In a note to "ruled by inactivity" he says: "*Wu-wei*, the phrase applied by the Taoists to the immobility of self-hypnosis." He explains "with his face due south" thus: "The position of the ruler. Shun was a divine sage (*shêng*) whose *tê* was so great that it sufficed to guide and transform the people."[57] Waley also says that Shun "is said to have ruled by *wu-wei* (non-activity), through the mere fact of sitting in a majestic attitude 'with his face turned to the South.' We have here the conception, familiar to us in Africa and elsewhere, of the divine king whose magic power regulates everything in the land. It is one which is common to all early Chinese thought, particularly in the various branches of Quietism that developed in the fourth century B. C. The *shêng*, however, only 'rules by non-activity' in the sense that his divine essence (*ling*) assures the fecundity of his people and the fertility of the soil. We find Shun assisted in his task by 'five servants,' who are clearly conceived of as performing the active functions of government."[58]

In my opinion, Confucius was not talking about "self-hypnosis"[59] or

---

an index: *Kokugo Sakuin* 國語索引, compiled by Suzuki Ryuichi 鈴木隆一 (Kyoto, 1934). This index does not list *wu-wei* as an expression, nor does it appear in any of the entries under *wu* 無 or *wei* 爲 (ibid., 181); *wu* 无 is not listed. There is one occurrence of the characters *wu wei*, but not the expression, in *Kuo-yü* (*Ssu-pu Pei-yao* ed.), 19.6a.

55. In addition to my own examination of the text, I have checked with *A Concordance to the Analects of Confucius*, Harvard-Yenching Institute Sinological Index Series, Supplement No. 16 (Peiping, 1940). In addition to the one case of the expression in *Lun-yü*, 15.4, the characters but not the expression occur in *Lun-yü* 6.11. (References to "*Lun-yü*" are given according to the numbering system used by Legge, Waley, and other translators.)
56. *Lun-yü*, 15.4. *Lun-yü Chu-su* 論語注疏, in *Shih-san Ching Chu-su*, 15.2b.
57. Arthur Waley, trans., *The Analects of Confucius* (London, 1936; reprint of 1945), 193.
58. Ibid., 18.
59. It is not clear from Waley's note (ibid., 193, n. 6) whether he meant to attribute this idea to Confucius or not.

the "magic power" of the "divine king." Such ideas became prevalent later, but they are quite out of context for Confucius.[60] Waley is more plausible when he points out that "the active functions of government" were performed by Shun's officials. Hsün-tzu 荀子, writing in the third century B. C., has a passage which seems clearly to be based upon and to interpret this passage, as follows: 人主者以官人爲能者 .... 人主得使人爲之 .... 何故必自爲之 .... 論德使能而官施之者聖王之道也 .... 則天子共己而已[61] "The abilities of a ruler appear in his appointment of (the proper) men to office. ... A ruler is able to cause others to perform (the functions of government) ... why must he personally perform them? ... To appraise virtue and employ the able in bestowing office is the way of the sage king. ... Thus the Son of Heaven need only correct his person."

The Han "Confucian" eclectic Tung Chung-shu 董仲舒 might well have been expected to interpret this passage in terms of the magical powers of the king, but in what is evidently an allusion to it he too explains that Shun could 垂拱無爲 "let fall (his robes), fold his hands, and do nothing" because the functions of government were carried on by his wisely chosen ministers.[62] The He Yen 何晏 commentary explains *Lun-yü* 15.4 similarly.[63]

This traditional Chinese interpretation of the passage is undoubtedly correct. Confucius would have liked, as much as Plato, to find a ruler imbued with philosophical principle, but in all his journeyings he never did. He came, therefore, to place his hope rather in ministers of virtuous character and proper education, to whom the ruler should turn over the administration of government. The ruler should set an example of character

60. I do not mean, of course, that the idea of divinity attaching to rulers did not exist before Confucius. Of course, it did, and was undoubtedly held by many in his own day. But in his attitude concerning the claims of the aristocracy to supernatural status, Confucius would seem to have partaken of the skepticism that became, among intellectuals at least, general in Chan-kuo times. Thus, for instance, he does not use the term "Son of Heaven" in any passage in the *Analects* that can be considered genuine, except in one quotation from the *Shih-ching* 詩經; see H. G. Creel, *Confucius, the Man and the Myth* (New York, 1949), 220, 321 (London, 1951), 239. After the skepticism of the Chan-kuo period, the idea of the divinity of the ruler became, in some measure, reestablished.
61. *Hsün-tzu (Ssu-pu Pei-yao* ed.), 7.6b–7b.
62. Wang Hsien-ch'ien 王先謙, *Ch'ien-Han-shu Pu-chu* 前漢書補註 (1900), 56.9b–10a. Tung later (ibid., 56.16a) quotes the beginning of this passage from the *Lun-yü* and explains that Shun for the most part merely continued the policies of his predecessor. The *Hsin-hsü* 新序, compiled by Liu Hsiang 劉向, also alludes to this passage with the explanation that Shun merely raised the worthy to office: *Liu Hsiang Hsin-hsü* 劉向新序 *(Ssu-pu Ts'ung-k'an* 四部叢刊 ed.), 4.1b.
63. *Lun-yü Chu-su,* 15.2b.

and conduct, and should select virtuous and able ministers, but having done so he should leave the governing to them, without interference. Government by *wu-wei* meant, for Confucius, that the ruler should "reign but not rule."[64]

Although *wu-wei* was used by Confucius, in this one passage that is transmitted to us, in a rather striking manner, the expression does not appear to have achieved currency rapidly. It does not occur in the *Mo-tzu* 墨子[65] nor in the *Meng-tzu* 孟子.[66] In fact it does not seem to be used again in any clearly datable Confucian work[67] until the *Hsün-tzu*. Since the *Hsün-tzu* was not written until around (and for the most part probably after) 300 B. C.,[68] it is too late to throw light on the early history of *wu-wei*. Quite significantly, in the two passages in which it appears in the *Hsün-tzu*[69] it is used in a manner not like that of Confucius, but rather in a way that is quite similar to its employment in Taoist works.[70]

We have now examined, I believe, all of the extant works which critical scholars would contend could be proved to have existed, in substantially their present form, before the composition of the earliest Taoist books.

64. For a fuller development of this point, with citation of evidence, see H. G. Creel, *Confucius, the Man and the Myth* (New York), 158–160; (London), 169–172.

65. *A Concordance to Mo Tzŭ*, Harvard-Yenching Institute Sinological Index Series, Supplement No. 21 (Peiping, 1948), does not list *wu-wei* as an expression. Its entries under *wu* show two occurrences of the characters *wu wei*, but they do not constitute the expression: *Mo-tzu* (*Ssu-pu Pei-yao* ed.), 9.9a, 10.14b.

66. *A Concordance to Meng Tzŭ*, Harvard-Yenching Institute Sinological Index Series, Supplement No. 17 (Peiping, 1941), does not list *wu-wei*; there are two instances of the characters but not the expression: *Meng-tzu Chu-su* 孟子注疏, in *Shih-san Ching Chu-su*, 8 *hsia*. 6a, 13 *shang*. 10a.

67. Two Confucian works that are not clearly datable are the *Ta-hsüeh* 大學 and the *Chung-yung* 中庸. I have found no instance of *wu-wei* in the *Ta-hsüeh*. It occurs once in the *Chung-yung*: *Li-chi Chu-su* 禮記注疏, in *Shih-san Ching Chu-su*, 53.6a. This passage uses *wu-wei* in a manner that has a distinctly Taoist flavor. It occurs in a section of the *Chung-yung* which Fung Yu-lan calls relatively late, and apparently would suppose to have been composed later than the *Meng-tzu*; see Fung, *A History of Chinese Philosophy*, I, 369–377.

68. Fung Yu-lan, *A Short History of Chinese Philosophy*, 143, says that the dates of Hsün-tzu "are not definitely known, but probably lay within the years 298 and 238 B. C." Ch'ien Mu, *Hsien-Ch'in Chu-tzu Hsi-nien*, 619 and chart facing 620, puts the extreme limits of his life between 340 and 245 B. C.

69. These occur among the entries under *wu* in *A Concordance to Hsün Tzŭ*, Harvard-Yenching Institute Sinological Index Series, Supplement No. 22 (Peking, 1950), 638–645. *Wu wei*, but not as the expression, also appears in *Hsün-tzu*, 1.12a.

70. *Hsün-tzu*, 15.8b, 20.3b. The latter occurrence is in an anecdote quoting Confucius, which is quite like the anecdotes in the *Chuang-tzu* that attribute Taoist sayings to him. It strongly resembles chapter 8 of the *Lao-tzu*; compare *Lao-tzu, shang*. 4b, and *Hsün-tzu*, 20.3b.

And we have found exactly five cases of the expression *wu-wei*. Four of
these are in the *Shih-ching*; of these, three occur in one poem and seem
to have no significance, and the remaining one has not very much, for
the later history of the term. The occurrence in the *Lun-yü*, on the other
hand, has great significance; it epitomizes Confucius' view that the ruler
should be one who sets a proper example and selects virtuous and able
officials, who "reigns but does not rule." But this Confucian use of the
term does not explain, nor does it even seem adequately to foreshadow,
the meaning of *wu-wei* in Taoist literature. Yet in the latter half of the
fourth century B. C. and the first half of the third there developed, with
no apparent antecedents, the Taoist *wu-wei* with all of its abstruse peculia-
rities. And this Taoist *wu-wei* became so influential that we find it, and
not the *wu-wei* of Confucius, in the Confucian book *Hsün-tzu*.

Has the search, then, been in vain? Is there no key in the literature;
if there was, has it been lost? I believe that in fact it did exist in a work
which is no longer extant, but that fragments of that work remain from
which we can glean a very considerable understanding of its content. I
refer to the book called *Shen-tzu* 申子,[71] attributed to Shen Pu-hai 申不害.

For some years I have been studying the philosophy of Shen Pu-hai,
who was prime minister of the small state of Han 韓 until his death in
337 B. C. In previous papers I have discussed his career and his thought.[72]
The book attributed to him circulated widely and was very influential in
Han times and even later, but it seems now to be lost. Numerous quotations alleged to be from it exist in other works,[73] but most scholars seem
either to have ignored them, or to have dismissed them as forgeries on
grounds that are, in my opinion, inadequate.[74] Kuo Mo-jo 郭沫若,

71. Not, it should be noted, to be confused with the *Shen-tzu* 慎子 attributed to Shen Tao
慎到.
72. See pp. 79–91, 92–120, and 121–159.
73. For the location of such quotations, see p. 97, n. 22.
74. Hu Shih 胡適, *Chung-kuo Che-hsüeh Shih Ta-kang, chüan shang* 中國哲學史大綱, 卷上,
15th ed. (Shanghai, 1930), 361–362, dismisses quotations attributed to the *Shen-tzu* on the
ground that they emphasize *fa* 法, which the *Han Fei-tzu* says Shen neglected. But the
contradiction is only apparent. The *fa* that Shen is criticized for neglecting has the
sense of "law." But in the Shen Pu-hai fragments, wherever the context makes the meaning
of *fa* clear, it always means "method," never "law." Ch'en Ch'i-t'ien 陳啓天, *Chung-kuo
Fa-chia Kai-lun* 中國法家概論 (Shanghai, 1936), 236–238, casts doubt upon all of the
quoted passages attributed to the *Shen-tzu*. Of the largest body of material, that quoted in
Ch'ün-shu Chih-yao 羣書治要, compiled by Wei Cheng 魏徵 (*Ssu-pu Ts'ung-k'an* ed.),
36.25b–27a, Ch'en holds that it is proved false by two references to Wu Huo 烏獲 and
Meng Pen 孟賁, as strong men, since (Ch'en believes) they did not make their reputations
as such until thirty years after the time of Shen Pu-hai. But I have made an extensive
study of references to these men in the literature, and it seems perfectly clear that they

however, seems to regard them as substantially genuine.[75]

With the help of my colleague, Professor T. H. Tsien, I have tried to collect all quotations attributed to the book of *Shen-tzu* and all direct quotations of Shen Pu-hai (it is not always possible to distinguish certainly between the two) in Chinese literature. The materials we have assembled total 1,347 characters. After studying this material from various points of view, while I do not suppose that all of it is certainly from Shen Pu-hai, I think that its relation to Shen Pu-hai is probably as close as is that of most early Chinese books to their reputed authors, and closer than that of some. More important for the present purpose, I think it probable that this material does emanate, in large part, from a time prior to the death of Shen Pu-hai in 337 B. C.[76] If this is true it antedates, according to most current critical opinion, both the *Chuang-tzu* and the *Lao-tzu*.

Do the Shen Pu-hai fragments indicate his philosophy to be based, as is so often alleged, on Taoism? They do not, though there is much that

were legendary paragons of strength who cannot be specifically referred to any such date; see *Chan-kuo Ts'e Chiao-chu* 戰國策校注 (*Ssu-pu Ts'ung-k'an* ed.), 3.45a, column 7, commentary, and *Shih-chi*, 5.63–64, commentary.

75. Kuo Mo-jo, *Shih P'i-p'an Shu* 十批判書 (Peking, 1954), 327–337. In my opinion, however, Kuo misunderstands much of the thought of Shen Pu-hai, and greatly underestimates its importance.

76. Among other methods of study, I have applied to these materials the criteria used in the study of the *Lieh-tzu* in Graham, "The Date and Composition of Liehtzyy." Insofar as they proved applicable, these criteria seem to indicate that — in the tested respects — the Shen Pu-hai fragments do not show evidence that they are not of pre-Han date. I have also applied to these fragments the criteria used by Karlgren in the study of early texts in Bernhard Karlgren, "On the Authenticity and Nature of the Tso Chuan," in Göteborgs Högskolas Årsskrift, XXXII (1926), 3, and further applied to the analysis of the *Shang-chün Shu* 商君書 in J. J. L. Duyvendak, trans., *The Book of Lord Shang* (London, 1928), 151–159. The result, which was quite surprising to me, was to show the Shen Pu-hai fragments to resemble the *Han Fei-tzu* more than any other of the texts analyzed by Karlgren and Duyvendak, and to a remarkable degree. Han Fei-tzu, it will be remembered, was born in the same state as Shen Pu-hai, some half a century after Shen's death. Of course, these things do not prove the fragments to be from the fourth century B. C. But for reasons that cannot be developed here, I believe that most of them bear a close relation to Shen's thought. There is one circumstance that tells heavily against these fragments having been forged. The now lost *Pieh-lu* 別錄 of Liu Hsiang said: "The doctrine of Shen-tzu is called *hsing-ming* 刑名" (*Ch'ien-Han-shu Pu-chu*, 9.1a, column 12, commentary). And *hsing-ming* is commonly described as a principal tenet of Shen Pu-hai. The *Shen-tzu* fragments do, I think, contain the idea denoted by *hsing-ming*, but *the term itself does not occur once in them*. Again, *Han Fei-tzu* (*Ssu-pu Pei-yao* edition), 17.5b–7a, uses the term *shu* 術, "methods," to describe the doctrine of Shen Pu-hai, and this is perhaps the character by which it is most frequently denoted in all of the literature. In the fragments, however, this character does not occur at all; it is replaced by *shu* 數, used in the same sense, and even this occurs only twice. It is hard to conceive that a forger or forgers, producing material to be attributed to Shen Pu-hai, would have completely omitted the expressions most commonly said to have denoted his principal tenets.

resembles the language of Taoist works. But these fragments are almost exclusively concerned with the philosophy of governmental administration. The one sure touchstone of an early Taoist work[77] is, in my opinion, the fact that *tao* 道 is used (not always, but some of the time) as a term denoting the sum total of reality. It is not so used, I think, in pre-Taoist, or early non-Taoist works. In the Shen Pu-hai fragments the character *tao* occurs ten times. It is never used to denote the sum total of reality; in five of the cases *tao* means "methods" or "policies" of governmental administration.[78]

Wu-wei occurs six times in the Shen Pu-hai fragments. In order to understand it, we must first know what *wei* meant to Shen, and why he was concerned about it. And to do this we must understand his situation.

A man of humble origin,[79] Shen became prime minister of the state of Han only some two decades after its ruler, and the rulers of Wei 魏 and Chao 趙, completed the process of dividing up the territories, and annihilating the state, of their overlord, the ruler of Chin 晉.[80] With this example before them, it would have been difficult for Shen to preach to the officials of Han about their duty to be loyal to their ruler. He never does so. The fragments show him greatly concerned about the danger that a ruler may be unseated, and giving much thought to methods by which his position may be made secure. But he never appeals to sentiment, religion, or traditional or familial loyalties. Instead he concentrates upon administrative methods by which a ruler may maintain his position and make his state strong and prosperous. Here we can consider only those methods that are associated with *wu-wei*.

Shen's conception of the proper role of a ruler is perhaps best summed up in the following passage from the *Shen-tzu*:

77. There is probably less reference to *tao* as meaning "the absolute" in later Taoist works concerned primarily with immortality, belonging to the school that I have called "Hsien Taoism" (see p. 7). But since Hsien Taoism does not seem clearly to have existed before Han times, such works are not in question in the present context.
78. *Ch'ün-shu Chih-yao*, 36.26b–27a. In one case (ibid., 36.26a), *tao* means "road." There are two instances of *T'ien tao* 天道, "Heaven's way": *Pei-t'ang Shu-ch'ao* 北堂書鈔, compiled by Yü Shih-nan 虞世南 (edition of 1888), 149.2b. *Ti tao* 地道 "Earth's way" occurs once: ibid, 157.2a. The one remaining instance is in a quotation of Confucius, which the Sung scholar Hsieh Chü 薛據 quoted as from the *Shen-tzu* in his *K'ung-tzu Chi-yü* 孔子集語 (edition of 1875), *shang*. 2b. Here Confucius speaks of having "heard the *tao*."
79. *Shih-chi*, 63.12, says of Shen: 故鄭之賤臣.
80. This final dismemberment took place in 376 B. C.; see *Shih-chi*, 39.94, 45.6. The chronology of the *Shih-chi* (45.7) indicates that Shen became prime minister in 351, but Ch'ien Mu (*Hsien-Ch'in Chu-tzu Hsi-nien*, 237–238) holds that in he fact assumed this office in 355.

鏡設精無爲而美惡自備衡設平無爲而輕重自得凡因之道身與公無事無事而
天下自極也[81]

[The ruler is like][82] a mirror, [which merely] reflects the light
[that comes to it, itself] doing nothing, and yet [because of its mere
presence], beauty and ugliness present themselves [to view]. [He is
like] a scale, [which merely] establishes equilibrium, [itself] doing
nothing, yet [the mere fact that is remains in balance causes] lightness
and heaviness to discover themselves. [The ruler's] method is [that of]
complete acquiescence. [He merges his] personal [concerns] with the
public [weal, so that as an individual] he does not act. He does not
act, yet [as a result of his non-action] the world [brings] itself [to a
state of] complete [order].

Here Shen pictures the ruler as a majestic arbiter, not actively interven-
ing in the government but presiding over it with complete impartiality.
Here and elsewhere, he strives to depict the ruler as at once inoffensive
and indispensable. The development of his concept of *wu-wei*, by Shen
Pu-hai, may well have been inspired by the statement of Confucius
concerning government through *wu-wei* by Shun.[83] Unlike other *Fa-chia*
books, the *Shen-tzu* (insofar as fragments of it are preserved) contains
nothing that seems specifically to attack Confucianism, and two passages
that are quoted from it refer to Confucius with approval.[84]

One might easily suppose that *wu-wei* meant, for Shen Pu-hai as for
Confucius, that the ruler should merely "reign but not rule"—but one
would be mistaken. If Shen Pu-hai got the inspiration for his concept from
Confucius, he drastically revised it, in accord with the conditions of his
time. A laissez-faire attitude would have been very dangerous for a

81. *Ch'ün-shu Chih-yao*, 36.27a.
82. In the preceding context, the subject is "the ruler." The first ten characters of this
passage are quoted as from the *Shen-tzu* in *T'ang-Sung Pai-K'ung Liu-t'ieh* 唐宋白孔六帖
(Ming Chia-ching ed.), 13.27a; they are there preceded by 豈不如.
83. Although the Shen Pu-hai fragments contain no mention of Shun, there are two
highly favorable references to Yao 堯, the legendary emperor who is supposed to have
preceded Shun and selected him to rule. Yao is described as using methods advocated
by Shen Pu-hai in two quotations from the *Shen-tzu* in: *Ch'ün-shu Chih-yao*, 36.26b-27a.
I-wen Lei-chü 藝文類聚, compiled by Ou-Yang Hsün 歐陽詢 and others (edition of 1879),
54.1b-2a.
84. These quotations were collected, as being from the *Shen-tzu*, into the Sung work,
Hsieh, *K'ung-tzu Chi-yü, shang.* 2ab. It must be admitted that they do not contain anything
that seems specifically related to the doctrines of Shen himself, and it may be that they
were merely put into the book when it was presumably compiled by members of his
school. The fact that they were included may however (though this argument cannot
be pressed too far) indicate that the school was not hostile toward Confucius.

Chan-kuo ruler, and no one knew this better than Shen. He emphasizes, quite as much as Confucius did, the necessity that the ruler must select and appoint able officials,[85] but he also insists that the ruler must exercise constant vigilance over their performance. According to Han Fei-tzu, Shen held that the ruler must "keep in his own hands the power of life and death".[86]

The policy of *wu-wei,* as Shen describes it, has two principal advantages for the ruler. One is that it leaves him free, as an executive, to supervise the government without becoming so involved in its details that he cannot perform his proper function, and loses perspective.[87] 明君如身臣如手 .... 君設其本臣操其末君治其要臣行其詳君操其柄臣事其常[88] "The intelligent ruler," the *Shen-tzu* says, "is like the trunk, the minister is like an arm. . . . The ruler plants the root, the minister manages the twigs. The ruler controls the principles, the minister carries them out in detail. The ruler holds the controls, the minister carries on routine functions."

While the ruler maintains firm control of the administration, he plays no active role in the carrying out of its functions. The *Shen-tzu* says: 鼓不與於五音而爲五音主有道者不爲五官之事而爲治主君知其道也臣[89] 知其事也一言十當百爲百當者人臣之事非君人之道也 [90] "The [sound of the] drum does not take part [as one] among the five notes, and yet it is their ruler.[91] One who has [the right] method does not perform the functions of the five officials,[92] and yet he is the master of the government. The ruler controls the policy, the ministers manage affairs. To speak ten times and ten times be right, to act a hundred times and a hundred times succeed—this is the business of one who serves another as a minister; it is not the way to rule."

---

85. *Han Fei-tzu,* 11.11b–12a, 17.5b.
86. Ibid., 17.5b.
87. This is the significance of the statement by Shen Pu-hai, which has sometimes been misunderstood, that is quoted in *Lü-shih Ch'un-ch'iu* 呂氏春秋 (*Ssu-pu Pei-yao* ed.), 17.7a.
88. *Ch'ün-shu Chih-yao,* 36.26a.
89. This *ch'en* appears in this passage as it is quoted by *Ch'ang-tuan Ching* 長短經, compiled by Chao Sui 趙蕤 (*Ts'ung-shu Chi-ch'eng* 叢書集成 ed.), 1.2. *Ch'ün-shu Chih-yao,* 36.26b, instead reads *kuan jen* 官人, but this is clumsy and spoils the style. Since the author was a careful stylist, *ch'en* seems the more probable reading.
90. *Ch'ün-shu Chih-yao,* 36.26b, with the emendation described in the preceding note. This passage appears elsewhere also, but in this paper I shall not detail textual variants or cite multiple sources unless they have special significance.
91. Presumably the sense is that the percussive sound of the drum does not correspond in pitch to any of the five notes, and yet it gives rhythm, emphasis, and definition to the music, thus "ruling" the five notes.
92. This probably means simply "the various officials." The term *wu kuan* was also used to designate the principal officials; see *Li-chi Chu-su,* 4.23b–26b.

Thus the policy of *wu-wei* enables the ruler truly to rule, because he never becomes immersed in the detailed administration of the government. But it has a second cardinal advantage. Shen was alert, as no intelligent man of his time could fail to be, to the dangers threatening a ruler, ranging from loss of actual control of the state to loss of his life. The ruler must, while eliciting the best efforts of his ministers, avoid placing his position or his person in jeopardy. Shen said: 上明見人備之其不明見人惑之其知見人飾[93]之不知見人匿之其無欲見人司之其有欲見人餌之故曰吾無從知之惟無爲可以規之[94] "If the ruler's intelligence is displayed men will prepare against it; if his lack of intelligence is displayed they will delude him. If his wisdom is displayed, men will gloss over [their faults to deceive] him; if his lack of wisdom is displayed they will hide [their shortcomings] from him. If his lack of desires is displayed, men will spy out[95] [what] his [true desires are]; if the fact that he has desires is displayed, they will [use their knowledge of them to] tempt[96] him. Therefore [the intelligent ruler] says, 'I cannot know them;[97] it is only by means of non-action that [I] can control[98] them.' "

Thus the ruler must refrain from taking the initiative, and from making himself conspicuous—and therefore vulnerable—by any overt action. The *Shen-tzu* says: 故善爲主者倚於愚立於不盈設於不敢藏於無竆竆端匿疏示天下無爲是以近者親之遠者懷之示人有餘者人奪之示人不足者人與之剛者折危者覆動者搖靜者安[99] "Therefore the skillful ruler avails himself of

93. This character appears as *huo* 惑 in the text of the *Han Fei-tzu* in the editions of the *Ssu-pu Pei-yao* (13.6a) and the *Ssu-pu Ts'ung-k'an* (13.5a), and in Wang Hsien-shen 王先愼, *Han Fei-tzu Chi-chieh* 韓非子集解 (1896), 13.7b. But Ch'en Ch'i-t'ien 陳啓天, *Han Fei-tzu Chiao-shih* 韓非子校釋, 2d ed. (Shanghai, 1941), 627, emends it to read *shih* 飾 in accord with three Ming dynasty texts, and I have followed this emendation. The repetition of *huo* at this point seems unlikely on the ground of rhetorical artistry, and could easily have resulted from scribal error. The meaning is not greatly altered in either case.
94. *Han Fei-tzu*, 13.6a. The quotation is prefaced by 申子曰, from which one might deduce that the book is quoted. But it is followed by 一曰申子曰, which rather makes it appear that this is a saying of Shen Pu-hai that circulated in different versions. The second version is similar to the first, and its last seven characters (including the *wu-wei*) are identical.
95. One Ming text writes *tz'u* 伺 here; see Ch'en, *Han Fei-tzu Chiao-shih*, 627. But many cases prove that *ssu* 司 was anciently used for *tz'u*, and carried its meanings; see *Shuo-wen Chieh-tzu Ku-lin* 說文解字詁林, edited by Ting Fu-pao 丁福保 (1928), 4012b–4013a.
96. Literally, "to bait," as a fish is tempted with a worm.
97. That is to say, the ruler's ministers and subjects are so numerous, and so much on the alert to discover his weaknesses and get the better of him, that it is hopeless for him as one lone man to try to learn their characteristics and control them by his knowledge. Similarly the *T'ai-p'ing Yü-lan* 太平御覽 (edition of 1892), 638.4b, quotes the *Shen-tzu* as saying: "The sage ruler depends upon methods, not upon [his] cleverness (*chih* 智)."
98. Taking *kuei* 規 in the sense of "to circumscribe." For the use of this character with the meaning of "to check on, to control," see *Ch'un-ch'iu Tso-chuan Chu-su*, 42.27.
99. *Ch'ün-shu Chih-yao*, 36.26b.

[an appearance of] stupidity, establishes himself in insufficiency, places himself in [a posture of] timidity, and conceals himself in inaction. He hides his motives and conceals his tracks.[100] He shows the world that he does not act. Therefore those who are near feel affection for him, and the distant think longingly of him [i.e., desire to become his subjects].[101] One who shows men that he has a surplus has [his possessions] taken from him by force, but to him who shows others that he has not enough, [things] are given. The strong are cut down, those in danger are protected. The active are insecure; the quiet have poise."

Superficially, this passage looks quite "Taoist." I suspect that, if it were quoted as being from the *Chuang-tzu,* it would be accepted without much question by all but those who are very familiar with that text. And yet, if we look at it closely, there is nothing specifically Taoist about it at all. It is simply an exposition of a practical technique by which, Shen Pu-hai maintains, a ruler may stay out of danger and even achieve a measure of popularity.

Wu-wei, as expounded by Shen Pu-hai, has something in common with the Japanese wrestling technique called *jūdō* 柔道, which is designed to enable the weak to overpower the strong. In *jūdō* one does not, or should not, take the lead in action, but remains quite relaxed, seeming to follow quite willingly the course taken by his opponent. But this passivity continues only until the opponent has, by taking the active role, placed himself in a disadvantageous position. When that moment arrives one acts, with all of the energy stored from his previous relaxation, and ends the contest (if his maneuver succeeds) at a single stroke.

So Shen Pu-hai tells us that the ruler, while not overtly active, never

100. I have been unable to find any way to interpret *su* 疏 in the context, and therefore reluctantly accept the suggestion of a marginal note in the *Ch'ün-shu Chih-yao* text that it should be emended to *chi* 跡. The two characters are sufficiently similar to make a copyist's error possible. This emendation may find some support in the occurrence, in a context having some analogy with this one, of the expression *ts'uan tuan ni chi* 竄端匿跡 in the *Huai-nan-tzu (Ssu-pu Ts'ung-k'an* ed.), 18.21b.
101. This is very reminiscent of *Lun-yü,* 13.16, which ends with 近者悅遠者來. Legge translates this whole passage thus: "The duke of She asked about government. The Master said, '*Good government obtains,* when those who are near are made happy, and those who are far off are attracted.'" This passage from Shen Pu-hai is very different in its tenor from the note that is struck repeatedly in the *Han Fei-tzu,* emphasizing the conflict between the interests of ruler and subjects and the undesirability of affection between them: *Han Fei-tzu,* 4.4b–5a, 14.4b–6a, 16.8ab. The Shen Pu-hai fragments do not substantiate the attitude of utter self-seeking malevolence that some scholars have attributed to Shen; notice for instance the passage cited above (*Ch'ün-shu Chih-yao,* 36.27a) in which he says that the ruler should "[merge his] personal [concerns] with the public [weal]."

ceases his vigilance and never removes his hand from the controls.[102] In general, however, "[the ruler's] method (*tao* 道) is [one of] complete acquiescence."[103] A time may come, nevertheless, when the ruler must intervene. But when that time does come, the prestige and power accumulated through his policy of watchful inaction are such that a single word suffices to rectify the situation. This is the meaning, I think, of the following passage from the *Shen-tzu:* 明君治國而晦晦而行行而止止故一言正 而天下治一言倚而天下靡[104] It is not easy to interpret this passage. In the light of the total context of our material on Shen Pu-hai, I venture the following translation:

> The brilliant ruler, in governing the state,[105] dims [his luster]. Dimming [his luster] he acts. [Although] acting, [his activity is so slight that he still seems] in repose. [Since he is thus virtually] in repose, therefore [everything he does has augmented import, so that if] his single word is correct, the whole world is well ordered, [but if] his single word is perverse, the whole world is ruined.

The meaning of *wu-wei*, as it appears in the Shen Pu-hai fragments, seems reasonably clear. There is nothing mystical, or mysterious, or "Taoist," about it. Did the use of *wu-wei* in this sense originate with Shen Pu-hai? We cannot certainly say. But if, as I believe, these fragments emanate substantially from a time prior to his death, it would seem that this conception does not appear in other literature now known to us that can be dated earlier.[106]

---

102. *Ch'ün-shu Chih-yao,* 36.26a–27a, *T'ai-p'ing Yü-lan,* 638.4b.

103. *Ch'ün-shu Chih-yao,* 36.27a.

104. *T'ai-p'ing Yü-lan,* 624.3ab. The last seven characters of this passage are also quoted in *Pei-t'ang Shu-ch'ao,* 29.2a.

105. Throughout this passage I take *er* 而 to be what might be called an adverbial postposition. It gives what precedes *er* adverbial force, modifying the verb that follows *er* by specifying the conditions under which the action takes place.

106. In addition to the works already considered, it may be pertinent to mention the *Chan-kuo Ts'e* 戰國策. To attach a specific date to any portion of this work would be very difficult, but most of its materials concern the Chan-kuo period and some may emanate from that time. There is not, to my knowledge, any complete concordance to this work, but the *Index du Tchan Kouo Ts'ö,* published by Université de Paris, Centre d'études sinologiques de Pékin (Peiping, 1948), does not cite *wu-wei.* I have searched this text and found three occurrences of *wu wei*: *Chan-kuo Ts'e* (*Ssu-pu Pei-yao* ed.), 5.3a, 18.2b, 29.10a. In the first two of these passages the characters do not constitute the expression. In the third it is present, used not in the sense of the Shen Pu-hai fragments but rather as it occurs in Taoist literature. This occurs in a speech addressed to King Chao of Yen (燕昭王), who reigned 311–279 B. C. Thus, even if this conversation is genuine, it dates from a time well after that of Shen Pu-hai, who died in 337.

The *Fa-chia* seems to have originated chiefly from a combination of the doctrines of two schools of thought founded on the one hand by Shen Pu-hai and on the other by Shang Yang,[107] who were contemporaries. It is generally agreed that the *Shang-chün Shu* was not written by Shang Yang, but in large part it does appear to represent the ideas of the wing of the *Fa-chia* of which he was the founder.[108] It is of interest, then, that in the *Shang-chün Shu* there is no single occurrence of *wu-wei*. Furthermore the administrative concept that is denoted by *wu-wei*, in the Shen Pu-hai fragments, is entirely absent from the *Shang-chün Shu*.[109]

Finally, the *Han Fei-tzu* explicitly attributes the use of *wu-wei*, in this sense characteristic of the Shen Pu-hai fragments, to Shen Pu-hai.[110] And the concept is quite in keeping with what we are told about his philosophy in other works. It is at least a plausible hypothesis, then, that the use of *wu-wei* in this sense originated with Shen Pu-hai.

If it be assumed that this is true, and that this sense of *wu-wei* preceded any datable occurrence of the Taoist concept of *wu-wei*, how could the development of the Taoist concept have been influenced by that of Shen Pu-hai? A number of scholars have recognized that Taoist thought represented, at least in part, a reaction against the kind of tight governmental controls over men that were favored by the *Fa-chia*.[111] And one tendency in Taoism (but not the only one) was to push individualism to the point of espousing anarchy. The eleventh chapter of the *Chuang-tzu* begins: "I have heard of letting the world alone; I have not heard of governing the world."[112]

The use of the expression *wu-wei* by such Taoists may have been a process, not unusual in debate, of reinterpreting the slogan of one's adversary and hurling it back at him. The *Fa-chia* (or the Shen Pu-hai branch of it) acclaimed *wu-wei* as a technique by which a ruler might maintain firm control of the state. But in fact, this was not complete inaction. Why not, Taoists of this highly individualistic sort asked, genuinely *wu-wei*, withdraw from all involvement in affairs? "The perfect man," the

107. See pp. 92–120.
108. See pp. 101–102. Chang Hsin-ch'eng 張心澂, *Wei-shu T'ung-k'ao* 偽書通考 (Changsha, 1939), 769–771. Duyvendak, *The Book of Lord Shang*, 131–159.
109. These statements are based upon my examination of the text of the *Ssu-pu Pei-yao* edition of the *Shang-chün Shu*.
110. *Han Fei-tzu*, 13.6a.
111. Hu, *Chung-kuo Che-hsüeh Shih Ta-kang, chüan shang*, 50–53. (It should be noted, however, that since Hu Shih believed Lao Tzu to be an older contemporary of Confucius, he did not suppose him to be reacting against the *Fa-chia*.) Fung, *A History of Chinese Philosophy*, I, 186–187, 226–230. Waley, *The Way and Its Power*, 86–88.
112. *Chuang-tzu*, 4.14a.

Chuang-tzu tells us, "does nothing (*wu-wei*), and the great sage originates nothing; that is to say, they merely contemplate the universe."[113]

This type of Taoism is what I suggested, in a paper published some years ago,[114] calling "contemplative Taoism." It advocated genuine detachment, true inactivity, with the sole aim of achieving serenity for the individual. A result of this was, such Taoists asserted, to bring the individual into harmony with, and thus to endow him with the virtues of, the *tao*, the majestic sum total of reality. But inevitably there were those who then wished to exploit these virtues—to use this power of the universe, concentrated within the person of the Taoist, to accomplish particular aims. Since the principal activity of the time was political, the motif of the use of these powers to achieve political ends was prominent. I have suggested calling this variety "purposive Taoism."

In "purposive" Taoism we find *wu-wei* used, where it relates to government, in a manner strongly reminiscent of that of Shen Pu-hai. At times the resemblance is detailed. For instance the *Chuang-tzu* says: 無爲而尊者天道也有爲而累者人道也主者天道也臣者人道也[115] "To be inactive and honored is the way of Heaven; to act and be involved [in affairs] is the way of man. The ruler [follows] the way of Heaven; the minister [follows] the way of man." Here we see the distinction drawn by Shen Pu-hai, between the *wu-wei* that is proper to the ruler, on the one hand, and the activity, *wei*, that is the function of his ministers, on the other. But often in the Taoist use of *wu-wei*, even as a technique of government, we find the addition of a mystical or cosmic touch that is never present in the Shen Pu-hai fragments. Thus the *Lao-tzu* says: 道常無爲而無不爲侯王若能守之萬物將自化[116] "The *tao* does nothing, and yet there is nothing that is not accomplished. If feudal lords and kings could maintain[117] it all things would transform themselves."

What would seem to be the influence of the Shen Pu-hai branch of the *Fa-chia* appears at many points in the *Lao-tzu* and the *Chuang-tzu*. Of especial interest is the first part of the thirteenth chapter of the *Chuang-tzu*, which is entitled *T'ien Tao* 天道. This first portion of the chapter, running to more than half of its length, seems to have little real connection with

---

113. *Chuang-tzu*, 7.23b.
114. Pp. 37–47.
115. *Chuang-tzu*, 4.22b.
116. *Lao-tzu, shang*, 21a (chap. 37).
117. *Shou* 守 seems to be used here in a dual sense, with the idea both that they should "preserve" undistorted the *tao* that is within them, and that they should "hold to" *tao* as a course of action.

the remainder.[118] Its basic theme is the role of *wu-wei* in connection with government.

Much of the argument of this first portion of the *T'ien Tao* chapter resembles that of the Shen Pu-hai fragments, though the language is definitely Taoist in flavor. It says repeatedly that the ruler must practice *wu-wei*, but it also emphasizes (somewhat surprisingly in a Taoist context) that his inferiors must *not* practice *wu-wei*, because activity is the proper role of a minister. 上必無爲而用天下下必有爲爲天下用[119] "Superiors must be without action in order to control the world; inferiors must be active in order to be employed in the world's business."

The allocation of functions between ruler and minister is described thus by the *T'ien Tao* chapter: 本在於上末在於下要在於主詳在於臣[120] "The foundation is the responsibility of the superior, the superstructure that of inferiors; principles are in the charge of the ruler, details are the domain of ministers." The same idea is stated thus in the *Shen-tzu*: 君設其本臣操其末君治其要臣行其詳[121] The resemblance is too detailed to be mere coincidence.

Yet if, as I believe, the *T'ien Tao* chapter of the *Chuang-tzu* borrows both ideas and terminology from the Shen Pu-hai branch of the *Fa-chia*, this does not in the least mean that it acknowledges that school to be superior, or even equal, to Taoism. Quite the reverse. It explains that various governmental techniques, including *shu* 數 and *hsing-ming* 刑名, are involved in carrying out the details of government, to be sure, but are entirely nonessential.[122] This is quite evidently an attack on the Shen Pu-hai school, which had among its cardinal tenets *shu* and *hsing-ming*.[123] *Shu* is used in the Shen Pu-hai fragments to mean "technique" of administration.[124] And *hsing-ming* 刑名 as used by the Shen Pu-hai school

118. This first portion runs from the beginning of the chapter, *Chuang-tzu*, 5.11b, to 5.16a, column 4, "K'ung-tzu" 孔子. While it includes several sections that may be regarded as independent, they are linked by the theme of the function of *wu-wei* in government. After this first section the theme is less clear and consistent.

Various scholars, from a time as early as the eleventh century, have doubted that this thirteenth chapter was written by Chuang-tzu; see Ch'ien Mu 錢穆, *Chuang-tzu Tsuan-chien* 莊子纂箋 (Hongkong, 1951), 103. Undoubtedly it was not written by the author of the earliest portion of the book. It seems to represent "purposive" Taoism, while the earliest portion is predominantly "contemplative."

119. *Chuang-tzu*, 5.13b.

120. *Chuang-tzu*, 5.14a.

121. *Ch'ün-shu Chih-yao*, 36.26a.

122. *Chuang-tzu*, 5.14a.

123. Actually, more than these two among the list given in the *Chuang-tzu* were linked with the Shen Pu-hai school, but it would be too complicated to go into the others.

124. *Shu* 數 occurs in the fragments only twice; see *T'ai-p'ing Yü-lan*, 638.4b, *Han Fei-tzu*,

meant, as I have shown in a previous paper, "performance and title." The idea was that the "performance" of an official, or of a candidate for office, was to be compared with the "title" and the duties of the office in question, to determine whether the individual measured up to the responsibility.[125]

"The men of old," the *T'ien Tao* chapter continues, "had *hsing-ming*[126] but they did not give it precedence. Those who, in antiquity, spoke of the Great *Tao*, only as the fifth step [in a series from the highest to successively lower concerns] referred to *hsing-ming,* and only as the ninth step mentioned rewards and punishments. Without preamble to speak of *hsing-ming* is to be ignorant of its basis; without preamble to speak of rewards and punishments is to be ignorant of their beginnings. Those who in their speech overthrow and controvert the *tao* (the proper order) are [only fit] to be governed by others; how can they rule? Those who without preamble speak of *hsing-ming* and of rewards and punishments possess the instruments, of government, but they do not know the way (*tao*) to rule. . . . They are what is called sophists, mere technicians."[127]

The fact that the *T'ien Tao* chapter is in large part an attack upon

---

16.6a. This character is quite clearly used instead of the character *shu* 術, which is more commonly employed to denote the "technique" of Shen Pu-hai, as in *Han Fei-tzu,* 17.5b. The sense of "technique" for *shu* 數, though somewhat rare, is well attested; it has the specific sense of administrative technique in *Shang-chün Shu* (*Ssu-pu Pei-yao* ed.), 5.13a. There is other evidence that this character was current in the Shen Pu-hai school. As one instance, *Lü-shih Ch'un-ch'iu,* 17.6a–8b, is an essay constructed around a quotation of Shen Pu-hai, and is clearly a production of his school; it is entitled *Jen Shu* 任數, "Rely on Technique."

125. For detailed demonstration of this, and evidence that *hsing* 刑 once had the now obsolete sense of "performance," see pp. 79–91. The term *hsing-ming* does not occur in the preserved fragments of the *Shen-tzu,* although the idea it expresses is to some degree implied; I suspect that it did occur in parts of the book that are now lost. That *hsing-ming* was a major doctrine of Shen Pu-hai was stated by Ssu-Ma Ch'ien (*Shih-chi,* 63.13) and by Liu Hsiang (Wang Hsien-ch'ien 王先謙, *Ch'ien-Han-shu Pu-chu* 前漢書補注 [1900], 9.1a, column 12, commentary); this is also very clearly implied in *Huai-nan-tzu,* 21.7b. Liu Hsiang, in the passage just cited, defined the sense in which *hsing-ming* was used by Shen Pu-hai, and we find the term used in this way in a passage in the *Han Fei-tzu,* 15.11a, which there is reason to believe emanated from his branch of the *Fa-chia.* The previous note pointed out that the school of Shen Pu-hai is undoubtedly responsible for the *Jen Shu* essay in the *Lü-shih Ch'un-ch'iu,* and in that essay (17.10b) we find the doctrine of *hsing-ming* stated but denoted by the alternate term often used for it, *ming-shih* 名實. And in the *Han Fei-tzu* this doctrine is directly attributed, using *ming-shih,* to Shen Pu-hai. For this latter passage see *Han Fei-tzu* (*Ssu-pu Ts'ung-k'an* ed.), 17.5a; the *Ssu-pu Pei-yao* text here (17.5b) substitutes *kuei* 貴 for *tse* 責, which is an obvious copyist's error.

126. *Chuang-tzu,* 5.15a, has *hsing* 形 rather than *hsing* 刑 here, but this is the result of an erroneous alteration of the text; see note 130, below.

127. *Chuang-tzu,* 5.15ab.

the Shen Pu-hai branch of the *Fa-chia*[128] has been obscured by two circumstances. First, the meaning of *hsing-ming* was lost, and has not been understood since an early date. Second, the text of the *Chuang-tzu* has been altered so that, whereas there were originally nine occurrences of *hsing-ming* 刑名 in this chapter, a number of the most current texts instead read 形名 (which is quite a different term)[129] in eight or even in all nine instances.[130]

In the *T'ien Tao* chapter of the *Chuang-tzu* we see an attempt—which was to prove quite successful—to take over *wu-wei* from the *Fa-chia*, and not only to make *wu-wei* a Taoist term but to wrest it away from the *Fa-chia* altogether. The argument is subtle.

The Shen Pu-hai fragments refer frequently to *tao*, but only as "methods" or "policies" of administration. But this, the author of the *T'ien Tao* chapter says, is not "the Great *Tao*." The Shen fragments say that a ruler must practice *wu-wei*, i.e., avoid overt activity, and that he can do this

128. The reference to "rewards and punishments" is presumably aimed at the branch of the *Fa-chia* stemming from Shang Yang, since the concept seems to be alien to the school of Shen Pu-hai. But this chapter of the *Chuang-tzu* is most centrally concerned with *wu-wei*, which as we have seen is not discussed in the *Shang-chün Shu*.

129. On the difference between, and the confusion of, these terms, see pp. 83–85.

130. To avoid repetition of the characters, *hsing-ming* 刑名 will be represented in the usual way, but *HSING-ming* will be used for 形名. The following texts have *hsing-ming* in the first occurrence, and *HSING-ming* in the other eight: *Chuang-tzu* (*Ssu-pu Pei-yao* ed.), 5.14a–15b. *Nan-hua Chen-ching* 南華眞經 (*Ssu-pu Ts'ung-k'an* ed.), 5.26b–29a. Ch'ien, *Chuang-tzu Tsuan-chien*, 105–107. The following have *HSING-ming* in all nine cases: Wang Hsien-ch'ien 王先謙, *Chuang-tzu Chi-chieh* 莊子集解 (1909), 4.3a–4a. *A Concordance to Chuang Tzŭ*, 34–35. Liu Wen-tien 劉文典, *Chuang-tzu Pu-cheng* 莊子補正 (Shanghai, 1947), 5 *chung*. 7a–10a. Kuo Ch'ing-fan 郭慶藩, *Chuang-tzu Chi-shih* 莊子集釋 (Peking, 1961), 468–473.

There is abundant evidence, nevertheless, that the text originally read *hsing-ming* in all nine cases. The context makes it clear that what is being discussed is a technique for personnel control, like that of Shen Pu-hai, and this was denoted by *hsing-ming*, not *HSING-ming*. What is being discussed is the same in all cases; there is no basis for the use of two different expressions that we find in some texts. The *Ch'ün-shu Chih-yao*, compiled in the T'ang dynasty, commonly abbreviates the texts it quotes, and in rendering this passage (37.24a–25a) it has only the first and the ninth occurrences, but both are given as *hsing-ming*. Because of religious conservatism, it is reasonable to suppose that texts in the Taoist canon might have undergone less alteration than others. And in fact we find *hsing-ming* in all nine cases in *Cheng-t'ung Tao-tsang* 正統道藏 (photolithographic reprint of 1447 ed.; Shanghai, 1923), *Ts'e* 350, *Nan-hua Chen-ching*, 3.12b–14a. Even more interesting is ibid., *Ts'e* 490, *Nan-hua Chen-ching K'ou-i* 南華眞經口義, 15.7a–11a. Here we find *hsing-ming* in the first, eighth, and ninth occurrences, and *HSING-ming* in the remainder. But although the second reads *HSING-ming*, the commentary on it reads *hsing-ming*. Quite evidently, although the character was changed in the text, the change occurred after the commentary was written and the commentary was not altered accordingly.

by means of various administrative techniques. Indeed, the *T'ien Tao* author says, the ruler must practice *wu-wei*, putting himself in tune with the sum total of reality, but such a ruler occupies a realm far too exalted to concern himself with petty techniques of administration. Those who do that are mere technicians, good enough to toil in the government service, but quite unfit to rule. Thus we have a clear distinction between those who practice *wu-wei*, who are enlightened Taoists, and those who concern themselves with the petty business of administration, that is, the *Fa-chia*.

We noted earlier that the manner in which the Taoist works use *wu-wei* in connection with government seems to violate common sense. It is hard to understand why it is that, as the *Lao-tzu* tells us, when the Sage, in governing, "practices inaction, as a consequence there is nothing that is not properly governed."[131] But this is much less mysterious if *wu-wei* first gained currency as a *Fa-chia* concept and was then taken over by the Taoists. For some of the *Fa-chia* connotation of *wu-wei*, as a thoroughly practical technique of administration, probably still adhered to the term even though the Taoists refashioned it for their own purposes.

The term *wu-wei*, as we find it in the *Chuang-tzu* and the *Lao-tzu*, seems in fact to denote two different things: (1) An attitude of genuine non-action, motivated by a lack of desire to participate in the struggle of human affairs. (2) A technique by means of which one who practices it may gain enhanced control over human affairs. Sense (1) is found in "contemplative," sense (2) in "purposive," Taoism. *Wu-wei* in sense (1) is basically and essentially Taoist; it did not derive from the doctrines of Shen Pu-hai except insofar as Taoism may have represented a reaction against the *Fa-chia*. But *wu-wei* in sense (2), as a technique of control and especially as a technique of government, does appear to have derived from the *wu-wei* of Shen Pu-hai.

Yet while *wu-wei* undoubtedly was used in these two different senses in Taoist literature, it would scarcely be possible to go through it and classify each occurrence as belonging to sense (1) or sense (2). The distinction between them tends to be blurred, for evident reasons. When the characters *wu-wei* were used to express the thoroughly Taoist idea of sense (1), the fact that this was (in a different sense) a *Fa-chia* term no doubt flavored its meaning. And when *wu-wei* was used by Taoists in a manner quite similar to that of Shen Pu-hai, the Taoist context gave it special connotations.

---

131. *Lao-tzu, shang,* 2b (chap. 3).

It is not easy to fix the chronology of the early development of Taoist doctrine, but we have some indications of it. They seem to show that Taoism moved progressively from being more "contemplative" to being more "purposive," that the use of the term *wu-wei* was rare at first but became progressively more frequent, and that as the use of *wu-wei* became more common it also came to be employed, in an increasing proportion of its occurrences, to denote a technique for the exercise of power, especially in government.

Current scholarly opinion dates the *Lao-tzu* as having been written (or compiled or edited) later than the earliest portions of the *Chuang-tzu*.[132] Concerning the dating of the various parts of the *Chuang-tzu* there is a variety of opinion. Traditionally the first seven chapters, constituting the *Nei-p'ien,* have been held to have been written by Chuang-tzu personally, but no doubt few would still agree to this simple position. Various passages of the *Nei-p'ien* are held by various scholars to be intrusive, while some later portions of the book are also considered equally authentic. Nevertheless it would probably be agreed that in general there are fewer problems, and less deviation from a consistent doctrine, in the *Nei-p'ien* than in other portions of the *Chuang-tzu*.[133] For a variety of reasons it seems quite possible that these first seven chapters may well, as has commonly been supposed, include the earliest portions of the book.

Wu-wei occurs only three times in these first seven chapters of the *Chuang-tzu.* Let us examine the passages in which it is found. The first one, speaking of a tree, says: 彷徨乎無爲其側逍遙乎寢臥其下‧[134] Fung Yu-lan translates this: "By its side you may wander in nonaction; under it you may sleep in happiness."[135] The second passage reads: 夫道有情有信無爲無形.[136] Fung translates this: "*Tao* has reality and evidence, but no action and form."[137] The third is: 彷徨乎塵垢之外逍遙乎無爲之業.[138]

132. Ch'ien, *Hsien-Ch'in Chu-tzu Hsi-nien,* 223–226. Fung Yu-lan, *A Short History of Chinese Philosophy,* 83, 87, 93–94, 104. Ku Chieh-kang, *Lun Shih-ching Ching-li Chi Lao-tzu Yü Tao-chia Shu* 論詩經經歷及老子與道家書, in *Ku-shih Pien,* IV, 57. Sun Tz'u-tan 孫次丹, *Po Ku-shih Pien Ti-ssu Ts'e Ping Lun Lao-tzu chih Yu-wu* 跋古史辨第四冊並論老子之有無, in *Ku-shih Pien,* VI (Shanghai, 1938), 91. Takeuchi Yoshio 武內義雄, *Rōshi Genshi* 老子原始, translated in Chiang Chia-an 江俠庵, trans. *Hsien-Ch'in Ching-chi K'ao* 先秦經籍考 (Shanghai, 1933), II, 304–306. Waley, *Three Ways of Thought in Ancient China,* 11, and Waley, *The Way and Its Power,* 86.
133. Hu, *Chung-kuo Che-hsüeh Shih Ta-kang, chüan shang,* 254. Fung, *Chuang Tzǔ,* 3. Chang, *Wei-shu T'ung-k'ao,* 712–734.
134. *Chuang-tzu,* 1.9b.
135. Fung, *Chuang Tzǔ,* 40.
136. *Chuang-tzu,* 3.5b.
137. Fung, *Chuang Tzǔ,* 117.
138. *Chuang-tzu,* 3.11b.

Fung's translation of this reads: "They stroll beyond the dirty world and wander in the realm of inaction."[139]

In none of these three passages does *wu-wei* figure as a technique of government, or of the exercise of power. None of them gives clear indication that *wu-wei* denotes a definitely formulated philosophical concept.

The main emphasis of the *Nei-p'ien* of the *Chuang-tzu* is on withdrawal from, nonparticipation in, the ordinary business of life. "The sage," we are told, "does not occupy himself with the affairs of the world."[140] But the benefits to be derived from such non-action are principally described in terms of serenity for the individual.[141] Only rarely is it suggested that such non-action may be a source of power for the ordinary person.[142] And this idea is never simply and directly formulated, or denoted by any particular expression, either *wu-wei* or any other.

In these first seven chapters the practice of government is not a prominent theme, but it occurs. One passage is translated thus by Fung Yu-lan: "When the sages set the world in order, they have no concern with what is outside human nature. They let every man follow his own proper nature, and go at that. Every man does what he really can do; that is all."[143] Two other passages speak of the value of non-action or limited action in government, but not in a very conclusive manner.[144]

Thus we do find, in the first seven chapters of the *Chuang-tzu*, two slightly different ideas which elsewhere in Taoist literature are denoted by *wu-wei*. One is the idea of complete nonparticipation in worldly affairs; the second is that of ruling by simply letting things alone and permitting them to develop of themselves. The three occurrences of *wu-wei* in these chapters may refer to the first of these ideas, but why is the term so rare? I suggest that the early Taoists may have intentionally avoided it, because of its *Fa-chia* associations. We have seen that chapter 13, *T'ien Tao*, seems to be an attempt to divorce *wu-wei* from these associations. Nevertheless, in the *Chuang-tzu* as a whole, eighteen chapters, more than one-half of the thirty-three, have no occurrence of *wu-wei* at all.[145]

139. Fung, *Chuang Tzǔ*, 124.
140. *Chuang-tzu*, 1.21b; Fung, *Chuang Tzǔ*, 60.
141. See, for instance, *Chuang-tzu*, 3.11b; Fung, *Chuang Tzǔ*, 125.
142. *Chuang-tzu*, 2.20a–22a, 3.19a; Fung, *Chuang Tzǔ*, 103–105, 141.
143. *Chuang-tzu*, 3.15b–16a; Fung, *Chuang-Tzǔ*, 134.
144. *Chuang-tzu*, 2.7a–8a, 2.20a–22a; Fung, *Chuang Tzǔ*, 79–81, 103–105. One passage is quite reminiscent of the retiring posture of the ruler advocated by Shen Pu-hai, but since it speaks of his "achievements" and "benefits" it does not seem, with any clarity at least, to involve non-action: *Chuang-tzu*, 3.17a; Fung, *Chuang Tzǔ*, 136.
145. *Wu-wei* occurs in the various chapters of the *Chuang-tzu* as follows: I, once. VI, twice. X, once. XI, five times. XII, five times. XIII, thirteen times. XIV, once. XV,

As compared with only three instances of *wu-wei* in the first seven chapters of the *Chuang-tzu,* it occurs fifty-three times in the last twenty-six chapters.[146] And in the *Lao-tzu,* which is generally agreed to represent a later phase of early Taoism, *wu-wei* occurs with more than two and one-half times its frequency in the *Chuang-tzu.*[147]

Wu-wei as denoting a technique of government does not appear in the first seven chapters of the *Chuang-tzu* at all. In its last twenty-six chapters, *wu-wei* figures as a governmental technique in thirty-four per cent of its occurrences.[148] In the *Lao-tzu, wu-wei* is a technique of government fifty per cent of the time.[149]

Not only does *wu-wei* occur with increasing frequency in Taoist literature, and in an increasing proportion of its appearances figure as a technique of government. But in the *Lao-tzu* we find *wu-wei* thoroughly naturalized as a major concept of Taoist philosophy. And in much of the *Lao-tzu* (this composite work does not make the same emphases in all of its parts) Taoism would seem to have undergone an about-face; from being a protest against the regimentation of the *Fa-chia,* it proclaims itself as the most powerful instrument for such regimentation.[150] This reflects the fact that in the *Lao-tzu* we find predominantly "purposive" Taoism, in which the Taoist seeks to use his power to control and govern the world.[151] Taoism has taken over, and partially remoulded, the *wu-wei*

---

three times. XVIII, nine times. XXI, once. XXII, eight times. XXIII, three times. XXIV, once. XXV, twice. XXXIII, once.

146. Thirteen of these occurrences, twenty-three per cent of the occurrences of *wu-wei* in the entire *Chuang-tzu,* occur in chapter 13, *T'ien Tao,* which as we have seen is devoted in considerable measure to taking over the *wu-wei* of the *Fa-chia* and converting it into a Taoist concept.

147. According to my count, the *Ssu-pu Pei-yao* edition of the *Lao-tzu* contains 5,275 characters. This accords well with the statement in *Shih-chi,* 63.6, that it contained "five thousand and more words." Since *wu-wei* occurs twelve times in the text, this is one occurrence for every 439 characters.

Cheng-t'ung Tao-tsang, Ts'e 495, *Nan-hua Chen-ching Chang-chü Yin-i* 南華眞經 章句音義, *Hsü* 序, 2b, says that the text of the *Chuang-tzu* contains 65,923 characters. I have made a rough calculation of the text published in *A Concordance to Chuang Tzŭ,* which comes within a few hundred characters of this figure. Dividing 65,923 by the number of occurrences of *wu-wei,* 56, there is one occurrence of *wu-wei* in the *Chuang-tzu* for every 1,177 characters.

Dividing, 1,177 by 439, we find that in a given quantity of text *wu-wei* occurs 2.68 times as frequently in the *Lao-tzu* as in the *Chuang-tzu.*

148. See pp. 54–55.

149. See p. 54.

150. So that *Lao-tzu, shang.* 2b (chap. 3), tells us that "the government of the sage empties the people's minds and fills their bellies, weakens their wills and strengthens their bones."

151. Thus Duyvendak, *Tao Te Ching,* 12, says that "the *Tao-tê-ching* addresses its message in the first place to the Saint as ruler." Similarly Waley, *The Way and Its Power,* 92, writes:

of Shen Pu-hai as a technique of administration. This was done so successfully that later scholars have supposed that the *Fa-chia* borrowed *wu-wei* from Taoism.

To recapitulate:

In the preserved Chinese literature earlier than the *Lun-yü*, the expression *wu-wei* occurs only four times, in contexts that bear little relation to its later significance. In the *Lun-yü* Confucius is quoted as using it to denote the idea that the ruler should "reign but not rule." *Wu-wei* does not occur again in any preserved text that can be dated as earlier than the *Chuang-tzu*. It figures, however, as an important administrative technique in various quotations from Shen Pu-hai, who died in 337 B. C. In the first seven chapters of the *Chuang-tzu, wu-wei* occurs only three times, and never as denoting a governmental technique. In the *T'ien Tao* chapter of the *Chuang-tzu* there is what appears to be an elaborate attempt to claim *wu-wei* as exclusively a Taoist concept, and to brand the *Fa-chia* as mere technicians unable to rise to its exalted sphere. In the last twenty-six chapters of the *Chuang-tzu, wu-wei* occurs fifty-three times, and denotes a technique of government one-third of the time. In the *Lao-tzu, wu-wei* occurs with two and one-half times its frequency in the *Chuang-tzu*, and has become an important and integral concept; in the *Lao-tzu* it is a technique of government in one-half of its occurrences.

Wu-wei as we find it in Taoism appears to have sprung from two sources. What was apparently the first, in point of time, was the *wu-wei* of Shen Pu-hai, denoting a particular complex of ideas concerning governmental administration. Quite different from this was the Taoist concept of "non-action," based in a desire to withdraw from and take no part in the struggle of human affairs. Although the term *wu-wei* was well suited to express the Taoist concept, it came into use in Taoism slowly, no doubt because of reluctance to use an expression associated with the *Fa-chia*. But as "purposive" Taoism developed, and Taoists became interested in the exercise of power, the term *wu-wei* was used increasingly, and more and more frequently in a manner resembling its employment by the *Fa-chia*, although embellished with characteristically Taoist overtones.

"The *Tao Tê Ching* is not in intention . . . a way of life for ordinary people. It is a description of how the Sage (shêng) acquires the power of ruling without being known to rule." (This is highly reminiscent of the inconspicuous posture of the ruler advocated by Shen Pu-hai.) And the *I-wen Chih* 藝文志 of the *Han-shu* (Wang, *Ch'ien-Han-shu Pu-chu, 30.38a) says that Taoism sets forth "the technique of the ruler on his throne."

5

The Meaning of 刑名 *Hsing-ming*

The expression *hsing-ming* 刑名 has been a puzzle (not always recognized as such) for many centuries. Giles defined it as "criminal law; punishments."[1] Couvreur's *Dictionnaire classique de la langue chinoise* (Siensien, 1930) does not list it under either character. The *Tz'ŭ-yüan* says: ". . . In former times the secretaries in government offices who had charge of the records of decisions in criminal matters were called *hsing-ming*."[2] The *Tz'ŭ-hai* offers two definitions.[3] The first quotes passages from three works and seeks to explain them by giving essentially the same definition as that of the *Tz'ŭ-yüan,* which is clearly inadequate for the purpose. The second definition, referring to a passage in *Hsün-tzŭ*, defines it as simply "names of punishments," but in fact the idiom *hsing-ming* does not occur there at all.[4]

This same passage is quoted by the *P'ei-wên Yün-fu,* together with two others, but none of them sheds much real light on the problem. The *K'ang-hsi Tzŭ-tien* does not quote the idiom under either character. Nor, as we shall see, are commentators much help. It is not surprising, then, that when all the usual sources of illumination fail translators have had difficulty with the expression.

For instance, in what evidently are occurrences of the idiom Chavannes translated *hsing-ming* as "les châtiments et les noms"[5] and Bodde

Reprinted with permission from *Studia Serica Bernhard Karlgren Dedicata,* ed. Søren Egerod and Else Glahn (Copenhagen, 1959), 199–211.

1. Herbert A. Giles, *A Chinese-English Dictionary,* 2d ed. (London, 1912), 577.
2. *Tz'ŭ-yüan* (Shanghai, 1915; reprinted 1923).
3. *Tz'ŭ-hai* (Shanghai, 1937).
4. See *Hsün-tzŭ (Ssŭ-pu Pei-yao* ed.), 16.1a. The two characters do occur together, meaning "names of punishments." But in English if we speak of "a love affair" meaning merely "a matter having something to do with love," we are not using the idiom "love affair."
5. *Les Mémoires historiques de Se-ma Ts'ien,* trans. Édouard Chavannes (referred hereafter to as *Mémoires historiques*) (Paris, 1895–1905), II, 186.

(presumably with the concurrence of Fung Yu-lan) rendered the character occurring as part of a series as "punishments, names."[6] Wilhelm similarly translates it as "die Strafen und die Bezeichnungen."[7] But this is strange when we put it together with the statement of the Ch'ien-Han-shu that Emperor Wên "was fond of the doctrines of hsing-ming,"[8] and remember that, as Dubs points out, this same emperor "ameliorated the severities of the law, abolishing mutilating punishments and other unnecessary cruelties," and that in his reign "capital punishment became a rare thing."[9] The usual renderings are of still less help when we read in the Han-fei-tzŭ that the ruler must "use hsing-ming to recruit ministers."[10] There are scores of such perplexing passages in Chan-kuo and Han literature.

Having spent many months in research on this problem, I certainly have no criticism of translators to whom it has given trouble. I merely hope that my work may be of some use to them in the future. In the course of extended research on the early background of the Chinese examination system, I became aware that hsing-ming was an important term, in Chan-kuo and Han times, concerned with personnel control and examination, and that its meaning has apparently become lost. I think that I can now explain it. In the process, many interesting side issues will have to be left unexplored, to be treated in a fuller study of the rise of the examination technique.

Probably the most revealing passage on hsing-ming is a quotation from the now lost Pieh-lu 別錄 of Liu Hsiang 劉向, which begins: "The doctrine of Shên-tzu 申子 is called hsing-ming."[11] Shên-tzu, i.e., Shên Pu-hai 申不害, was a prime minister of the state of Han 韓 who died in 337 B. C.[12] Fung Yu-lan described him as "the leader of the group [in the Legalist school] which emphasized shu 術, that is, statecraft or methods of government."[13]

6. Fung Yu-lan, A History of Chinese Philosophy, trans. Derk Bodde (Princeton, 1952–1953), I, 320. The preface says (p. xii) that "Dr. Fung Yu-lan . . . read the manuscript and carefully checked it with the original."

7. Frühling und Herbst des Lü Bu We, trans. Richard Wilhelm (Jena, 1928), 259. For the text see Lü-shih Ch'un-ch'iu (Ssŭ-pu Pei-yao ed.), 16.17a.

8. Wang Hsien-ch'ien 王先謙, Ch'ien-Han-shu Pu-chu 前漢書補注 (referred to hereafter as Han-shu) (1900), 88.3b.

9. Pan Ku, The History of the Former Han Dynasty, trans. Homer H. Dubs (referred to hereafter as Dubs, Han-shu) (Baltimore, 1938–1955), I, 218–219.

10. Han-fei-tzŭ (Ssŭ-pu Pei-yao ed.), 15.11a.

11. Han-shu, 9.1a (col. 12); Dubs, Han-shu, II, 300, n. 1.2.

12. Takigawa Kametaro 瀧川龜太郎, Shih-chi Hui-chu K'ao-chêng 史記會註考證 (referred to hereafter as Shih-chi) (Tokyo, 1932–1934), 45.7–8.

13. Fung Yu-lan, op. cit., I, 319.

From a number of statements about Shên Pu-hai, and numerous quotations from his now lost work called *Shên-tzŭ*,[14] we get a fairly clear picture of his ideas. The terms by which we attempt to pigeonhole Chinese thinkers are of dubious usefulness, but if we employed them we should have to say that the ideas of Shên Pu-hai show both Confucian and Taoist characteristics. A quotation from his book says that if a ruler acts as he should "the near will feel affection for him, and the distant will yearn toward him."[15] This is almost a paraphrase of the words of Confucius in *Lun-yü*, 13.16, but stands in complete opposition to the dictum of Han-fei-tzu that "gaining the people's hearts" has no place in good government, which must be so strict that the people will consider their ruler an oppressor.[16] The *Han-fei-tzŭ* criticizes Shên for trusting solely to *shu*, methods, while neglecting *fa*, laws,[17] and Shên's book is quoted as saying that a ruler ought to "use methods (*shu*) and lack punishments (*hsing*)," controlling his subordinates by means of persuasion.[18] Thus it appears very improbable that the *hsing* in the *hsing-ming* of Shên Pu-hai meant "punishments."

Shên argued that if the government were organized by the proper methods the ruler personally need do little; he could be "without action," *wu wei* 無爲.[19] This sounds "Taoist,"[20] but we should not forget *Lun-yü*,

14. Hu Shih called this work a forgery, and said that quotations from it found in other works "do not seem to have been written by Shên Pu-hai"—*Chung-kuo Chê-hsüeh Shih Ta-kang* 中國哲學史大綱, *chüan shang* 卷上 (Shanghai, 15th ed., 1930), 362–363. While I find much of Hu's argument concerning the "so-called Legalist school" excellent, I think he has overlooked the fact that in the passage he quotes attributed to the *Shên-tzŭ* the character *fa* 法 should (in the light of other passages elsewhere quoted from this work) clearly be translated as "methods," not as "laws." The numerous passages that I have seen quoted from this work seem remarkably consistent with what we are told of Shên Pu-hai. It should be noted, too, that it was evidently a brief work, such as even a statesman might have found time to write. Attesting to his authorship, see: *Shih-chi*, 45.8 (col. 1, commentary), 63.13, 63.14 (cols. 2–3, commentary), *Han-shu*, 30.40b.

15. This quotation from the *Shên-tzŭ* occurs in a T'ang dynasty work, Wei Chêng 魏徵, *Ch'ün-shu Chih-yao* 羣書治要 (*Ssŭ-pu Ts'ung-k'an* ed.), 36.26b.

16. *Han-fei-tzŭ*, 19.12b–13a. This section of the work seems to be universally accepted as written by Han-fei-tzŭ. See: Ch'ên Ch'i-t'ien 陳啓天, *Han-fei-tzŭ Chiao-shih* 韓非子校釋, 2d ed. (Shanghai, 1941), 1. Derk Bodde, *China's First Unifier* (Leiden, 1938), 40, n. 1. Jung Chao-tsu 容肇祖, *Han-fei-tzŭ K'ao-chêng* 韓非子考證 (Shanghai, 1936), 1.2.

17. *Han-fei-tzŭ*, 17.5b–6a. This section of the work is accepted by most critics as being by Han-fei-tzŭ; see Ch'ên Ch'i-t'ien, *Han-fei-tzŭ Chiao-shih*, 88.

18. This quotation from the *Shên-tzŭ* was quoted from the *Hsin-hsü* 新序 (a work usually attributed to Liu Hsiang) by the commentator P'ei Yin 斐駰, of the fifth century A. D., in his commentary on the *Shih-chi*; see *Shih-chi*, 63.14 (cols. 2–3). I have not been able to locate this passage in the *Ssŭ-pu Ts'ung-k'an* edition of the *Hsin-hsü*, but it is common for passages to have dropped out of ancient texts in transmission.

19. Wei Chêng, *Ch'ün-shu Chih-yao*, 36.26b–27a.

15.4, in which Confucius says that Shun governed "without action," *wu wei*.

Specific descriptions of the "methods" of Shên almost always concern personnel control, what we should call management of the bureaucracy. A passage preserved in the *T'ai-p'ing Yü-lan* reads: "Shên-tzŭ said, 'The ruler must have discriminating methods and correct and definite[21] principles, just as one suspends a balance and weight to measure lightness and heaviness, in order to unify and organize his ministers.'"[22] The *Han-fei-tzŭ* says: "Shên Pu-hai talked of 'methods.'... His 'methods' were (for the ruler to) confer office according to ability, to demand reality (*shih* 實) [here presumably meaning performance] according to the name (*ming* 名) [here presumably meaning the official's title], to keep in his own hand the power of life and death, and to test (*k'ê* 課) the ability of the various officials; these are the things that the ruler must personally do."[23] And the *Pieh-lu* of Liu Hsiang said: "The doctrine of Shên-tzŭ is called *hsing-ming*. *Hsing-ming* is to use *ming* to demand *shih*, thus honoring the ruler and humbling the minister, exalting superiors and curbing inferiors."[24]

Hsing-ming, then, is equivalent to *ming-shih* 名實.[25] But *ming-shih*, "name and reality," is a term that was used in numerous senses in Chan-kuo times, and we are concerned with it only as it occurs in connection with personnel control. It is so used in a number of works. It is by no means always easy to determine the value of *ming* in such passages; at times it seems intentionally to be used in more than one sense

20. The fact that various ideas attributed to Shên Pu-hai resemble Taoism does not prove them anachronistic. Such ideas were developing in his time, and no "school" had a copyright on them. Ssŭ-Ma Ch'ien said that "the doctrine of Shên Pu-hai was based on Huang Lao 黃老," probably meaning the Yellow Emperor and Lao Tzŭ (*Shih-chi*, 63.13). But this has little probative value; it is a cliché that he uses with regard to various individuals. I have seen no mention of Lao Tzŭ in any quotation from Shên Pu-hai, and it is improbable that the Yellow Emperor was associated with Taoism until well after his time; see p. 18.

21. I use both "correct" and "definite" to translate the single character *chêng* 正, since both are implied here.

22. *T'ai-p'ing Yü-lan* (1892), 638.4b

23. Wang Hsien-shên 王先慎, *Han-fei-tzu Chi-chieh* 韓非子集解 (1896), 17.7b. The *Ssŭ-pu Pei-yao* edition (17.5b) has an obvious typographical error here. On the authorship of this section see note 17, above.

24. *Han-shu*, 9.1a (col. 12)–1b (col. 1). To understand the end of this passage we must remember the Chan-kuo preoccupation with the problem of the ruler who desires to get and maintain control of the state, bringing order out of the existing chaos.

25. This fact is recognized by Ch'ên Ch'i-t'ien, who fails however to understand *hsing-ming* correctly if I am right; see his *Han-fei-tzŭ Chiao-shih*, 89, n. 4.

simultaneously. Sometimes it means "speech," so that the idea is to compare the statements of an officer, or of one who aspires to office, with the "reality" of his actions.[26] *Ming* also means "reputation," which again is compared with "real" conduct.[27] And, perhaps of most interest for our purpose, *ming* sometimes means "title" or even "official title," which is again contrasted with "real" performance.[28] A passage in the *Lü-shih Ch'un-ch'iu* says: "The hundred officers carefully perform their functions and none dares to be negligent or dilatory, so that title (*ming*) and actual performance (*shih*) guarantee each other."[29]

Turning again to *hsing-ming*, it is obvious that it has the term *ming* in common with *ming-shih*. And in *hsing-ming* we do find *ming* used in all the ways that it is in *ming-shih*, though I believe the sense of "title" or "official title" is most common. But what, then, does *hsing* mean? It evidently corresponds with *shih*, reality. A number of scholars have recognized that in this context *hsing* cannot mean punishments. Instead they interpret it as being simply another way of writing the character *hsing* 形, "form" (hereafter this character will be romanized as *HSING*). Thus our problem would be solved very simply, by the formula: *hsing-ming* 刑名 is equivalent to *HSING-ming* 形名.[30]

This solution although widely accepted is certainly erroneous, as will be shown. Yet a number of accidents have conspired to make it almost diabolically plausible. *Hsing* and *HSING* are used interchangeably.[31] *Hsing-ming* is used at least once where the reading should obviously be *HSING-ming*.[32] And we sometimes find *HSING-ming* used in passages where it is very difficult to determine from the sense whether this is correct, or the reading should be *hsing-ming*.[33] Furthermore a case can be made for always reading *hsing-ming* as *HSING-ming*. We have already seen that *hsing-ming* corresponds to *ming-shih*, and that *ming-shih* has the sense (in this context) of "title and performance." *Hsing* should then

26. This may be related to the sense of "written character" which *ming* has. For *ming-shih* in this sense see: *Han-fei-tzŭ*, 4.13a. *Lü-shih Ch'un-ch'iu*, 17.11b, 18.1a.
27. See: *Han-fei-tzŭ*, 4.14b, 16a, 17a. *Lü-shih Ch'un-ch'iu*, 13.10a.
28. See: *Han-fei-tzŭ*, 2.2b, 14.7b. *Kung-Sun Lung Tzŭ* (*Ssŭ-pu Pei-yao* ed.), 8a–9a.
29. *Lü-shih Ch'un-ch'iu*, 17.10b. See also ibid., 17.1b–2a.
30. Wang Ming-shêng 王鳴盛, *Shih-ch'i Shih Shang-chüeh* 十七史商榷 (1787), 5.1b–2a. *Shih-chi*, 63.3a (col. 5f., commentary). Dubs, *Han-shu*, II, 300, n. 1.2.
31. For instance, the same passage occurs (with very slight differences) in the *Kuan-tzŭ* and in the *Han-fei-tzŭ*, but the former has *hsing* where the latter has *HSING*; *HSING* is evidently correct. Compare *Kuan-tzŭ* (*Ssŭ-pu Pei-yao* ed.), 1.8b–9a, with *Han-fei-tzŭ*, 16.7b.
32. *Chan-kuo Ts'ê* (*Ssŭ-pu Pei-yao* ed.), 19.4b.
33. For instance, see: *Han-fei-tzŭ*, 1.10a, 2.10b. *Lü-shih Ch'un-ch'iu*, 19.6a.

mean something like "performance." *HSING* may have the sense of "to appear, to become manifest." Thus *HSING-ming* could, it may be argued, mean something like "official title and the performance which is the real manifestation of what it implies." Thus *HSING-ming* would be equivalent to *ming-shih*, which is equivalent to *hsing-ming*.

This theory has been so persuasive that it has even led to the alteration of text. The contemporary scholar Ch'ên Ch'i-t'ien, in his very useful edition of the *Han-fei-tzŭ*, explains that where the expression *hsing-ming* occurs, "even though the characters *HSING* and *hsing* were anciently interchangeable, in order to eliminate the possibility of misunderstanding I have changed [*hsing*] to *HSING*."[34] Insofar as I have observed, he has altered every occurrence of *hsing-ming* in the text. Ch'ên does at least tell us in notes what he has done. There is reason to believe, however, that other scholars (and perhaps copyists) have been making the same "correction" in texts for centuries, without feeling any necessity to indicate the fact.[35] Thus the original reading of many passages has probably been irretrievably lost.[36]

34. Ch'ên Ch'i-t'ien, *Han-fei-tzŭ Chiao-shih*, 758, n. 6.

35. There is room for suspicion that this has happened everywhere that we find *HSING-ming* where the sense calls for *hsing-ming*. But suspicion is not, of course, proof. There is proof, however, in the case of at least one passage in the *Chuang-tzŭ*. This concept is treated at length in *Chuang-tzŭ* (*Ssŭ-pu Pei-yao* ed.), 5.14a–15b. The expression occurs nine times in this passage. From the context it should clearly read *hsing-ming*, but it does so read only in the first instance, while in the latter eight it reads *HSING-ming*. Yet in the first and last instances it is embedded in exactly the same sequence of eight characters, so that the identity is beyond question. Furthermore, this same passage is quoted in abbreviated form in the T'ang work of Wei Chêng, *Ch'ün-shu Chih-yao*, 37.23a–25a. Unfortunately the abbreviation omits all but the first and last occurrences of the expression, but both of these read *hsing-ming*, which makes it appear almost certain that the text available to the T'ang compilers so read in all nine cases. It would appear, therefore, that in the latter eight occurrences *hsing-ming* had been altered to *HSING-ming* in the Ming text which is used by the *Ssŭ-pu Pei-yao*, and also used by the *Ssŭ-pu Ts'ung-k'an* (see 5.25b–29a). Even more interesting evidence is supplied by a text in the Taoist canon; see the *Chêng-t'ung Tao-tsang* 正統道藏 (photolithgraphic reprint of 1447 ed.) (Shanghai, 1923), *Ts'ê* 490, *Nan-hua Chên-ching K'ou-i* 南華眞經口義, 15.7a–11a. In this Ming text, of the nine occurrences the first, eighth, and ninth read *hsing-ming*, while the second through the seventh read *HSING-ming*. But the commentary, in referring to the second and third occurrences, repeatedly renders them as *hsing-ming*; obviously the text has been altered here, but the "correction" has not been made in the commentary. And the commentary quite clearly interprets this as the *hsing-ming* concerned with personnel control, even though it does say that the character "*hsing* is equivalent to *HSING*."

36. This has all but happened with the passage discussed in the previous note. Wang Hsien-ch'ien 王先謙, *Chuang-tzŭ Chi-chieh* 莊子集解 (1909), 4.3a–4a, gives *HSING-ming* in all nine cases without the slightest indication that any text ever read otherwise. The same is true of the Harvard-Yenching Institute publication, *A Concordance to Chuang Tzŭ* (Peiping, 1947), 34–35, although this work is generally excellent in giving textual variations.

However convenient, the widely accepted theory that our problem results merely from the substitution of one form of the same character for another will not stand. There are passages in which *HSING* and *ming*, "form" and "name" or "appearance" and "name," are discussed in conjunction, but these are quite different from the contexts in which we find *hsing-ming*.[37] Since as we have seen *hsing-ming* is used analogously with *ming-shih*, *hsing* must perform a function like that of *shih*, "reality." But *HSING*, "form" or "appearance," is not necessarily the same as reality at all, as early Chinese texts tell us explicitly. In fact, we find both *HSING* and *ming* cited as *contrasting* with reality,[38] and the *Han-fei-tzŭ* points out that appearance is not a safe guide to *shih*, "reality."[39]

We have seen evidence (and will see more) that *hsing* as equivalent to *shih*, "reality," has the sense of "performance." Does the character *hsing* 刑 have any such meaning? It does, though this sense has become obsolete and all but forgotten. In two passages in the *Li-chi*, *hsing* is used in a sense that Couvreur renders, correctly I think, as "exécuter, accomplir."[40] In one passage in the *Shu-ching* 書經 it has the meaning of "behavior."[41] In the *Mo-tzŭ* we find the passage *chu chih luan hsing chêng* 助治亂刑政, "to help to control disorder and to administer government," where *hsing* quite clearly stands as a verb meaning "to administer."[42] Thus there is ample justification for interpreting *hsing-ming* as meaning "performance and title."

In Chan-kuo times there was an intense preoccupation with the problem of finding competent men to serve as officials, and of controlling them while they served. If one observes the manner in which the term *hsing-ming*

37. *Chuang-tzŭ*, 5.18a. *Lü-shih Ch'un-ch'iu*, 5.4a. *Huai-nan-tzŭ* (*Ssŭ-pu Pei-yao* ed., referred to hereafter as *Huai-nan-tzŭ*), 16.1a. Fung Yu-lan, *A History of Chinese Philosophy*, I, 192, says that one school of philosophers "during the Warring States period was generally known as the School of Forms and Names (*hsing ming chia* 刑名家), or as the 'Dialecticians.' . . ." Fung quite correctly says that in the one passage he cites in support of this, *Chan-kuo Ts'ê*, 19.4b, *hsing* is a substitution for *HSING*. But this is the only passage that I have been able to find anywhere that speaks of either a "*HSING*-ming school" or a "*hsing-ming* school," in such manner that it might be supposed to be that of the Dialecticians. No doubt the term occurs elsewhere, but its usage does not seem to be general.
38. *Chuang-tzŭ*, 5.18a. *Lü-shih Ch'un-ch'iu*, 5.4a. *Huai-nan-tzŭ*, 16.1a.
39. *Han-fei-tzŭ*, 19.10b–11a.
40. Couvreur, *Dictionnaire classique de la langue chinoise*, 83. *Shih-san Ching Chu-su* (Nanchang, 1815), *Li-chi Chu-su*, 34.13b, 36.9a.
41. *Yao-tien* 堯典, par. 12. See Bernhard Karlgren, "The Book of Documents," in *Bulletin of the Museum of Far Eastern Antiquities*, Stockholm, no. 22 (1950), 2, 4.
42. *Mo-tzŭ* (*Ssŭ-pu Pei-yao* ed.), 3.9b. The expression *hsing chêng* occurs some twenty-seven times in the *Mo-tzŭ* and twice in the *Hsün-tzŭ*. In most of these cases it seems impossible to be sure whether it means "administration of government" or whether the two characters together comprise an expression meaning "government."

was used, it is clear that it denoted a technique for doing these things. It has already been noted that, in his edition of the *Han-fei-tzŭ*, Ch'ên Ch'i-t'ien changes *hsing-ming* to *HSING-ming*. Nevertheless he understands the meaning of the expression almost exactly as I do.[43] So, I think, did Liu Hsiang, writing in the Former Han period when the expression was still current. As we have seen, Liu said: "The doctrine of Shên-tzŭ is called *hsing-ming*. *Hsing-ming* is to demand actual performance (*shih*) on the basis of the title (*ming*) held, thus honoring the ruler and humbling the minister, exalting superiors and curbing inferiors."[44] That is, this was the practice of comparing an officer's title with his performance to determine whether they corresponded.[45] This would naturally result in emphasizing the high position of superiors, and in compelling subordinates to act as such. Such comparison of title with performance would also provide a check on an officer's discharge of his duties.[46]

As the term *hsing-ming* was used in Ch'in and Han times it evidently denoted a system for the organization and control of the corps of officials. This is its most probable sense in the passage on a stele set up by Ch'in Shih-huang which reads: "The Sage of Ch'in, taking charge of the government, for the first time established *hsing-ming*."[47] The *Huai-nan-tzŭ* says that at the period in which Shên Pu-hai lived "the various officials [of the state of Han] were at cross-purposes and in confusion; they did not know what practices to follow. The books on *hsing-ming* therefore came into being."[48] This clearly implies that these books dealt with the duties of officials.

43. Ch'ên Ch'i-t'ien, *Han-fei-tzŭ Chiao-shih*, 89, n. 4.

44. *Han-shu*, 9.1a (col. 12)–1b (col. 1).

45. The reader will have noticed the similarity to the concept of *cheng-ming* 正名, "the rectification of names," the process of making names correspond to reality. This term was sometimes used very much as *hsing-ming* was; see, for instance, the use of both terms in *Lü-shih Ch'un-ch'iu*, 16.17a. Although the concept of *chêng-ming* is traditionally attributed to Confucius, it in fact arose after his time in much the same context of so-called Legalist ideas as that which produced *hsing-ming*; see H. G. Creel, *Confucius, the Man and the Myth* (New York, 1949), 221, 321–322; (London, 1951), 240. On *chêng-ming* as a Legalist concept see Fung Yu-lan, *A History of Chinese Philosophy*, I, 323–325.

46. We have already observed that *ming* sometimes had the sense of "speech," so that *hsing-ming* might have the sense of the comparison of a minister's, or prospective minister's, claims with his actual performance; see *Han-fei-tzŭ*, 15.11a. It seems probable, however, that in Ch'in and Han works *ming*, in this expression, more commonly denoted an official title. This also seems to be its sense in the *Han-fei-tzŭ* in such passages as 1.11b and 2.12a.

47. *Shih-chi*, 6.62. For the differing translation of Chavannes, see *Mémoires historiques*, II, 186. Later in this same inscription, and in another erected earlier, Ch'in Shih-huang uses the related term *ming-shih*; see *Shih-chi*, 6.40, 6.63. Li Ssŭ, who was his prime minister, is quoted as repeatedly recommending to his heir the methods of Shên Pu-hai; see *Shih-chi*, 87.28–34.

48. *Huai-nan-tzŭ*, 21.7b.

Emperor Hsüan of Han, who reigned 73–49 B. C., considered one chapter of the book of Shên Pu-hai particularly important; he was fond of reading it and ordered one of his officials to correct its text.[49] And the *Han-shu* tells us that the officials of Emperor Hsüan *i hsing-ming shêng hsia* 以刑名繩下 "used *hsing-ming* to control their subordinates" (literally, "to keep them in line").[50]

The lively discussion, in Chan-kuo times, of methods for the recruitment, testing, and control of officials had direct and important influence upon the institution of civil service examinations in Han times. The abundant evidence for this that is available cannot be cited here. It is interesting, however, to note the way in which the term *hsing-ming* occurs in connection with Han examinations.

The earliest formal written examination of which there seems to be a clear and unimpeachable record, anywhere in the world, was given at the court of the Han emperor Wên in the year 165 B. C.[51] Both the *Shih-chi* and the *Han-shu* tell us that Emperor Wên was "fond of the doctrine of *hsing-ming*."[52] Two scholars who were advisers to his heir were well-known students of *hsing-ming*.[53] One of them, Ch'ao Ts'o 鼌錯, made the highest grade in the examination of 165.

Ch'ao Ts'o was a student of "[the doctrines of] Shên [Pu-hai] and Shang [Yang], and of *hsing-ming*."[54] Under Emperor Ching he rose to high office. The *Shih-chi* says: "The *Yü-shih-tai-fu* Ch'ao Ts'o became celebrated among his contemporaries for his practice of *hsing-ming*. He repeatedly admonished Emperor Ching, saying, 'The feudal lords are the guardrails and props of the emperor. That subjects are to the ruler as sons to the father has been the rule from antiquity to the present. But now the great states monopolize power and establish separate governments, not looking to the capital for orders.' "[55] Here Ch'ao Ts'o was applying *hsing-ming* to the Han feudal nobles, saying that they had the title, *ming*, of subordinates, and that they should conduct themselves, *hsing*,

---

49. We have this on the authority of Liu Hsiang. See: *Han-shu*, 9.1a (col. 12)–1b (col. 1). *T'ai-p'ing Yü-lan*, 221.5b.
50. *Han-shu*, 9.1a.
51. For details on this examination, including the text of the emperor's question and of the winning answer, see *Han-shu*, 49.17a–22a.
52. *Shih-chi*, 121.6-7. *Han-shu*, 88.3b. The latter passage is an exact copy of the former, but it is worthwhile to cite both because Pan Ku sometimes omits statements by Ssŭ-Ma Ch'ien from passages he is copying, apparently because he disagrees.
53. *Shih-chi*, 101.15–17, 103.17. *Han-shu*, 46.9a, 49.8a.
54. *Shih-chi*, 101.15. *Han-shu*, 49.8a.
55. *Shih-chi*, 23.6.

accordingly. He was perhaps the chief author of the plan whereby the Han feudal states were eventually destroyed.[56]

The earliest regular and extensive use of examination, in China or anywhere else, seems to have been in the *T'ai-hsüeh* 太學 or "Imperial University," established by the Han Emperor Wu in 124 B. C.[57] This step was apparently first suggested by the famous Han Confucian Tung Chung-shu 董仲舒, who also recommended that the students be "frequently examined in order to compel them to exert their abilities."[58] The university was not actually inaugurated, however, until after a very similar suggestion by a scholar more favored by Emperor Wu, Kung-Sun Hung 公孫弘. He recommended that all students in the proposed institution be examined annually and, if successful, given government office in accord with their performance in examination.[59] This plan was put into operation. As a milestone in the development of the Chinese examination system this event deserves more notice than it has sometimes received.

The Chan-kuo discussions of personnel control and testing had clear and direct influence on the writings, concerning these subjects, of both Kung-Sun Hung[60] and Tung Chung-shu.[61] I have not, however, found the term *hsing-ming* in the extant writings of either man. One reason for this may be the official bans laid down, early in the reign of Emperor Wu, against scholars recommended for government service who practiced this doctrine. In 141 B. C. those who were versed in "the words of Shên Pu-hai" were among those dismissed,[62] and in the period from 135 to 132 the prime minister discriminated against, among others, those who followed the doctrine of *hsing-ming*.[63] For other reasons also, which we shall consider shortly, it is not surprising that Tung Chung-shu, a sincere though extremely eclectic Confucian, should have avoided the term.

With Kung-Sun Hung the case is different. Both he and his master, Emperor Wu, made great public show of Confucianism. But it is clear that Wu (once he had thrown off the influence of the Confucian ministers who were ascendant for a time after he came to power at the age of

56. See Dubs, *Han-shu*, I, 292–297.

57. Dubs, *Han-shu*, II, 24, 54.

58. *Han-shu*, 56.12a.

59. *Shih-chi*, 121.10–11. *Han-shu*, 88.4b–5a. Dubs, *Han-shu*, II, 54.

60. *Han-shu*, 58.2b–3b, 7a.

61. *Han-shu*, 56.11a, 13b. Tung Chung-shu, *Ch'un-ch'iu Fan-lu* (*Ssǔ-pu Pei-yao* ed.), 6.5b, 9a; 7.1a–2b, 9a–11b; 17.3a.

62. Dubs, *Han-shu*, II, 28.

63. *Shih-chi*, 121.8. *Han-shu*, 88.3b. For the period in which T'ien Fên was prime minister, see *Shih-chi*, 22.19–20.

fifteen) was familiar with and favorable to Legalist ideas and practices.[64]
So was Kung-Sun Hung,[65] and we might reasonably expect to find the
term *hsing-ming* in some of his writing. The chapter on literature in the
Han-shu lists a work called *Kung-Sun Hung,* in ten *p'ien* 篇.[66] One passage
from this work was quoted by the *T'ai-p'ing Yü-lan* (81.7a), so that it
may have been extant as late as the tenth century A. D., but it is now
lost. It is mentioned, however, in a passage in the *Hsi-ching Tsa-chi* 西京
雜記, which says: "Kung-Sun Hung wrote the *Kung-Sun Tzŭ,* discussing
matters having to do with *hsing-ming,* and said that every character
was worth a hundred pieces of gold."[67] While the date of the *Hsi-ching
Tsa-chi* is uncertain,[68] there would seem to be little reason to doubt that
this book by Kung-Sun Hung did in fact discuss *hsing-ming.*[69]

The influence of the Chan-kuo works on the Chinese examination
system can be traced to a late date. For instance, we read in the *Han-fei-tzu*
that the methods of Shên Pu-hai included *hsün ming êr tsê shih* 循名而責實,
"in accordance with the title demanding real [performance],"[70] and in
a Ch'ing dynasty document we read that the Yung Chêng Emperor
(1723–1735) *hsün ming tsê shih.*[71] Yet the term *hsing-ming* seems to have
dropped out of usage. I have not found it in any document later than

64. Although Wu was a terror to some of his ministers, he treated Chang Ch'ü 張歐,
well known as a practitioner of *hsing-ming,* very well indeed; see: *Shih-chi,* 103.17–18.
Han-shu, 46.9–10a.
65. For documentation on the Legalist tendencies of Kung-Sun Hung and Emperor Wu,
see H. G. Creel, *Confucius, the Man and the Myth* (New York, 1949), 234–242; (London,
1951), 254–263.
66. *Han-shu,* 30.31b.
67. *Hsi-ching Tsa-chi* (*Ssŭ-pu Ts'ung-k'an* ed.), 3.5a.
68. One tradition ascribes it to Liu Hsin 劉歆 of the first centuries B. C. and A. D., but
while much of its material is probably of early date it appears to have been compiled
considerably later; see Chang Hsin-ch'êng 張心澂, *Wei-shu T'ung-k'ao* 偽書通考
(Changsha, 1939), 544–547.
69. If the statement in the *Hsi-ching Tsa-chi* was written early, it should be correct.
And it is improbable that it was written very late, because the meaning of *hsing-ming*
became lost and it is unlikely that anyone would have connected it, at a late date, with
Kung-Sun Hung. The passage quoted from the *Kung-Sun Tzŭ* in *T'ai-p'ing Yü-lan,*
81.7a, says, "Shun, pasturing sheep at the Yellow River, met Yao and was raised to be
Son of Heaven," which is certainly within the realm of "matters having to do with
hsing-ming."
70. Wang Hsien-shên 王先愼, *Han-fei-tzŭ Chi-chieh* 韓非子集解 (1896), 17.7b. The
Ssŭ-pu Pei-yao edition (17.5b) has a very obvious typographical error here.
71. Quoted in Têng Ssŭ-yü 鄧嗣禹, *Chung-kuo K'ao-shih Chih-tu Shih* 中國考試制度史
(published by the Examination Yüan of the Chinese Government, 1936), 292. This
extremely valuable book is excessively rare. I am deeply indebted to Dr. Têng for his
kindness in lending me his personal copy for this research. [This book was reprinted in
Taipei, Taiwan, in 1967.]

Former Han, except in historical accounts and discussions of its occurrence in early works. At least three reasons for its disappearance are fairly obvious.

First, *hsing-ming* was associated with Legalism. Not only Shên Pu-hai but also Shang Yang 商鞅 and Han-fei-tzu were named as students of it.[72] The interesting question of what was the actual relationship between Legalism and *hsing-ming* must be reserved for another paper, but this association was enough to make it distasteful to Confucians. As the examinations came to be based, in the Imperial University and elsewhere, on the Confucian classics, it is not surprising that Confucians did not seek to find the origins of examination in concepts with such associations, and did not themselves use a term which so clearly had such associations.

Second, we have direct evidence that in Han times the doctrine of *hsing-ming* was regarded as being in opposition to that of the *Ju* 儒, "Confucians."[73] This is not surprising. Confucius, and many if perhaps not all Confucians, believed that an official must in the last analysis follow his own conscience and criticize his ruler fearlessly if he believes him in the wrong.[74] But the doctrine of *hsing-ming* could be used to demand of subordinates a supine acquiescence in the policies of their superiors,[75] and the *Han-shu* links it with the execution of high ministers under Emperor Hsüan (73–49 B. C.) for the crime of criticism.[76]

Finally, although the character *hsing* employed in *hsing-ming* did not, in that context, mean "punishment," that was the most usual sense of the character, in Han times as now. This fact must have enhanced the association of *hsing-ming,* for many Confucians, with Legalism, and caused them to shun it. The writings of Tung Chung-shu are instructive. They discuss personnel testing and control in a manner sometimes hardly distinguishable from that of such works as the *Han-fei-tzŭ*.[77] Tung does not hesitate to use the term *ming-shih,* but I have not found *hsing-ming* in any of his preserved writings. And Tung does, significantly, inveigh repeatedly against reliance upon the use of *hsing,* punishments.[78]

---

72. *Shih-chi,* 63.13, 14; 68.2.

73. *Shih-chi,* 121.6–7, 8. *Han-shu,* 9.1, 88.3b. Dubs, *Han-shu,* II, 300.

74. *Lun-yü,* 11.23, 13.15, 14.8, 14.23.

75. The implication of *Shih-chi,* 103.17–18 and *Han-shu,* 46.9a–10a seems clearly to be that practitioners of *hsing-ming* were usually martinets.

76. *Han-shu,* 9.1. Dubs, *Han-shu,* II, 300.

77. *Han-shu,* 56.11a, 13b. Tung Chung-shu, *Ch'un-ch'iu Fan-lu,* 6.5b, 9a; 7.1a–2b, 9a–11b; 17.3a.

78. *Han-shu,* 56.4b–5b, 11b. Tung Chung-shu, *Ch'un-ch'iu Fan-lu,* 11.6b; 12.3b–4a, 6b. This does not mean that he would eliminate *hsing.* He would not (see ibid., 13.1a, 17.4b), but he does seek to diminish its status from that which the Legalists would give it.

In view of the well-known conservatism of Chinese usage, the abrupt way in which *hsing-ming* all but vanishes from the literature is remarkable. The Harvard-Yenching Institute index to the *Han-shu* lists four passages in which it occurs, and there is at least one other.[79] But the index to the *Hou-Han-shu* does not list the expression at all.[80] Although *hsing-ming* was clearly a well-known doctrine practiced at the Chinese court as late as the middle of the first century B. C.,[81] by the third century A. D. when the commentator Chin Shao 晉灼 sought to elucidate the *Han-shu* he completely misunderstood it.[82]

To recapitulate: The expression *hsing-ming*, literally meaning (most commonly) "performance and title" and denoting a technique for personnel control, played a significant role in Chan-kuo, Ch'in, and Han times. It was an important part of the background out of which the Chinese examination system developed. But the practitioners of this technique were adversaries of the Confucians, and as Confucianism became nominally dominant the term seems to have disappeared. The term *hsing-ming* scarcely exists in literature written after the Former Han dynasty, and its meaning became unknown even to historians.

79. William Hung et al., *Combined Indices to Han Shu and the Notes of Yen Shih-ku and Wang Hsien-ch'ien* (Peiping, 1940), 727. This index does not undertake, of course, to be complete. See also *Han-shu*, 9.1a.
80. *Combined Indices to Hou-Han-shu and the Notes of Liu Chao and Li Hsien* (Peiping, 1949), 799.
81. See: *Han-shu*, 9.1a. Dubs, *Han-shu*, II, 299–300.
82. *Han-shu*, 9.1a (cols. 11–12). For the approximate date of Chin Shao, see *Han-shu*, *chüan shou* 卷首, 25b.

6

The *Fa-chia* 法家 : "Legalists" or "Administrators"?

In the opinion of a great many scholars, concern with law is an essential characteristic of the *Fa-chia* 法家.[1] This has led to the usual practice of calling the school "Legalists" or "the School of Law." Joseph Needham put this opinion in extreme form when he wrote that "the Legalists laid all their emphasis on positive law (*fa*). . . "[2]

Not a few scholars, on the other hand, have held that the central concern of the *Fa-chia* has not been law but rather methods of administration, of which the use of law is only one.[3] Some have suggested the use of names other than "Legalist" for the school, designed to make clear its concern with administration.[4]

Reprinted with permission from *Studies Presented to Tung Tso Pin on His Sixty-fifth Birthday, The Bulletin of the Institute of History and Philology, Academia Sinica,* Extra Volume No. 4, Taipei, Taiwan, China, 1961, 607–636. I am indebted to my colleague Dr. Tsien Tsuen-hsuin 錢存訓 for help with many problems encountered in the course of this research, especially regarding matters of bibliography.
1. See: The preface by Wang Hsien-ch'ien 王先謙 to Wang Hsien-shên 王先愼, *Han-fei-tzŭ Chi-chieh* 韓非子集解 (1896). Liang Ch'i-ch'ao 梁啓超, *Hsien-Ch'in Chêng-chih Ssŭ-hsiang Shih* 先秦政治思想史, in *Yin-ping-shih Chuan-chi* 飲冰室專集, 50 (Shanghai, 1936), 132–154. Ch'ên Ch'i-t'ien 陳啓天, *Chung-kuo Fa-chia Kai-lun* 中國法家概論 (Shanghai, 1936), 4–5. Lü Chên-yü 呂振羽, *Chung-kuo Chêng-chih Ssŭ-hsiang Shih* 中國政治思想史 (Shanghai, 1947), 127–130, 190–191. J. J. L. Duyvendak, *The Book of Lord Shang* (London, 1928), 66–130. Derk Bodde, *China's First Unifier* (Leiden, 1938), 197. Karl Bünger, "Die Rechtsidee in der chinesischen Geschichte," in *Saeculum,* III (Munich, 1952), 196, n. 16.
2. Joseph Needham, *Science and Civilization in China* (Cambridge, 1954–1956), II, 544.
3. Hu Shih 胡適 even denied the existence of a "so-called *Fa-chia*": *Chung-kuo Chê-hsüeh Shih Ta-kang* 中國哲學史大綱 (15th ed.; Peking, 1930), I, 360. See also: Chang Ping-lin 章炳麟, *Chang-shih Ts'ung-shu* 章氏叢書 (1919), *Chien-lun* 檢論, 9.4a. Arthur Waley, *Three Ways of Thought in Ancient China* (London; 2d impression, 1946), 199, 232. Fung Yu-lan 馮友蘭, *A Short History of Chinese Philosophy* (New York, 1953), 157.
4. Alfred Forke, *Geschichte der alten chinesischen Philosophie* (Hamburg, 1927), 441. O. Franke, *Geschichte des chinesischen Reiches* (Berlin and Leipzig, 1930–1948), I, 215. Marcel Granet, *La Pensée chinoise* (Paris, 1934), 458. Erich Haenisch, *Politische Systeme und Kämpfe im alten China* (Berlin, 1951), 17–19.

This paper will undertake to show that to call the *Fa-chia* "Legalist" is to misconstrue its nature and to distort its role in Chinese history. This error seems to have been the result of undue prominence that has been given to the school of Shang Yang 商鞅, one of the two fourth-century schools from which the *Fa-chia* principally developed. It laid its emphasis on harsh penal law as the chief instrument of government. The other school, founded by Shên Pu-hai 申不害, was indifferent if not opposed to such use of law; its emphasis was rather on the role of the ruler, and the methods by which he could organize and control the bureaucracy.

History has exaggerated the role of the school of Shang Yang and its ideas, while that of Shên Pu-hai is almost forgotten. Yet there is clear evidence that the latter school played an important role well into Former Han times, and possibly even later. It is by no means certain that the impact of the ideas of Shang Yang upon Chinese institutions has been as great as that of the philosophy of Shên Pu-hai.

When Ssu-Ma T'an 司馬談 used the name *Fa-chia* for this school, apparently for the first time, he may not have intended *fa* 法 to mean merely "law." He was clearly aware that the school had two emphases,[5] and may have availed himself of the fact that *fa* 法 means both "law" and "method." It has both of these senses (sometimes simultaneously) in *Fa-chia* literature, and even in the *Shang-Chün Shu* 商君書.[6] "Method" seems to be the sense in which Shên Pu-hai used *fa*, in all of the quotations of his words known to me. The *Han-fei-tzu* 韓非子 quotes Shên as saying: "What is called 'method' (*fa*) is to examine achievement [as the ground for] giving rewards, and to use ability as the basis upon which to bestow office."[7]

The strong feeling against the *Fa-chia* that has prevailed for more than two thousand years is no doubt partly responsible for the fact that we know very little about its early history. It was probably never a "school" in the same sense as were the Confucians and the Moists. Various early thinkers are named, with different degrees of reason, as its early members or forerunners. The various tendencies that came to typify it seem to have first been pulled together and fully expounded in the *Han-fei-tzu*. It is generally agreed that only a part of that work can have been written by

---

5. Takigawa Kametaro 瀧川龜太郎, *Shih-chi Hui-chu K'ao-chêng* 史記會注考證 (Tokyo, 1932-1934)(referred to hereafter as *Shih-chi*), 130.8, 12.

6. *Shang-Chün Shu* (*Ssŭ-pu Pei-yao* 四部備要 ed.), 3.6a, 4.2a, 14a. Duyvendak, *The Book of Lord Shang*, 294.

7. *Han-fei-tzŭ* (*Ssŭ-pu Pei-yao* ed.), 11.11b–12a.

Han-fei-tzu personally,[8] but it is believed that he probably did write the section that contains the following passage:[9]

問者曰申不害公孫鞅此二家之言孰急於國應之曰是不可程也人不食十日
則死大寒之隆不衣亦死謂之衣食孰急於人則是不可一無也皆養生之具也
今申不害言術而公孫鞅爲法術者因任而授官循名而責實操殺生之柄課羣
臣之能者也此人主之所執也法者憲令著於官府刑罰必於民心賞存乎愼法
而罰加乎姦令者也此臣之所師也君無術則弊於上臣無法則亂於下此不可
一無皆帝王之具也[10]

A questioner asked, "As between the doctrines of the two schools of Shên Pu-hai and Kung-Sun Yang [Shang Yang], which is more vital to the state?" In reply it was said, "This cannot be determined. If a man does not eat for ten days he will die. If he does not wear clothing when the cold weather is at its height he will also die. If it is asked whether clothing or food is more vital to a man, the reply must be that he cannot get along without either one. Both are instruments for maintaining life. Now Shên Pu-hai speaks of *shu* 術 (method), while Kung-Sun Yang practices *fa* 法 (law). What is called *shu* is to bestow office according to the capacity [of the candidate]; to demand actual [performance] in accordance with the title [of the office held];[11] to hold fast the handles of [the power of] life and death; and to examine into the abilities of all of his ministers; these are the things that the ruler keeps in his own hand. [According to the doctrine of] *fa*, laws and decrees are promulgated to the government offices; the inevitability of [deserved] punishment is [impressed] upon the minds of the people; rewards are reserved for those who are careful [to respect] the laws, and punishment is visited upon those who violate orders; these are [the precepts] which the ministers take as their models. If the ruler does not have *shu* he will be overshadowed[12] above; if the ministers lack *fa* they will be insubordinate below. Neither one of these can be dispensed with. Both are instruments of emperors and kings."

8. See: Jung Chao-tsu 容肇祖, *Han-fei-tzŭ K'ao-chêng* 韓非子考證 (Shanghai, 1936). Ch'ên Ch'i-t'ien 陳啓天, *Han-fei-tzŭ Chiao-shih* 韓非子校釋, 2d printing (Shanghai, 1941).
9. See Ch'ên Ch'i-t'ien, *Han-fei-tzŭ Chiao-shih*, 88. In an article written in 1927 Jung Chao-tsu stated that he suspected that this *Ting-fa* chapter was not by Han-fei-tzŭ; see *Ku-shih Pien* 古史辨, IV, ed. Lo Kên-tsê 羅根澤 (Peking, 1933), 674. But in his book published in 1936 he stated at length that after further study he had become convinced that it did appear to come from his hand; see Jung Chao-tsu, *Han-fei-tzŭ K'ao-chêng*, 3.23a–24b.
10. Wang Hsien-shên, *Han-fei-tzŭ Chi-chieh*, 17.7b.
11. The expression *hsün ming êr tsê shih* is used with a variety of meanings in the *Fa-chia* literature. This is the one that seems most appropriate here.
12. Reading *pi* 蔽 for *pi* 弊. See Ch'ên Ch'i-t'ien, *Han-fei-tzŭ Chiao-shih*, 90. Karlgren says

Here the *Han-fei-tzŭ* describes two "schools" of thought which in fact do appear to have coalesced to become the *Fa-chia*.[13] The one that is said to stem from Shang Yang, emphasizing penal law, is that which receives almost all the emphasis in scholarly writing on the *Fa-chia*. The one stemming from Shên Pu-hai is much less well known. Yet notice what this passage says it concerns: "to bestow office according to the capacity [of the candidate]; to demand actual [performance] in accordance with the title [of the office held]; to hold fast the handles of [the power of] life and death; and to examine into the abilities of all of his ministers; these are the things that the ruler keeps in his own hand." Here, in the fourth century B. C. (Shên Pu-hai died in 337), we have at least the seeds of civil service examination and merit rating, and of imperial government through a systematically controlled bureaucracy.

Shên Pu-hai is perhaps less well known than any other figure of comparable importance in Chinese history. In my opinion the impact of his ideas upon Chinese institutions has been much greater than that of the ideas of Shang Yang. Yet in the *Shih-chi*, Ssu-Ma Ch'ien 司馬遷 devotes all of a long biographical chapter (chapter 68) to Shang Yang, while covering the life and works of Shên Pu-hai in a notice consisting of exactly sixty-eight characters.[14]

A book attributed to his authorship and known as *Shên-tzŭ* 申子 was widely distributed and read in Han times.[15] It was listed, along with the *Shang-Chün Shu* and other works, in the *Fa-chia* section of the *Han-shu I-wên-chih* 漢書藝文志.[16] The *Sui-shu Ching-chi-chih* 隋書經籍志, completed

that the latter character occurs as a loan for the former in the *Chan-kuo Ts'ê* 戰國策; see Bernhard Karlgren, "Grammata Serica Recensa," in *Bulletin of the Museum of Far Eastern Antiquities*, no. 29 (Stockholm, 1957), p 100. This reading also receives some support from the use of the former character in a somewhat analoguous passage preserved from the lost book of Shên Pu-hai; see Wei Chêng 魏徵, *Ch'ün-shu Chih-yao* 羣書治要 (*Ssŭ-pu Ts'ung-k'an* 四部叢刊 ed.), 36.25b. The sense is that unless the ruler has effective methods for keeping his ministers under control, they will grasp power and get the upper hand; this is a frequent theme in sayings of Shên Pu-hai that are preserved to us.

13. It is commonly said that there was a third school which coalesced into the *Fa-chia*, of more or less comparable importance, headed by Shên Tao 慎到 and emphasizing *shih* 勢, meaning "power," "authority," and "position." See for instance Fung Yu-lan, *A History of Chinese Philosophy*, trans. Derk Bodde, rev. ed. (Princeton, 1952), I, 318–326. Although I formerly accepted this, I now find it implausible. I have seen no evidence in the Chan-kuo or Han literature that there was actually any "school," based on the ideas of Shên Tao, comparable in any way to those based on the ideas of Shên Pu-hai and Shang Yang.

14. *Shih-chi*, 63.12–13.

15. Ibid., 63.13 (quotation of Liu Hsiang 劉向 in the commentary), 63.28–29. Wang Hsien-ch'ien 王先謙, *Ch'ien-Han-shu Pu-chu* 前漢書補注 (1900) (referred to hereafter as *Han-shu*), 6.1b, 9.1ab (quotation of Liu Hsiang in the commentary).

16. *Han-shu*, 30.40b.

in A. D. 656, still listed the *Shang-Chün Shu* but stated that the *Shên-tzŭ*, which had been extant in the Liang dynasty (502–556), was lost.[17] The bibliographical sections of both of the T'ang histories again listed the work,[18] and it appears in a library catalogue written around 1700, but since that time it seems to have vanished completely.[19]

There are however a number of passages in books of varying date that purport to be quotations from the *Shên-tzŭ*. I have collected and collated all of these that I can locate; they number fifteen. Some of them exist in as many as three versions of which no single one is entirely usable, but in every case it has been possible to arrive at a good text. The longest of these fifteen passages includes five hundred thirty-five characters; together they number eight hundred eighty-one characters.[20]

Various scholars have called in question the genuineness of some or all of these passages that purport to be quotations from the lost work of Shên Pu-hai.[21] Space does not permit discussion of these problems here, but it is my opinion that the evidence—of those who cite any—against these materials is unconvincing. Of the fifteen passages I think that six, totaling one hundred thirty-six characters, may or may not be correctly attributed to Shên Pu-hai.

In my opinion it is highly probable that the other nine passages, totaling seven hundred forty-five characters, come to us from Shên Pu-hai himself. Although these quotations are found in a wide variety of works, of different periods, they are extraordinarily consistent. The style is distinctive and remarkable, of a cryptic terseness quite unlike that of most Chan-kuo philosophical works. The ideas, as difficult to understand as the style, belong to a coherent system. Above all, this material bears the stamp of a personality. And it agrees completely with what we are told about Shên and his ideas in other books.

I have translated all of these quotations from the book of Shên Pu-hai—with great difficulty, for some of them are as cryptic as the text of the *I-ching* 易經. In the near future I shall publish this material, with the

17. *Êr-shih-ssŭ Shih* 二十四史 (Shanghai, *T'ung-wên Shu-chü* 同文書局, 1884) (all references to standard histories later than Han are to this edition), *Sui-shu* 隋書, 34.5b.
18. *Chiu T'ang-shu* 舊唐書, 47.7a. *T'ang-shu* 唐書, 59.14b.
19. For the bibliographic history of this book, see Yen K'ê-chün 嚴可均, *T'ieh-ch'iao Man-kao* 鐵橋漫稿 (1885 ed.), 5.20a. My colleague Dr. Tsien Tsuen-hsuin has made great efforts to locate a copy of the *Shên-tzŭ*, but without success. A work that has eluded his bibliographical ingenuity is not likely, I feel, to be found unless by a lucky chance.
20. [It should be noted that the 1,347 characters mentioned on p. 62 include not only this material but also direct quotations of Shen Pu-hai.] This work attributed to Shên Pu-hai should not, of course, be confused with the extant work *Shên-tzŭ* 慎子, which is attributed to Shên Tao.

necessary notes and with my evidence for believing it genuine.[22] Here it is possible only to summarize Shên's views as these materials reveal them.

The *Shih-chi* tells us that Shên Pu-hai became chancellor of the state of Han 韓 in 351 B. C., and held that office until he died in 337.[23] It was only a half century earlier that the state of Han had come into existence when its ruler, a retainer of Chin 晉, had joined with two other retainers in partitioning Chin. Both this and other circumstances of his life focused the attention of Shên Pu-hai upon the danger that a ruler's ministers, who must function effectively if there is to be a government at all, will become so effective as to usurp his power.

"One who murders the ruler," Shên says, "and takes his state does not necessarily [force his way in by] climbing over difficult walls and battering in barred doors and gates. [He may be one of the ruler's own ministers, who gradually] limits what the ruler [is permitted] to see, and restricts what he [is permitted] to hear, getting [control of] his government and taking over his power to command, [so that in the end the minister] possesses the [ruler's] people and seizes his state."[24]

The ruler must therefore prevent any single minister from gaining pre-eminent power. On the other hand, he must not inhibit his ministers;

21. Hu Shih, *Chung-kuo Chê-hsüeh Shih Ta-kang,* I, 361–363. Ch'ên Ch'i-t'ien, *Chung-kuo Fa-chia Kai-lun,* 237–238. Duyvendak appears to question these materials when he says (*The Book of Lord Shang,* 73): "It is of course not likely that either Shên Pu-hai or Lord Shang wrote anything themselves, but it may be supposed that the books to which their names were attached were evolved in the favorable atmosphere created by King Hui's protection of scholars."
22. As has already been mentioned, these quotations from the book of Shên Pu-hai occur, in some cases, in differing versions that require collation. The quotations themselves are found in the following works: Wei Chêng 魏徵 (T'ang dynasty), *Ch'ün-shu Chih-yao* 羣書治要 (631; *Ssŭ-pu Ts'ung-k'an* ed.), 36.25b–27a. *Ch'ün-shu Chih-yao* as it is reproduced in the *Yüeh-ya-t'ang Ts'ung-shu* 粵雅堂叢書 (1853), 36.22a–23b, and in the *Lien-yün-i Ts'ung-shu* 連筠簃叢書 (1848), 36.20a–21b. Ma Tsung 馬總 (T'ang dynasty), *I-lin* 意林 (*Ssŭ-pu Pei-yao* ed.), 2.10b. Chao Sui 趙蕤 (T'ang dynasty), *Ch'ang-tuan Ching* 長短經 (*Ts'ung-shu Chi-ch'êng* ed.), 3.67. *T'ang-Sung Pai-K'ung Liu-t'ieh* 唐宋白孔六帖 (Ming Chia-ching ed.), 13.27a. *Ch'u-hsüeh-chi* 初學記 (edition of 1883), 25.17b. *I-wên Lei-chü* 藝文類聚, ed. Ou-Yang Hsün 歐陽詢 (A. D. 557–641) (edition of 1879), 1.2a, 19.2b, 20.8b, 54.1b–2a, 54.3a. *T'ai-p'ing Yü-lan* 太平御覽 (completed in A. D. 983) (edition of 1892), 2.3a, 37.7b, 390.6a, 401.6b, 402.6a, 432.6b, 624.3ab, 638.4b. *Liu-ch'ên-chu Wên-hsüan* 六臣註文選, ed. Hsiao T'ung 蕭統 (501–531) (*Ssŭ-pu Ts'ung-k'an* ed.), 20.30a, 39.5a. *Pei-t'ang Shu-ch'ao* 北堂書鈔 comp. Yü Shih-nan 虞世南 (A. D. 558–638) (edition of 1888), 29.2a, 45.9b, 149.2b, 157.2a. Hsieh Chü 薛據 (Sung dynasty), *K'ung-tzŭ Chi-yü* 孔子集語 (edition of 1875), *shang* 2ab.
23. *Shih-chi,* 15.7–8, 63.12. This dating is called in question in Ch'ien Mu 穆錢, *Hsien-Ch'in Chu-tzŭ Hsi-nien* 先秦諸子繫年 (rev. ed.; Hongkong, 1956), 237–238. I have not yet gone closely into the question of chronology.
24. *Ch'ün-shu Chih-yao,* 36.25b–26a.

he needs their help. "The intelligent ruler causes all his ministers to advance together, like the spokes of a wheel. . . ."[25] In other words, they are to act as a team, a simile much used in *Fa-chia* literature.

The ruler holds firm control over his team of ministers by means of a number of techniques, including examination and merit rating. He is careful, however, not to compete with his ministers. The ruler concerns himself with principles, policies, large matters; he leaves the carrying out of government business entirely to his ministers. "The ruler holds the controls, the ministers carry on routine functions."[26] Such a ruler does not flaunt his power nor make a show of cleverness. Thus he may seem to be almost completely inactive. Yet although he speaks little, "if his single word is correct, the whole world is well ordered, [but if] his single word is perverse, the whole world is ruined."[27]

The ruler is thus a majestic arbiter, who does not jeopardize his prestige by frequent speech or action, but reigns while leaving it to his ministers to rule.

鏡設精無爲而美惡自備衡設平無爲而輕重自得凡因之道身與公無事無事而天下自極也[28]

[The ruler is like] a mirror, [which merely] reflects[29] the light[30] [that comes to it, itself] doing nothing, and yet [because of its mere presence] beauty and ugliness present themselves [to view. He is like] a scale, [which merely] establishes equilibrium, [itself] doing nothing, and yet [the mere fact that it remains in balance causes] lightness and heaviness [to] discover themselves. [The ruler's] method is [that of] complete acquiescence. [He merges his] personal [concerns] with the public [weal, so that as an individual] he does not act. He does not act, yet [as a result of his mere presence] the world [brings] itself [to a state of] complete [order].[31]

25. Ibid., 36.25b.
26. Ibid., 36.26a.
27. *T'ai-p'ing Yü-lan*, 624.3ab.
28. *Ch'ün-shu Chih-yao*, 36.27a.
29. For this translation of *shê* 設 see *Shuo-wên Chieh-tzŭ Ku-lin* 說文解字詁林, ed. Ting Fu-pao 丁福保 (1928), 1012a, where *shê* is defined as *shih ch'ên* 施陳, "to set forth."
30. For this meaning of *ching* 精, see *Lü-shih Ch'un-ch'iu* 呂氏春秋 (*Ssŭ-pu Pei-yao* ed.), 3.9b.
31. To anyone seeing only this one passage, the translation may seem extremely conjectural. In fact however these words come at the end of five hundred thirty-five characters of text, which provide a great deal of contextural guidance. Other quotations from Shên Pu-hai also throw light on this one. Complete evidence for my translation will be given in my full treatment of Shên Pu-hai.

The use of *tao* 道 here for "method" and of *wu-wei* 無爲 for "non-action" may seem to make this passage Taoist, and Shên Pu-hai has indeed been said to have been a Taoist.[32] After considering the evidence, I am satisfied that he was not. The *Fa-chia* is generally supposed to have borrowed the idea of *wu-wei* from the Taoists, but I now believe that this is most improbable. It will be recalled that in *Lun-yü* 論語, 15.4, Confucius is quoted as having said: 無爲而治者其舜也與 "Was it not Shun who governed by means of *wu-wei*?" Confucius and Shên Pu-hai seem to have been using the expression similarly, and in a sense somewhat different from that of the Taoists.

This conception of the ruler's role as a supreme arbiter, who keeps the essential power firmly in his grasp but is for the most part content to reign while leaving all of the details of ruling to his ministers, has had deep influence upon the theory and practice of the Chinese monarchy. Dubs writes that up until the reign of Han Wu-ti (140–87 B. C.) the Han practice had been that the emperor "confines his own activity chiefly to the appointment and dismissal of his high officials. . . . This custom, which made the emperor chiefly the personnel manager of the government, was plainly a Legalistic . . .[33] practise."[34]

It should be noted that, although the role of Shang Yang in laying the foundations of the *Fa-chia* is generally emphasized while that of Shên Pu-hai is almost forgotten, all of the evidence indicates that this immensely

---

32. *Shih-chi,* 63.13.

33. Here Dubs adds in parentheses: "(and Taoistic)." I could agree to this only with very elaborate qualification. The relationship between the *Fa-chia* and Taoism is a problem too complex for discussion here.

34. Pan Ku, *The History of the Former Han Dynasty,* trans. and annotated by Homer Dubs, 3 vols. (Baltimore, 1938–1955) (referred to hereafter as: Dubs, *Han-shu*), II, 8. Immediately following the words quoted above, Dubs continues: "It was called 'governing by non-activity' and was strongly advocated by Han Fei and by Chuang-tzu. . . . Since the Ch'in government adopted Legalist practises and the early Han rulers adopted Ch'in practises, this imperial abnegation of ruling power came almost certainly to the Han dynasty from the Ch'in, along with many other governmental institutions and offices." In my opinion it is incorrect to describe the conception of the ruler's role that is held by the *Fa-chia* as one of "imperial abnegation of ruling power." In the words of Shên Pu-hai and in the *Han-fei-tzŭ* we read repeatedly that the ruler is not to occupy himself with the details of governing, but the intent seems clearly to be not to diminish but to enhance his power. Over and over again we are told that he must keep a tight grip on the power—"hold fast the handles of life and death." Nor would "imperial abnegation of ruling power" seem a suitable description of the practice of Ch'in Shih-Huang. In Han times also, it seems to me that *Fa-chia* ideas were associated with firm control by the emperor, not the reverse. It is very true, however, as Dubs indicates on the page following these observations, that in the Han period the question of what ideas belonged to the *Fa-chia* and what were "Confucian" sometimes became almost hopelessly confused.

important conception of the ruler's role stemmed principally from Shên Pu-hai, and not at all from Shang Yang.

We have already seen that the *Han-fei-tzŭ*, in a section that may well come from the philosopher Han-fei-tzŭ himself, describes the "two schools" of Shên Pu-hai and Shang Yang. The doctrines of Shên are called *shu* 術 and described as concerned almost exclusively with the manner in which the ruler governs by selecting capable ministers, making certain that they perform their duties, and taking care to hold the controlling power in his own hands. At the same time the doctrines of Shang Yang are called *fa* 法, and described as concerned with law, rewards, and punishments.[35] This same section also criticizes Shên Pu-hai for neglecting *fa*—"he did not take firm control of the laws and unify the statutes and decrees." Shang Yang on the other hand is criticized on the ground that he "lacked *shu*," so that he did not provide the ruler with any method for supervising and controlling his ministers.[36]

An impressive body of testimony in early works bears unanimous witness that this was, in fact, the nature of the doctrines and methods of Shang Yang. The *Shih-chi* describes them at length in chapter 68, devoted to his biography,[37] and twenty-eight passages in five other pre-Han and Han works comment on them in greater or less detail.[38] In every one of these works Shang Yang is associated with law, and most of them emphasize his dependence on harsh penal law. Not one of them indicates that he was concerned with the organization or control of the bureaucracy —except as such control might be secured by penal law, and then only as a part of the general reign of law.

Just the opposite picture emerges from discussions, in early works, of the doctrines of Shên Pu-hai as an individual. These include twelve passages in six pre-Han and Han works.[39] All of them link Shên Pu-hai

35. Wang Hsien-shên, *Han-fei-tzŭ Chi-chieh*, 17.7b.

36. Ibid., 17.8a–9a.

37. It is true that the *Shih-chi* does, at the beginning of his biography, say that Shang Yang "when young was fond of the study of *hsing-ming* 刑名"; see *Shih-chi*, 68.2. And *hsing-ming* was, as we shall see below, the name of a technique for personnel control. But nothing in the biography adds substance to this. The *hsing-ming* doctrine is repeatedly attributed, in various works, to Shên Pu-hai but almost never to Shang Yang.

38. *Han-fei-tzŭ*, 4.11b–12a, 13b–14b; 9.2a, 8b–9a; 17.5b–7a. *Chan-kuo Ts'ê* (*Ssŭ-pu Pei-yao* ed.), 3.1ab, 5.11a–12a. *Huai-nan-tzŭ* 淮南子 (*Ssŭ-pu Pei-yao* ed.), 6.10a; 10.12a; 11.14b; 16.14b; 20.16b, 18a; 21.7b. *Yen-t'ieh Lun* 鹽鐵論 (*Ssŭ-pu Ts'ung-k'an* ed.), 2.1a, 2a, 3b, 4b, 5b, 15a; 5.11a, 11b, 21b; 7.11a; 10.2a, 5a, 10b. *Shih-chi*, 67.22–23 (this reference is a quotation, by a commentator, from the *Hsin-hsü* 新序 of Liu Hsiang 劉向).

39. *Han-fei-tzŭ*, 11.11b–12a; 13.1b, 6a, 8a; 16.6a, 6b; 17.5b–7a. *Lü-shih Ch'un-ch'iu*, 17.7ab. *Chan-kuo Ts'ê*, 26.1b. *Huai-nan-tzŭ*, 21.7b. *Shih-chi*, 63.14. *Han-shu*, 9.1ab. The last two references are to quotations, in commentaries, from works of Liu Hsiang.

with government through control of the bureaucracy. None of them identifies him with the use of penal law. I know of no pre-Han reference that does. Four passages in works of Han date do, but significantly in every one of these cases he is spoken of *together with Shang Yang*.[40]

It is clear that already in former Han times some scholars were no longer aware that the doctrines of Shên and Shang differed. But Liu Hsiang wrote:

申子之書言人主當執術無刑因循以督責臣下其責深刻故號曰術[41]

Shên-tzŭ's book says that a ruler of men ought to use technique rather than punishment, relying on persuasion[42] to supervise and hold responsible[43] his ministers and subordinates; his holding responsible is very strict. Therefore [his doctrine] is called *shu* (method).

The best way to compare the ideas of Shang Yang and Shên Pu-hai would be to compare their writings, but this is unfortunately impossible. We have seen that only fragments of the *Shên-tzŭ* remain. While we have the *Shang-Chün Shu*, perhaps no critical scholar could be found who would suppose it, in its present form at least, to have been written by Shang Yang. Duyvendak concluded that "the present Book of Lord Shang is a com-pilation of paragraphs of different styles, some of which are older than the others; the older ones contain probably the mutilated remnants of the

---

40. *Huai-nan-tzŭ*, 6.10a, 11.14b. *Yen-t'ieh Lun*, 10.5a. *Han-shu*, 56.11a.

41. *Shih-chi*, 63.14.

42. *Yin hsün* 因循 is hard to translate. The two characters are interpreted as meaning "to follow after" or "to imitate." I think it better to render them here in the sense of "relying on going along with," hence "relying on persuasion." One who persuades does not directly oppose those he would influence; rather he agrees, "goes along with" them initially, or at least seems to. And this sense accords with the philosophy of Shên Pu-hai as we know it.

43. This translation of *tu tsê* 督責 is at variance with some interpretations. A memorial of Li Ssŭ 李斯, quoted in the *Shih-chi*, implies that the practice of *tu tsê* derived from Shên Pu-hai and Han-fei-tzŭ (*Shih-chi*, 87.29), and the commentary of Ssŭ-Ma Chên 司馬貞 explains it (ibid., 87.28) thus: 督者察也察其罪責之以刑罰也 "*Tu* means 'examine'; examine into guilt, and punish it by means of punishment." This clearly reflects the common opinion that the *Fa-chia* is concerned only with penal law, and just as clearly it is wrong. The sense that *tsê* 責 has here is illuminated by a quotation by another commentator from another work by Liu Hsiang, which is also describing the doctrine of Shên Pu-hai (*Han-shu*, 9.1a). It reads in part: *i ming tsê shih* 以名責實 "in accord with the title to demand actual [performance]." One of the preserved passages from the book of *Shên-tzŭ* (*Ch'ün-shu Chih-yao*, 36.26a) uses *tsê* 責 in the sense of *chai* 債, "to be in debt." The idea is that the minister is indebted to the ruler who has entrusted an office to him, and owes the ruler service in return. That is, he is "responsible." Bodde (*China's First Unifier*, 39) translates *tu tsê* as "supervising and holding responsible," which in my opinion is clearly correct.

original book that has been lost; the later ones date, on the whole, from the third century."[44] Chinese scholarly opinion is somewhat similar.[45]

On reading the *Shang-Chün Shu* one is struck by a difference between it and the *Han-fei-tzŭ*. Those parts of the latter text that have most claim to the authorship of Han-fei-tzŭ[46] do speak of law a good deal, but they are concerned even more with the role of the ruler and methods by which he may control the bureaucracy. In the *Shang-Chün Shu*, on the other hand, the preponderant emphasis as regards governmental method is on law, and on control by means of rewards and punishments. While there is some discussion of control of the bureaucracy[47] most of it is on a very simple level. In line with the emphasis of this work on agriculture and war, we find it said that men should be permitted to buy office with grain[48] and that office and rank should be awarded for exploits on the battle-field.[49] The method chiefly advocated for personnel control is simply that of punishment and reward.

In a word, the governmental measures advocated in the *Shang-Chün Shu* are just about what we should expect from Shang Yang, as his ideas are described by other sources. Yet the composite style of that work, and the fact that it mentions events that occurred after his death, make it impossible that the book as we have it could have been written by Shang Yang. It probably does, however, represent with some fidelity the views of the "school" that was based on his doctrines, of which the *Han-fei-tzŭ* tells us.[50] That school gave heavy emphasis to penal law. If we are to speak of a Legalist school in China we should reserve the term, in my opinion, for the school of Shang Yang, and for it alone.

The book to which the name of Shên Pu-hai was attached no longer survives, but the fragments that remain correspond very closely with

---

44. Duyvendak, *The Book of Lord Shang*, 159.

45. Chang Hsin-ch'êng 張心澂, *Wei-shu T'ung-k'ao* 偽書通考 (Changsha, 1939), 769–771.

46. On the authorship of the various parts of this text see: Ibid., 773–783. Ch'ên Ch'i-t'ien, *Han-fei-tzŭ Chiao-shih*. Jung Chao-tsu, *Han-fei-tzŭ K'ao-chêng*.

47. *Shang-Chün Shu*, 2.6ab, 9b–10a; 3.1a, 2b, 9a, 9b, 10b, 13a; 4.5ab, 9a, 11b; 5.1a–3b, 10a–12a, 13a, 14b–18a.

48. Ibid., 3.9b.

49. Ibid., 4.5ab; 5.1a–3b.

50. The *Shang-Chün Shu* certainly embodies ideas that came into the school later than the time of Shang Yang. Two passages that deal with control of the bureaucracy in some detail (2.6ab, 2.9b–10a) are so unusual in this text, and make such use of terms common in the school of Shên Pu-hai, that I suspect they represent influence from the latter school. Another longer section (5.10a–12a) that also deals with personnel control is puzzling. The text seems to be somewhat corrupt. This passage seems to deplore the use of many officials. It does not seem characteristic either of the school of Shang Yang or of that of Shên Pu-hai.

what other works tell us of his ideas and probably give us a fairly good conception of his doctrine. In all of the fragments that I have been able to find there is no mention of penal law,[51] nor of the use of rewards and punishments. And ninety per cent of this material is concerned with the ruler's role and the methods by which he may control the bureaucracy.[52]

This difference between the doctrines of Shang Yang and Shên Pu-hai is confirmed by a memorial written by Li Ssǔ that is quoted by Ssǔ-Ma Ch'ien. As chancellor of Ch'in Shih-Huang, Li Ssǔ was no doubt the most effectively practicing member of the *Fa-chia* in all history. In this memorial he mentions Shang Yang twice and Shên Pu-hai four times. He mentions Shang Yang in connection with law and only with law.[53] He mentions Shên Pu-hai in connection with methods for control of the bureaucracy, and only in this connection.[54] And Han-fei-tzǔ is named in connection with both.[55]

It seems quite clear that the *Fa-chia* stemmed, in large measure at least, from two schools of thinkers. One of these, founded by Shang Yang, laid major emphasis on penal law. The other, founded by Shên Pu-hai, concerned itself with the ruler's role and with control of the bureaucracy; it was little interested in, and may even have been opposed to, the application of harsh penal law. Han-fei-tzǔ combined the two tendencies, and it is the combination that is commonly known as the *Fa-chia*.

Before continuing with its history we must consider the term *hsing-ming* 刑名. It was used in Han times to refer to the doctrine of Shên Pu-hai,[56] and to the techniques for control of the bureaucracy that appear to stem from him. Its meaning has, however, long been lost. How completely this is so is indicated for instance by the fact that Duyvendak, one of the most

51. The character *fa* 法 does occur, but we have already seen that the *Han-fei-tzǔ* quotes Shên Pu-hai as using it in the sense of "method"; see Wang Hsien-shên, *Han-fei-tzǔ Chi-chieh,* 11.18b. And that seems to be its sense for him, wherever context makes it clear.
52. This ninety per cent includes all of the fragments which, for a variety of reasons, I feel thoroughly satisfied did emanate from Shên Pu-hai, or represent his ideas.
53. *Shih-chi,* 87.30, 33.
54. Ibid, 87.28, 29, 33, 34.
55. Ibid., 87.29, 30, 33, 34.
56. This term does not, in fact, occur in any of the fragments of the *Shên-tzǔ* that I have found, but the idea it denotes is very clearly present in them. It has already been noted that the *Shih-chi* says that Shang Yang "when young was fond of the study of *hsing-ming,*" but that this appears improbable; see note 37, above. The *Shih-chi* says that the doctrine of Shên Pu-hai "emphasized *hsing-ming*" (*Shih-chi,* 3.13), and the *Pieh-lu* 別錄 of Liu Hsiang said, "The doctrine of Shên-tzǔ is called *hsing-ming*" (*Han-shu,* 9.1a). In the Han period the term was, as we shall see below, persistently associated with the same people who were identified as students of the doctrine of Shên Pu-hai.

thorough and careful students of the *Fa-chia,* translated *hsing-ming* as "criminal law."[57]

In another paper I have reconstructed what was, I am convinced, the original sense of *hsing-ming.*[58] It is not possible here to reproduce the evidence, which is there presented in full, but only to summarize the conclusions. The character *hsing* in this expression does not mean "punishment," nor is *hsing-ming* 刑名 an alternative way, as it is often said to be, of writing *hsing-ming* 形名. Instead *hsing* 刑 here has the sense, now obsolete but preserved in a few early texts, of "performance" or "administration."[59] As *hsing-ming* is most commonly used, *ming* has the sense of "title," the name of the office that is bestowed upon an official.[60] Thus a particular office has its title and the duties that pertain to it, constituting its *ming.* The *hsing,* "performance," of a man being considered for the office is inquired into by the ruler. If *hsing* and *ming* correspond, he is the man for the post. And the same technique served to check on officials actually in office. They held a certain title, *ming.* Did their performance, *hsing,* correspond to it? By comparing *hsing* and *ming* it was possible to determine whether an official was or was not fulfilling his duty.

Although the meaning of *hsing-ming* seems to have been forgotten rather early, Liu Hsiang at the end of the Former Han still understood it. He wrote:

申子學號刑名刑名者以名責實尊君卑臣崇上抑下 [61]

The doctrine of Shên-tzǔ is called *hsing-ming.* [The practice of] *hsing-ming* is to demand actual [performance] in accord with the title [which each official holds, thus] honoring the ruler and humbling the ministers, exalting superiors and curbing inferiors.

Hsing-ming was, then, a technique by which the ruler could maintain firm control of the government while leaving all of the running of it to his ministers. For the ruler prescribed the functions of each official, who must

57. Duyvendak, *The Book of Lord Shang,* 8. For the Chinese text, see *Shih-chi,* 68.2.
58. Pp. 79–91.
59. For examples see: *Mo-tzǔ* 墨子 (*Ssŭ-pu Pei-yao* ed.), 3.9b. Bernhard Karlgren, "The Book of Documents," in *Bulletin of the Museum of Far Eastern Antiquities, Stockholm,* no. 22 (1950), 2, 4.
60. *Ming* is also sometimes used in the sense of the words the man in question utters, i.e., his claims. Ch'ên Ch'i-t'ien, although interpreting *hsing* 刑 as an alternative reading of *hsing* 形, agrees with my understanding of the force of *hsing-ming*; see his *Han-fei-tzǔ Chiao-shih,* 89. He says that the *Fa-chia* uses *hsing-ming* in the same manner as *ming-shih* 名實, and that "*ming* denotes either words or official position, while *shih* denotes either conduct or official functions."
61. *Han-shu,* 9.1ab.

perform them in exactly the manner laid down. As Shên Pu-hai said, "The ruler is like a shout, the minister is like an echo. The ruler plants the root, the minister manages the twigs. The ruler holds the controls, the minister carries on routine functions."[62] This method of tight centralized control conflicted, of course, with the Confucian idea as we find it in Confucius and Mencius that the minister should exercise a large degree of autonomy, following his own best judgment and the dictates of his conscience.[63]

It is well known that the Ch'in dynasty made use of the legalistic practices advocated by that branch of the *Fa-chia* that stemmed from Shang Yang. The influence of Shên Pu-hai is less commonly recognized. We have noted, however, the memorial in which Li Ssŭ repeatedly recommended the method of "supervising and holding responsible" which he attributed to Shên Pu-hai.[64] It is obvious that the Ch'in administration, with power tightly held by the emperor, had some similarity to that which Shên Pu-hai had advocated. And a stele set up by Ch'in Shih-Huang in 211 B. C. bore the words: 秦聖臨國始定刑名 [65] "The Sage of Ch'in [i.e., Ch'in Shih-Huang], taking charge of the government, for the first time established *hsing-ming*." I understand this to be a claim that he had for the first time set up a systematic technique for the organization and control of the bureaucracy.[66]

It is in the Former Han dynasty that the influence of the Shên Pu-hai wing of the *Fa-chia* on some key individuals, and the crucial bearing of their activities on the history of Chinese institutions, become clear. Unfortunately these points could be developed properly only in a complete account that is beyond the scope of this paper; here it is possible only to summarize the most important facts.

It is well known that the governmental institutions of the Han dynasty were taken over from those of Ch'in, with relatively little change.[67] Many of the men who formed them had been Ch'in officials. That being the case, it is more than probable that they held *Fa-chia* principles. Yet I have found no statement that this was true of any of the men close to Han Kao-tsu.

---

62. *Ch'ün-shu Chih-yao*, 36.26a.
63. See, for instance: *Lun Yü* 論語, 11.23, 13.15, 14.23. *Mêng Tzŭ* 孟子, 1(2).8, 1(2).9, 2(2).5, 5(2).9, 7(1).31.
64. *Shih-chi*, 87.28, 29, 33, 34.
65. *Shih-chi*, 6.62.
66. Édouard Chavannes, *Les Mémoires historiques de Se-ma Ts'ien* (Paris, 1895–1905) (referred to hereafter as *Mem.Hist*), II, 186, here translated *hsing-ming* as "les chatiments et les noms," a natural error but, I think, an error. Later in this same inscription, and in another erected earlier, Ch'in Shih-Huang used the related term *ming-shih*; see *Shih-chi*, 6.40, 6.63.
67. *Shih-chi*, 23.5–6. *Han-shu*, 23.12a. Dubs, *Han-shu*, II, 8–9.

This is not surprising. Because Han had supplanted Ch'in, Han officials during the early Han reigns made a great point of displaying their detestation for everything connected with the "lost Ch'in" dynasty.[68] And Han officials who had formerly served Ch'in undoubtedly felt their position to be ambiguous. Even if they held *Fa-chia* views, it is unlikely that they would have talked about them.

It is not until the fourth Han reign, that of Emperor Wên (179–157 B.C.), that there seems to be mention of *Fa-chia* ideas as playing a recognized role. Wên himself, we are told, "was basically fond of the doctrine of *hsing-ming* 刑名."[69] And in his actions there was a great deal that, coincidentally or not, accorded quite precisely with the policy of cautious, unobtrusive firmness that Shên Pu-hai recommended to the ruler.

Emperor Wên particularly favored four men who had *Fa-chia* connections. One of these was a Governor Wu 吳 of Honan (his given name is unknown). Wu was a fellow townsman of the Ch'in chancellor, Li Ssǔ, and had studied with him. It will be recalled that Li advocated the doctrines of Han-fei-tzǔ, Shang Yang, and Shên Pu-hai. Emperor Wên made Wu his Commandant of Justice, the chief legal officer of the empire.[70]

Wu told Emperor Wên that he had a protégé named Chia I 賈誼 who although he was only twenty-three years old was very learned. Wên made him a *po-shih* 博士. Chia I never seems to have proclaimed the *Fa-chia* origins of some of his ideas—he was unpopular enough anyway. It is quite clear, moreover, that both Confucian and Taoist ideas were also important in his philosophy. This combination is normal, of course, for a "Han Confucian," which is what Chia I is generally reputed to be. But the influence of the Shên Pu-hai branch of the *Fa-chia* is sharply clear. Ssǔ-Ma Ch'ien called him an exponent of the doctrines of Shên Pu-hai and Shang Yang.[71] This was partially erroneous; he was no advocate of the ideas of Shang Yang, as we shall see.[72]

It would have been difficult for Chia I to be a sincere Confucian and a sincere adherent of the Shang Yang branch of the *Fa-chia*, for this group attacked the Confucian virtues and sometimes even Confucius himself. But this is not true, insofar as I know, of any individual known as a member of the Shên Pu-hai school. There are no such attacks in any of the preserved

68. *Han-shu*, 23.12b.
69. *Shih-chi*, 121.6–7. *Han-shu*, 88.3b.
70. *Shih-chi*, 84.20–21.
71. *Shih-chi*, 130.59.
72. It is interesting that Pan Ku, in copying this passage (*Han-shu*, 62.15a), substituted the name of Han-fei-tzǔ for that of Shang Yang, no doubt because he realized that the latter was implausible.

fragments of the book of Shên Pu-hai. One of those fragments is in fact a good "Confucian" saying ascribed to Confucius.[73]

There is, however, ample evidence of the affinity of many of the ideas of Chia I with those of the Shên Pu-hai school. And at least two passages in his *Hsin-shu* 新書 [74] are so similar to preserved fragments of the book of Shên Pu-hai that it seems clear that Chia I must have been familiar with it.[75]

A basic difference between the typical "Confucian" position and that of the *Fa-chia* concerned the locus of the authority to make policy. The Confucian view was that the ruler should select wise and virtuous ministers, and then let them govern as they saw fit. As Mencius indicated, he should no more presume to tell his ministers how to govern than he would try to tell a lapidary how to cut jade.[76] But Shên Pu-hai had said that the ruler should determine the structure and the policies of the government, hold everything firmly in his own control, and permit his ministers only to implement the policies he has set.[77] And the *Fa-chia* elaborated various methods, *shu,* by which this could be done.

In this regard Chia I is clearly of the *Fa-chia* opinion. He advised Emperor Wên to teach his heir "to depend upon methods (*shu* 術), to cause him to be able to supervise the functions of the many officials and to understand the usages of government."[78] Some of Wên's other ministers opposed this.[79] In fact the more orthodox Confucians had a tendency to consider such matters as the details of the organization and administration of the government beneath the notice not merely of the ruler, but of ministers as well; they would have left them to underlings.[80] This was not the view of Chia I. He drew up elaborate plans for reorganizing the bureaucracy and revising the laws and other institutions, which Emperor Wên started to put into effect.

The Han empire, in its early decades, was not a centralized state. Han Kao-tsu had parceled much of the country out to a number of relatives, who as vassal kings ruled their domains with full authority within their

73. Hsieh Chü 薛據, *K'ung-tzǔ Chi-yü* 孔子集語 (edition of 1875), *shang* 2ab.
74. Although the authenticity of parts of this work has been attacked, it seems probable that what we have now is essentially the work as it existed at an early date, with such losses and alterations as are normal. See Chang Hsin-ch'êng, *Wei-shu T'ung-k'ao,* 634–637.
75. Compare: *Hsin-shu* (*Ssǔ-pu Pei-yao* ed.), 9.5a, with *T'ai-p'ing Yü-lan,* 402.6a. *Hsin-shu* 8.3a with *Ch'ün-shu Chih-yao,* 36.26b–27a.
76. *Mêng-tzǔ,* 1(2).9.
77. *Ch'ün-shu Chih-yao,* 36.25b–27a.
78. *Hsin-shu,* 5.1a.
79. *Han-shu,* 49.8a.
80. *Yen-t'ieh Lun,* 2.11ab, 3.3ab.

borders. This situation conflicted with the conception of strong centralized rule held by Chia I, and he warned Emperor Wên that he must weaken his vassals before they grew strong enough to rebel. When Wên started to put the plans of Chia I into operation, and talked of making him one of his highest officials, the group of ministers and nobles who had chosen Wên to be emperor, after the extermination of the Lü family, became alarmed. They had selected Wên because he was a young man reputed to be of very mild disposition,[81] but he was clearly getting out of hand. The chancellor, who had played the chief role in making Wên emperor, demanded that Chia I be dismissed. The emperor yielded, and sent Chia I to be Grand Tutor to one of the vassal kings. A short time later Wên dismissed the chancellor, with public assurances of the highest imperial esteem. A few years later Wên recalled Chia I to the court and made him Grand Tutor to one of his sons. While Chia I occupied this position Wên repeatedly asked for, and received, his detailed advice on the organization and conduct of the government.[82]

The third of these men whom Emperor Wên favored, Ch'ao Ts'o 鼌錯, is generally recognized to have been a member of the *Fa-chia*.[83] Ssǔ-Ma Ch'ien said that he "was famous throughout the world for his practice of *hsing-ming*," [84] and that he had studied the doctrines of Shên Pu-hai and Shang Yang.[85] No doubt he had, but it seems clear that those of Shên made the deeper impression; there is no evidence that he stressed penal law as Shang did, and he criticizes Ch'in for its use of "cruel punishments."[86]

The career of Ch'ao Ts'o had some resemblance to that of Chia I. On the basis of his learning he became an officer at the court of Emperor Wên, and proposed a number of changes in the laws and regulations. When Wên administered the first examination known to history, in 165 B. C., to a group of scholars, Ch'ao urged Wên, in his answer, to take firm personal control of the government. Wên graded Ch'ao's paper first.[87]

Ch'ao Ts'o continued with even greater emphasis the insistence that Chia I had made on the necessity for weakening the growing power of the vassal nobles. He was made an attendant of the heir apparent, who was greatly impressed with his ideas. After Wên's death, under Emperor

81. *Han-shu*, 4.19a, 38.6a.
82. *Shih-chi*, 10.24, 84.20–36. *Han-shu*, 4.11a, 48.
83. *Han-shu*, 30.41b.
84. *Shih-chi*, 23.6.
85. Ibid., 101.15, 130.59.
86. *Han-shu*, 49.20b.
87. *Han-shu*, 49.21b-22a.

Ching (156–141 B. C.), Ch'ao Ts'o became "the power behind the throne." He changed a number of laws and regulations, and moved to weaken the vassal states decisively.[88]

The fourth *Fa-chia* scholar at the court of Emperor Wên was Chang Ch'ü 張歐, who "used the doctrine of *hsing-ming* to serve the heir apparent."[89] It is highly significant that Wên entrusted three men of *Fa-chia* principles—Chang Ch'ü, Chia I, and Ch'ao Ts'o—to be mentors to his sons.

Just as there were no "pure" Confucians in Han times, neither can we expect "pure" adherents of *Fa-chia* ideas. And it is still less likely that we should find men who belong exclusively either to the Shên Pu-hai or to the Shang Yang wing of the *Fa-chia*. Han-fei-tzŭ had merged them, and we might expect this association to continue. It is nevertheless a surprising fact that each of these individuals active during the reign of Emperor Wên, who were influenced by the doctrines of Shên Pu-hai, seems to have been definitely opposed to the harsh use of penal law as an instrument of government that was advocated by Shang Yang.

Emperor Wên himself was famous for his clemency. Dubs says that in his reign "capital punishment became a rare thing. He ameliorated the severities of the law, abolishing mutilating punishments and other unnecessary cruelties."[90] The Governor Wu who was Chia I's patron, although a student of Li Ssŭ, is praised for the fact that he was able to achieve good government "without going to the point of severity."[91] Chia I blamed Shang Yang and Ch'in for their dependence upon punishment,[92] and in language clearly patterned after that of Confucius contrasted "driving the people by means of laws and decrees" with the better practice of "guiding them by means of virtue."[93] Ch'ao Ts'o did, it is true, have something to say in favor of reward and punishment as an instrument of government[94] — so did many whose Confucianism is never called in question[95] — but he also blames Ch'in for its use of cruel punish-

88. *Shih-chi*, 101.15–21. *Han-shu*, 49.8a–25a.
89. *Shih-chi*, 103.17.
90. Dubs, *Han-shu*, I, 218. It has been suggested that Wên's clemency has been exaggerated; this may be true, but it was nonetheless real. See: *Han-shu*, 32.12b–14b, 51.31a.
91. *Han-shu*, 59.1a.
92. *Han-shu*, 48.18b, 25a–27a.
93. Compare *Han-shu*, 48.27a with *Lun-yü*, 2.3.
94. *Han-shu*, 49.16b.
95. *Kuo-li Pei-ching Ta-hsüeh Wu-shih-chou-nien Chi-nien Lun-wên Chi* 國立北京大學五十週年紀念論文集 (Peking, 1948): Ch'ü T'ung-tsu 瞿同祖, *Chung-kuo Fa-lü chih Ju-chia Hua* 中國法律之儒家化, 2.

ments, and praises Wên for mitigating them.[96] Chang Ch'ü, known for his practice of *hsing-ming,* was so famed for his leniency that Ssŭ-Ma Ch'ien, who did not praise easily, lauded his "love for men."[97]

While Emperor Ching was heir apparent he had two mentors who practiced the doctrines of Shên Pu-hai, and when he came to the throne he made Ch'ao Ts'o his most influential minister. And the "rebellion of the seven kingdoms" was put down in his reign; this was the most decisive single step taken, during Former Han times, to consolidate power in the hands of the emperor. These things would seem to associate Ching with the *Fa-chia.* At the same time, Ching repeatedly acted to reform criminal procedures so as to prevent injustice and to lighten punishments.[98]

It is clear that not one of these individuals we have considered, who were influenced by the philosophy of Shên Pu-hai during the reigns of Wên and Ching, was a "Legalist" as that term is ordinarily understood.

The situation changed during the long and important reign of Emperor Wu (140–87 B. C.). When he came to the throne at the age of fifteen his chief ministers were Confucians. In giving appointments to office and promotions they discriminated against students of *hsing-ming* and of the doctrines of Shên Pu-hai, Shang Yang, and Han-fei-tzŭ, while favoring Confucians.[99] The number of "Confucians" immediately multiplied; as Ssŭ-Ma Ch'ien commented, "the world's scholars turned around to face the wind."[100] This is undoubtedly an important part of the reason why we find so few individuals after that date who openly espouse *Fa-chia* ideas, while more and more of these ideas find their way into the doctrine known as "Han Confucianism." Ideas of the Shên Pu-hai school can be clearly traced not only in the writings of such a dubious Confucian as Emperor Wu's chancellor Kung-Sun Hung 公孫宏[101] but even in those of the most famous Confucian of the Former Han dynasty, Tung Chung-shu 董仲舒.[102]

Tung Chung-shu may well not have known where these ideas came from. Kung-Sun Hung probably did; Emperor Wu liked him because his *Fa-chia* ideas were masked behind an extremely respectable show of

96. *Han-shu,* 49.20b.
97. *Shih-chi,* 103.17–19.
98. *Han-shu,* 5.7a–8b, 23.14b–15a.
99. *Han-shu,* 6.2a, 88.3b.
100. *Shih-chi,* 121.8.
101. *Han-shu,* 58.2b–4a. The *Hsi-ching Tsa-chi* 西京雜記 (*Ssŭ-pu Ts'ung-k'an* ed.), 3.5a, says that "Kung-Sun Hung wrote the *Kung-Sun-tzŭ,* discussing matters having to do with *hsing-ming.*"
102. *Han-shu,* 56.13ab. Tung Chung-shu, *Ch'un-ch'iu Fan-lu* 春秋繁露 (*Ssŭ-pu Pei-yao* ed.), 1.7ab; 6.4b–5b, 8b–9a; 7.1ab; 17.1a–4b.

Confucianism.[103] As Wu grew older and increasingly authoritarian he found *Fa-chia* ideas increasingly to his liking, but he continued to patronize Confucianism because it was popular. It is well recognized that while "the triumph of Confucianism" is commonly dated from his reign, it was in fact characterized by "legalistic" practices and the harsh application of penal law.[104] Officials who served late in his reign condemned Confucius[105] and praised Shang Yang, Li Ssŭ, and the Ch'in dynasty[106] in a manner that had perhaps been unknown since the beginning of Han. It would seem, however, that it was the Shang Yang branch of the *Fa-chia* that was dominant under Wu. Undoubtedly there was influence from the Shên Pu-hai wing, but it would appear that his policies were relatively little used and his name seldom mentioned.[107]

It was during the reign of Wu that Ssŭ-Ma T'an gave its name to the *Fa-chia*.[108] And the stigma of "cruel punishments" that has commonly attached to it undoubtedly derives in part from the tendency to associate the *Fa-chia* with the reign of Emperor Wu, as well as with the Ch'in dynasty.

The last time that the philosophy of Shên Pu-hai played a recognized role in government in Han times, insofar as I am aware, was in the reign of Emperor Hsüan (63–49 B. C.). Hsüan conducted himself as almost a model emperor according to the ideas of Shên Pu-hai, making no overt show of power but quietly and firmly consolidating his authority and dealing effectively with those who threatened it.[109] The *Han-shu* tells us that his officials *i hsing ming shêng hsia* 以刑名繩下 "used *hsing-ming* to maintain strict control over their subordinates."[110] And Liu Hsiang

103. *Shih-chi*, 112.4.
104. *Shih-chi*, 30.13–14, 112.4 *Han-shu*, 23.15ab. Dubs, *Han-shu*, II, 11–12, 24–25. Duyvendak, *The Book of Lord Shang*, 127. Esson M. Gale, *Discourses on Salt and Iron*, XXIV, XXX.
105. *Yen-t'ieh Lun*, 5.2a, 3b, 5b–7b, 21a; 10.15b. The official side in this debate was upheld by the chancellor and the *yü-shih tai-fu* 御史大夫 and their aids (ibid,. 1.1a). While the debate took place six years after the death of Wu, these two highest officials had begun their terms while he was alive (*Han-shu*, 19 *hsia* 26a–28b).
106. *Yen-t'ieh Lun*, 2.1a–4b. 4.7a.
107. Emperor Wu's emphasis on war, economic measures, and penal law has some resemblance to that of the *Shang-Chün Shu*. Organization of the bureaucracy does not seem to have been a dominant interest, and Wu's open despotism contrasts sharply with the policy advocated by Shên Pu-hai. In the *Yen-t'ieh Lun* Shang Yang is mentioned twenty-nine times, as opposed to a single casual reference to Shên Pu-hai. Even Han-fei-tzŭ is mentioned only twice. If we may judge from this work, Shang Yang is the *Fa-chia* figure in whom interest centered at this time.
108. *Shih-chi*, 130.8, 12.
109. Dubs, *Han-shu*, II, 187.
110. *Han-shu*, 9.1a.

says that Hsüan was particularly fond of reading the chapter of Shên Pu-hai's book called "Ruler and Ministers," and commissioned one of his attendants to correct its text.[111] Yet Hsüan was emphatically no "legalist." On the contrary he personally gave much attention to mitigating the rigors of the law and was considered a model of justice and clemency.[112] Dubs writes of his reign that "never before [during the Former Han] was the government . . . so kindly disposed to the people."[113]

From that time down to our own day it is only rarely that the book or the philosophy of Shên Pu-hai is mentioned. Yet research might show that at some times they were not without influence. We read for instance that the *Shên-tzŭ* was among the books most intensively studied by Chu-Kê Liang 諸葛亮 (A. D. 181–234),[114] and that the Sui emperor Wên (reigned A. D. 590–604) withdrew his favor from the *Ju* 儒 ("Confucians") and gave it to "the group [advocating] *hsing-ming* and authoritarian government" (刑名執政之徒).[115] Nevertheless real understanding of the philosophy of Shên Pu-hai must have been rare, for the few scholars who have mentioned his name have commonly bracketed him together with Shang Yang or Han-fei-tzŭ as an advocate of harsh penal law.[116] Scholars of our own day seldom mention Shên Pu-hai; if they do they usually note that his doctrines differed from those of Shang Yang, but they almost never recognize the historic importance of those doctrines.

The virtual disappearance of the school of Shên Pu-hai from the historical record poses a problem. Why, from Han times to our own day, has the *Fa-chia* commonly been represented as "Legalist," having its center of gravity in dependence upon harsh penal law as the chief instrument of government? Why has the important role played by the school of Shên Pu-hai, which emphasized governmental organization and methods for control of the bureaucracy, been all but expunged from the record?

One reason was probably genuine confusion. The book of Shên Pu-hai, to judge from the fragments that remain, was very hard to read and understand, while the *Shang-Chün Shu* and the *Han-fei-tzŭ* are easy. Another

111. *Han-shu*, 9.1ab. *T'ai-p'ing Yü-lan*, 221.5b.

112. *Han-shu*, 8.10a–11a; 23.15b–16a. Dubs, *Han-shu*, II, 188–189.

113. Dubs, *Han-shu*, II, 180.

114. Ch'ên Ch'i-t'ien, *Chung-kuo Fa-chia Kai-lun*, 85.

115. *Sui-shu*, 75.2b.

116. *Han-shu*, 23.12a. Kê Hung 葛洪, *Pao-p'u-tzŭ* 抱朴子 (*Ssŭ-pu Pei-yao* ed.), *wai* 14.3b–4a. Wang Fu-chih 王夫之, *Chiang-chai Wén-chi* 薑齋文集 (*Ssŭ-pu Ts'ung-k'an* ed.), 1.2b–5b. Yü Yüeh 俞樾, *Ch'un-tsai-t'ang Ts'ung-shu* 春在堂叢書 (edition of 1902), *Pin-méng-chi* 賓萌集, 1.14b–15b.

circumstance that made for misunderstanding was the fact that the character *hsing* 刑, which occurred in the term *hsing-ming*, commonly meant "punishment" or "law."

It also seems certain that opponents of the *Fa-chia*, who were very numerous, deliberately promoted confusion. They believed, with Confucius and Mencius, that officials of the government should be permitted by the ruler, as men of intelligence and virtue, to act with considerable discretion according to their own moral judgments. But the school of Shên Pu-hai saw them as parts of a vast bureaucratic organism, parts that must do no more than carry out the orders of the controlling central intelligence if chaos were to be avoided. Most officials would naturally chafe under such a regime, yet they could not easily oppose the principle of control by the ruler openly. It was quite popular and respectable, however; to oppose "legalism," the harsh use of penal law. The easiest way to discredit all members of the *Fa-chia*, then, was to call them "Legalists," and brand them as followers of such execrated figures as Shang Yang, Li Ssŭ, and Ch'in Shih-Huang. And this was done.

Let us look, finally, at the achievements of the *Fa-chia*. It is generally agreed that they lie principally in two areas: that of jurisprudence, and that of the organization and conduct of the government. In the field of jurisprudence the contribution was considerable,[117] and we may safely credit this to the wing of the *Fa-chia* that descended from Shang Yang. Yet the doctrines of this school regarding law were never really accepted into the main stream of Chinese thinking; the testimony of ancient literature[118] and the judgments of modern scholars coincide on this.[119] The role of law and jurisprudence has been far less prominent in China than in the West.

It is in connection with the organization and regulation of centralized, bureaucratic government that the *Fa-chia* made its most important contribution. Wang Yü-ch'üan 王毓銓 states that the governmental machinery of the Chinese empire, for two thousand years, was essentially that developed by Ch'in, with modifications but no change in the basic structure.[120] And it is widely recognized that the traditional structure of

117. Jean Escarra, *Le Droit chinois* (Peking and Paris, 1936), 57, 92–93. Bünger, "Die Rechtsidee in der chinesischen Geschichte," 200–201. A.F.P. Hulsewé, *Remnants of Han Law*, I (Leiden, 1955), 4–11.
118. *Huai-nan-tzŭ*, 20.9b–10a. *Yen-t'ieh Lun*, 2.1a–5b. *Han-shu*, 22, 23.
119. Duyvendak, *The Book of Lord Shang*, 128–130. Escarra, *Le Droit chinois*, 55–57. Bodde, *China's First Unifier*, 197–199.
120. Wang Yü-ch'üan, "An Outline of the Government of the Former Han Dynasty," in *Harvard Journal of Asiatic Studies*, XII (Cambridge, Mass, 1949), 134.

China's government was in large part created by the *Fa-chia*.[121]

Of course no such complex institutional structure could be exclusively the creation of any one individual or any one school. Similarly, when we speak of the doctrines of the Shên Pu-hai or the Shang Yang wing of the *Fa-chia*, this does not of course refer to the ideas of these individuals alone but also to those of their many successors who developed their philosophies. Yet we have seen that these two somewhat different doctrines did persist, and it is convenient to call them after their founders.

Since Shang Yang was a chancellor of the state of Ch'in, and is credited with having reformed its government,[122] it is reasonable to credit his school with a share in the organization of the administration of the Ch'in dynasty. Yet we should not forget the testimony of Han-fei-tzŭ. He was born only some sixty years after the almost simultaneous deaths of Shang Yang and Shên Pu-hai.[123] As a prince of the ruling house of the state of Han, which Shên Pu-hai served as its chancellor, Han-fei-tzŭ had every opportunity to know his doctrines. And since the state of Ch'in adjoined Han directly to the west, he should have had little difficulty in obtaining information about Shang Yang.

It will be recalled that Han-fei-tzŭ, while criticizing Shên Pu-hai for lacking *fa*, "law," blamed Shang Yang because he did not have *shu*, which he defined as being methods for organizing and controlling the bureaucracy.[124] And we have seen that this judgment concerning the nature of Shang Yang's doctrines is concurred in by virtually every early work that discusses them. Even the *Shang-Chün Shu*, which apparently includes doctrines developed by his successors in his school, is devoted chiefly to war, economic measures, and penal law, while having relatively little to say about the organization and methods of government. Li Ssŭ, who as chancellor to Ch'in Shih-Huang must have had a share in shaping the Ch'in government, refers to Shên Pu-hai and not to Shang Yang as the author of methods for the control of the bureaucracy.[125] And Ch'in

121. E. A. Kracke, Jr., *Civil Service in Early Sung China—960–1067* (Cambridge, Mass, 1953), 28. Hulsewé, *Remnants of Han Law*, I, 5, 11. Bünger, "Die Rechtsidee in der chinesischen Geschichte," 202–204.

122. *Shih-chi*, 68.7–11. To what extent we should actually believe that the reforms attributed to Shang Yang were his personal achievements has been much debated; see Ch'i Ssŭ-hê 齊思和, *Chan-kuo Chih-tu K'ao* 戰國制度考, in *Yen-ching Hsüeh-pao* 燕京學報, XXIV (Peking, 1938), 159–219.

123. See Ch'ien Mu, *Hsien-Ch'in Chu-tzŭ Hsi-nien*, 617–620. Ch'ien estimates their dates as follows: Shên Pu-hai, 400–337 B. C. Shang Yang, 390–338 B. C. Han-fei-tzŭ, 280–233 B. C. But only the death date of any of these men is certainly known.

124. *Han-fei-tzŭ*, 17.5b.

125. *Shih-chi*, 87.28, 29, 33, 34.

Shih-Huang, in one of his inscriptions, said of himself that he, "taking charge of the government, for the first time established *hsing-ming*."[126] It appears not unreasonable, therefore, to suppose that the school of Shên Pu-hai had some share in forming the centralized bureaucratic government of Ch'in.

We have more detailed information for the reigns of the Han emperors Wên and Ching. Dubs (*Han-shu*, I, 218) writes that Wên's reign "was a period of beginnings. . . . It was the first really long reign in the dynasty and it established many of the practices of the dynasty." We have seen that Wên studied *hsing-ming* and that Chia I, a student of the doctrines of Shên Pu-hai, was highly favored by him at the beginning of his reign. Encouraged by the emperor, Chia I drew up complete plans for revising the institutions of the government and reorganizing the bureaucracy, plans which Wên began to put into effect. Because pressure from a group of ministers compelled the emperor to dismiss Chia I from the court for a time it has been said that these plans were not used, but this is a gratuitous assumption.[127] And we know that the emperor later recalled Chia I and thereafter repeatedly asked him to criticize the conduct of the government, whereupon Chia "repeatedly offered memorials discussing in detail those governmental matters concerning which he desired reforms or the establishment [of new practices]."[128] Wên also received suggestions for reforms from Ch'ao Ts'o, another student of the doctrines of Shên Pu-hai. When Ching became emperor, Ch'ao Ts'o put many of these changes into practice.[129]

In the reign of Emperor Wu *Fa-chia* doctrines, though supposedly repressed, in fact had great influence. As we have seen, however, the school of Shang Yang rather than that of Shên Pu-hai seems to have been dominant at this period. The reign was beyond doubt very important, but it seems possible that its great length and flamboyance have fostered the impression that its role in the shaping of Chinese institutions was even greater than in fact it was. The *Shih-chi* would give all the credit for curbing the power of the vassal states to measures taken in Wu's reign,[130]

126. *Shih-chi*, 6.62.
127. See the quotation in Hulsewé, *Remnants of Han Law*, I, 429, and *Han-shu*, 22.4a. The manner in which materials from Chia I's writings of various periods are juxtaposed without regard to chronology indicates that this account in the *Han-shu* was not written with the greatest care. See Hulsewé, *Remnants of Han Law*, I, 433, 445, n. 29.
128. *Han-shu*, 48.9a.
129. *Shih-chi*, 101.17.
130. *Shih-chi*, 11.17. Whether this chapter is the work of Ssŭ-Ma Ch'ien has been debated; see *Mem.Hist.*, II, 496. Chavannes seems to give insufficient weight to steps that had been taken previously; see *Mem.Hist.*, I, LXXXIX–XCI.

yet in fact these were chiefly further developments of similar steps taken under Wên and Ching, without which they would hardly have been possible. Again there is a tendency to locate the significant beginnings of the examination system in Wu's reign.[131] Certain developments of it under Wu, such as the basing of examinations on the classics and the establishment of the Imperial University, were of the utmost importance. But the practice itself had much earlier origins that are not always given due weight.

Undoubtedly modifications of government structure were made under Wu that had lasting effects, but this does not seem to have been one of his chief interests. Dubs observes that "much that Emperor Wu did had to be undone in order that the dynasty might retain popular approval."[132]

We have seen that Emperor Hsüan used the method of *hsing-ming* to control his officials, and was a close student of the book of Shên Pu-hai. Dubs calls him "the best ruler in the whole Former Han period" and says that "never before was the government so well-administered."[133] His heir, who became Emperor Yüan, disapproved of Hsüan's use of the methods of Shên Pu-hai, and clashed with him over it.[134] It is significant that the weakening and deterioration of the central government in Former Han began under Emperor Yüan.[135]

It would seem clear, then, that a not inconsiderable share of that formation of the structure of China's traditional government that was the work of the *Fa-chia* must be attributed to the school of Shên Pu-hai. It remains to examine two specific points. The first is the origin of the examination system.

Although there are excellent studies of the history of the examination system, little attention has been given to its origin. This is highly important, because the technique of examination itself—in government, in schools, or anywhere—seems to have been unknown outside of China until a rather late date. In fact it is possible that the use of examination in the West was inspired by the Chinese example.[136] How then did this technique begin in China?

131. *Mem.Hist.*, I, XCI–XCIV.
132. Dubs, *Han-shu*, II, 25.
133. Dubs, *Han-shu*, II, 180, 190.
134. *Han-shu*, 9.1ab.
135. Dubs, *Han-shu*, II, 279. Wang, "An Outline of the Central Government of the Former Han Dynasty," 135.
136. Oral examinations seem to have first appeared in European universities in the thirteenth century, while written examinations seem to have been unknown in Europe until the seventeenth century. See: The article "Examinations" in the *Encyclopaedia Britannica*, eleventh edition. Têng Ssǔ-yü 鄧嗣禹, "Chinese Influence on the Western Examination System," in *Harvard Journal of Asiatic Studies*, VII (Cambridge, Mass., 1943), 267–312. I have done further research which confirms Têng's findings.

It is commonly supposed that it originated with Confucians, but the Confucian contribution would seem to be only the principle that the most capable and virtuous men should be selected for office. But examination is a technique for objectively measuring the possession by one or more men of certain qualities predetermined to be necessary. The earliest suggestion of such a technique of which I am aware occurs in connection with the doctrines of Shên Pu-hai. It will be recalled that the *Han-fei-tzǔ* said that according to Shên the ruler should "bestow office according to the capacity [of the candidate]" and "examine into the ability of all of his ministers."[137] And elsewhere that work speaks of "using *hsing-ming* to recruit ministers."[138]

The testing of both prospective and practicing officers is much discussed in the *Fa-chia* literature of Chan-kuo times, and we might expect that the Ch'in bureaucracy would have been recruited by examination. And in fact we find two statements that men in Ch'in times *shih li* 試吏 "took the tests for officials."[139] It seems to be impossible to determine whether or not these were written examinations.[140]

The earliest written examination of which we have clear evidence is that given by Emperor Wên in 165 B. C. There is much more to link it with the Shên Pu-hai wing of the *Fa-chia* than the mere fact that Wên was fond of the doctrine of *hsing-ming*. Chia I (who died before this examination was given) repeatedly recommended examination to Wên, saying, "Scholars who have not yet held office can be tested (*shih* 試)."[141] Ch'ao Ts'o proposed to Wên that he should stimulate his heir's studies by personally examining him on them from time to time.[142]

It is not only under Wên that the ideas of the Shên Pu-hai branch of the *Fa-chia* appear in connection with examination. The establishment of the Imperial University was proposed by both Kung-Sun Hung and Tung Chung-shu.[143] Both are considered Confucians, yet when they discuss examination they constantly use the terminology of the school of Shên Pu-hai.[144]

137. *Han-fei-tzǔ*, 17.5b.
138. Ibid., 15.11a.
139. *Shih-chi*, 95.19; Dubs, *Han-shu*, I, 29. This is Dubs's translation. Where the latter passage occurs (with the addition of one character) in the *Shih-chi* (8.5) Chavannes translates it differently (*Mem.Hist.*, II, 326), but Dubs is undoubtedly correct.
140. The fact that one of the men was Han Kao-tsu does not preclude this, for although no scholar he was not illiterate; see *Shih-chi*, 93.10.
141. *Hsin-shu*, 9.7a. See also: ibid., 6.8a. *Han-shu*, 48.23a.
142. *Han-shu*, 49.8a–9a.
143. *Han-shu*, 56.12a, 88.3b–6a.
144. *Han-shu*, 56.11a–13b, 58.2b–7a. Tung chung-shu, *Ch'un-ch'iu Fan-lu*, 6.9a, 7.1a–2b, 17.3a.

It seems clear, therefore, that its doctrines played no inconsiderable role in the establishment of that immensely important institution, the Chinese examination system.

Our final point to consider is the triumph of the central government over the vassal kingdoms, which was an essential prelude to the transformation of the empire into a centrally controlled, bureaucratically governed empire. To realize its importance, we must remember that when Emperor Wên came to the throne in 180 b. c. nothing of the kind had existed in China (at least since the early years of the Western Chou dynasty) except for the fifteen short years of Ch'in. Han Kao-tsu had had to parcel out much of the country to vassal kings, and they not only had full authority within their domains but were taking an increasingly independent attitude toward the central government.

The position of Wên was most delicate. His title to the throne was not unquestionable, and some of the men who had put him on it regretted doing so when he proved to have a mind of his own. One of his nephews rebelled against Wên in the third year of his reign,[145] and in his sixth year his half brother took the title of "Eastern Emperor" and was restrained from dividing the empire only by force.[146] The ruler of one state, Wu, was as rich as the emperor,[147] and the defiance and warlike preparations of some of the states were scarcely disguised. Both Chia I and Ch'ao Ts'o repeatedly warned Wên that he must act to divide the vassal states into smaller territories, and to weaken their rulers, before it was too late.[148] Wên however followed a cautious policy, refraining from overt action that might push matters to the breaking point. But he did gradually partition one state after another, and move vassal rulers about the empire, implementing the advice of Chia I as unobtrusively as possible.[149]

After Wên's death, when Ch'ao Ts'o enjoyed the full confidence of Emperor Ching, he insisted that it was time to act. "They are plotting rebellion," he said. "If you take territory from them they will rebel; if you do not, they will also rebel. If you deprive them of territory and they rebel sooner the disaster will be small; if you do not and they rebel later it will be great." Ch'ao charged several of the vassal kings with crimes, for which they were punished by the loss of parts of their territories.[150] Revolt followed swiftly.

145. *Han-shu*, 4.11b–12a.
146. *Han-shu*, 4.13a, 27 *hsia shang* 3a.
147. *Han-shu*, 24 *hsia* 6b.
148. *Han-shu*, 48–11a–15a, 32a–35b 49.22a.
149. *Han-shu*, 4.10a, 16a; 14.3b.
150. *Han-shu*, 35.6b.

Some scholars both ancient and modern have condemned Ch'ao Ts'o for precipitate and ill-advised action.[151] Yet there is little doubt that he was right in asserting that if the central government were to retain its control, much less extend it, the vassal kings must be curbed even though this should provoke rebellion. As matters stood the issue was extremely close. Just how close may be judged from the fact that only one money-lender had enough faith that the imperial armies would be victorious to be willing to lend money to outfit them, even though interest amounting to *ten times the principal* was offered and paid.[152] Before the fighting was over, more than a hundred thousand heads are said to have been cut off.[153]

Every one of the seven states involved in this rebellion had been seriously weakened by the twenty-four years of gradual attrition that their power had suffered as a result of the policies of Emperor Wên, Chia I, and Ch'ao Ts'o. If those policies had not been in operation, there can be little doubt that the vassal states would have been able to maintain and increase their power. This would have confirmed the traditional pattern, which for nearly a millennium had been broken only by the fifteen short years of Ch'in, of China as an association of autonomous or semiautonomous states.

The work of Emperor Wên, Chia I, and Ch'ao Ts'o was decisive in making possible the development of the Chinese state as we think of it: a centrally controlled, bureaucratically administered monarchy.[154]

It has been demonstrated—it is hoped, to the reader's satisfaction—that the *Fa-chia* has been composed principally of persons predominantly influenced by one or both of two streams of thought. One of these, apparently stemming principally from Shang Yang, stressed penal law and is properly denominated "Legalist." The other, which seems to have developed chiefly on the basis of the ideas of Shên Pu-hai, gave its chief emphasis to the role of the ruler and to the organization and operation of bureaucratic government; it tended to be indifferent to penal law,

---

151. *Shih-chi*, 11.17. *Yen-t'ieh Lun*, 2.6a–7a. Gale, *Discourses on Salt and Iron*, 50, n. 1.
152. *Han-shu*, 91.11b.
153. Ibid., 5.4b.
154. For appreciative appraisals of their roles, see: Dubs, *Han-shu*, I, 292–297. Chien Po-tsan 翦伯贊, *Chung-kuo Shih-kang* 中國史綱 (Shanghai, 1946–1947), II, 356–361. The *Shih-chi* (23.6) very interestingly associates the practice of *hsing-ming* by Ch'ao Ts'o with his campaign to curb the independence of the vassal kings. Although the argument is not completely spelled out, it is apparently that they have the name (*ming*) of subjects, and ought therefore to match it with the performance (*hsing*) proper to a subject.

and some of its exponents were even "anti-legalistic." Although these two streams of thought were combined at an early date, we still in Han times find some individuals who seem to be predominantly under the influence of one or the other.

Since the school based on the ideas of Shên Pu-hai had the interests it did, it would be reasonable to suppose that it might have had some influence upon the establishment of the role of the Chinese emperor in the government, and upon the development of the bureaucracy and other governmental institutions. We have seen that in fact some individuals influenced by this school made important contributions in these connections. We have also seen evidence that these individuals were not "legalists."

It is entirely correct, therefore, to say as is often said that the basic structure of China's traditional government was in large measure shaped by the *Fa-chia*. But it is not correct to say, as is sometimes said, that this was done by "Legalists." To do so is seriously to warp our understanding of important forces underlying the whole course of the history of Chinese government.

7

The Beginnings of Bureaucracy in China: The Origin of the *Hsien*

Accounts of China's contributions to world culture have progressed far beyond the "paper and gunpowder" stage, but even today they seldom emphasize the Chinese role in developing techniques essential to what is known as "the modern, centralized, bureaucratic state." This is somewhat curious, since complex organization on a vast scale is more characteristic of our age than any other activity, and it is in precisely this field that the Chinese have probably made their most important contribution.

As early as the beginning of the Christian Era the Chinese Empire showed many similarities to the superstate of the twentieth century. The importance of sheer size in stimulating the development of bureaucracy has often been remarked,[1] and in territorial terms the Chinese Empire is the largest state that has endured for many centuries. When the Roman Empire attained its largest size, that of China was already larger.[2] Far more than the Roman Empire, and more than any comparable state

Reprinted with permission from the *Journal of Asian Studies*, XXIII (1964), 155–184. The research on which this paper is based has been furthered by the suggestions and assistance of scholarly friends so numerous that it is impossible to mention them all. A few are named in the text and in the notes. Special acknowledgement must be made of the help on this particular paper of Professors T. H. Tsien, E. A. Kracke, Jr., C. Y. Hsü, and Muhsin Mahdi. Professors Fred Eggan and Sol Tax kindly advised me on points concerned with anthropology, and read and criticized my first draft of the paper. Miss June Work, my research assistant, has made a major contribution to its preparation.

1. *From Max Weber: Essays in Sociology*, trans. H. H. Gerth and C. Wright Mills (New York, 1946), 209 (referred to hereafter as: Weber, *Sociology*). Arthur K. Davis, "Bureaucratic Patterns in the Navy Officer Corps," *Social Forces*, XXVII (1948), 145.
2. Gibbon wrote that the Roman Empire "was supposed to contain above sixteen hundred thousand square miles"; see Edward Gibbon, *The History of the Decline and Fall of the Roman Empire*, ed. J. B. Bury, (New York: Heritage Press, 1946), I, 21. The area known as "China Proper" comprises some fifteen hundred thousand square miles, and the Chinese Empire was far more extensive than this as early as 100 B. C. In population, however, the Roman Empire appears to have greatly exceeded the contemporary Chinese Empire.

before modern times, it was administered by a centralized bureaucratic government.[3] Centrally controlled officials of the imperial and provincial governments, around the beginning of the Christian Era, are said to have numbered 130,285.[4]

In a process of which the rudiments can be discerned in the fourth century B. C. and which can be documented beginning with 165 B. C.,[5] an increasing number of these officials were selected by civil service examinations. These examinations brought into the government many men of quite humble origin.[6] An increasing proportion of officeholders

3. Any careful comparison of the governmental systems of the Chinese and Roman empires, in the centuries just before and after the beginning of the Christian Era, makes it evident that in terms of *centralized administration* China was far more developed. No doubt the Roman territories were under more firmly centralized *control*, guaranteed by the formidable and highly mobile Roman armies. But most of the business of local administration was left by the Romans (no doubt wisely in terms of their objectives) to the cities that dotted the Empire. See M. Rostovtzeff, *The Social and Economic History of the Roman Empire*, 2d ed. (Oxford, 1957) (referred to hereafter as: Rostovtzeff, *Roman Empire*), I, 187, 192–194, 252; Émile Belot, *Histoire des chevaliers romains* (Paris, 1866, 1873), II, 77; Arthur E. R. Boak, *A History of Rome to 565 A.D.* (New York, 1923) (referred to hereafter as: Boak, *Rome*), 198–199. Max Weber has commented on "the lack of a bureaucratic apparatus" under the Roman Republic; see Weber, *Sociology*, 211. Even in the Roman Empire, no bureaucratic structure comparable in scope and complexity to that of contemporary China was developed. Certainly the Byzantine Empire had a large and complicated bureaucracy. But that empire was, in the first place, only a fraction of the size of the Chinese. And Byzantium inherited from Rome the emphasis that gave military officials precedence over civilians. This fact, together with the necessities of defence, gave rise to the organization into districts called *themes*, each controlled by a military governor who administered it somewhat in the manner of a "vice-emperor"; see *Cambridge Medieval History* (referred to hereafter as: *Camb. Med. Hist.*), IV (New York and Cambridge, 1927), 731–734; *Byzantium*, ed. Norman H. Baynes and H. St. L. B. Moss (Oxford, 1949; reprint of 1953), 290. While these military governors were usually held in check by the emperor, this organization did not resemble that of the modern centralized bureaucratic state to the same degree as did that of China, which was normally controlled by civilian bureaucrats. Concerning other factors that tended to operate against complete centralized control of the Byzantine Empire, see Ernst H. Kantorowicz, " 'Feudalism' in the Byzantine Empire," in *Feudalism in History*, ed. Rushton Coulborn (Princeton, 1956) (referred to hereafter as: Coulborn, *Feudalism*), 151–166.

4. See: Wang Hsien-ch'ien, *Han-shu Pu-chu* (1900) (referred to hereafter as: *Han-shu*) 19A.31. Wang Yü-ch'üan, "An Outline of the Central Government of the Former Han Dynasty," in *Harvard Journal of Asiatic Studies* (referred to hereafter as *HJAS*) XII (1949) (referred to hereafter as: Wang, "Han Government"), 136–137.

5. See pp. 116–118.

6. It has commonly been supposed that examination did not become important in connection with the bureaucracy until the seventh century A. D. It is true that the pattern of examination that continued without essential change to the twentieth century was established only at that time, but a variety of examinations played an increasingly important role in connection with the Han bureaucracy. The examinations for men recommended as "Filial and Incorrupt" are commonly said not to have been "open"

were educated in an imperial university that was expressly founded, in 124 B. C., for the purpose of inculcating in future officials the values and attitudes desired by the government.[7] Many of them were career bureaucrats from an early age. As early as the Han dynasties (206 B. C.– 220 A. D.) the Chinese bureaucrat, far more than his counterpart in ancient Egypt,[8] Rome,[9] or even Byzantium,[10] depended for his professional advancement upon his evaluation by other officials on the basis of relatively objective criteria: grades obtained in examinations, experience and seniority, voluminous records of his performance in office, and merit ratings.[11] The central government kept itself informed of local

---

because the candidates had to be recommended, and it is assumed that the officials would have recommended only their relatives and members of powerful families. But a crucial fact is often overlooked: those recommended had to pass the examinations. If a candidate proved conspicuously incapable, both the candidate *and the recommender* might be punished very severely; see *Han-shu*, 17.4a, 19B.17a, 88.5a. The result was that, since officials were compelled to make recommendations, they had to find men of ability regardless of birth or wealth, and there is concrete evidence that numerous men of humble origin in fact did enter the bureaucracy. For an excellent discussion of this situation see Ch'ien Mu 錢穆 , *Chung-kuo Li-tai Cheng-chih Te-shih* 中國歷代政治得失 , 2d ed. (Hongkong, 1954) (referred to hereafter as: Ch'ien, *Te-shih*), 10–14.

7. *Han-shu*, 88.4a–6a. Ch'ien, *Te-shih*, 10–14.

8. The impressive bureaucracy of ancient Egypt, concerning which voluminous records have survived, does not seem to have included any apparatus for the objective weighing of merit. See Adolf Erman, *Aegypten und Aegyptisches Leben im Altertum*, revised by Hermann Ranke (Tübingen, 1923), especially 55–145. John A. Wilson, *The Culture of Ancient Egypt* (Chicago, Phoenix Books edition, 1957), 49, writes that the pharaoh "as a god, *was* the state," and that the evidence indicates that the officials were "appointed by him, responsible to him alone, and holding office subject to his divine pleasure." See also "The Question of Feudal Institutions in Ancient Egypt," by William F. Edgerton, in Coulborn, *Feudalism*, 120–132.

9. In the course of a fairly extensive study of Roman administration, I have been able to find no evidence of the systematic use of objective criteria for the control of official careers, either under the Roman Republic or the Empire. It appears that the emperor made all appointments, promotions, and dismissals at the imperial pleasure. See: Boak, *Rome*, 268. *The Development of the Civil Service*, by various authors (London, 1922), 16. Rostovtzeff, *Roman Empire*, I. 47, 185–186.

10. To what extent anything resembling what we know as "civil service examination" may ever have been practiced in the Byzantine Empire is a difficult problem, which must be reserved for discussion in my as yet uncompleted history of the institution of examination. In any case there does not seem to have been much use of objective criteria in the actual management of the bureaucracy; Charles Diehl writes (*Camb. Med. Hist.*, IV, 726–727) that the Byzantine Emperor "kept a close supervision over administrative affairs, appointing and dismissing officials at his pleasure, and advancing them in the complicated hierarchy of dignities according to his caprice." And the manual on statecraft that has come down to us from the hand of a Byzantine emperor shows very little concern with impersonal or objective criteria; see Constantine Porphyrogenitus, *De Administrando Imperio*, Greek text edited by Gy. Moravcsik, English translation by R. J. H. Jenkins (Budapest, 1949).

11. See: Ch'ien, *Te-shih*, 10–14. Wang, "Han Government" passim.

conditions by means of various systems of inspection and a voluminous flow of reports and statistics.[12] It estimated its income and budgeted its expenditures.[13] Like some governments of our own day, it sought to control economic activity and even at times to regulate prices.[14]

All this does not mean that the ancient Chinese state was "just like" those of our own day. Of course it was not. But I believe that anyone who examines the evidence carefully must agree that the pattern of Chinese government, as early as Han times, showed remarkable resemblances to the type of centralized bureaucratic government that is considered peculiarly modern. This might seem doubtful to one whose conception of the Chinese bureaucracy and its functions were derived principally from the well-known studies of Max Weber. It is an unfortunate fact, however, that Weber's work on China was not based on a body of erudition comparable with that which underlay his studies of Occidental institutions. Weber himself acknowledged not only that he was not a Sinologist but that he did not even have the advice of one. In publishing his principal study of Chinese culture he wrote that he did so "with misgivings and with the greatest reservation."[15] This awareness of his limitations did not, however, restrain Weber from attempting to make highly original interpretations of Chinese texts, producing results that are sometimes plainly contrary to fact.[16] Another complication, for which Weber is of course in no way to blame, is the fact that much of the most important research on early China has been done since Weber died in 1920. Yet despite all handicaps his almost incredible genius produced, even in this field, some insights of great usefulness and uncanny accuracy. For these

12. See: Wang, "Han Government," 145–146 and passim. Ch'ien, Te-shih, 2–10.
13. Han-shu, 24A.3b, 9b–10a, 20a; 24B.8a; 84.9a. Wang, "Han, Government," 145–146. In contrast, Rostovtzeff (Roman Empire, I, 515) says: "The Roman state never had a regular budget, and when it was faced with financial difficulties, it had no fixed and stable reserve to draw upon . . . the usual way of getting money, according to the principles of the city-state, was to demand it from the population either by means of extraordinary taxation or by means of requisitions and confiscations." These latter devices were not unknown in Han China, but they were unusual abuses rather than normal policy. Concerning the Roman lack of interest in the principles of public finance, see G. H. Stevenson, Roman Provincial Administration (Oxford, 1939; 2d impression, 1949), 133.
14. Han-shu, 24A, 24B. Nancy Lee Swann, Food and Money in Ancient China (Princeton, 1950).
15. Max Weber, Gesammelte Aufsätze zur Religionssoziologie, I (Tübingen, 1920), 278. Max Weber, The Religion of China, trans. Hans H. Gerth (Glencoe, Illinois, 1951), 252.
16. In connection with Weber's interpretations of passages in the Analects, it should be noted that he explicitly (The Religion of China, 250) cites the translation of James Legge in the Chinese Classics as his source. He writes (ibid., 143): "On the one hand, when viewed from the perspective of Confucian reasons of state, religion had to be 'upheld for the people.' The order of the world, according to a word of the Master, could not be

we can only be grateful. But these contributions, and Weber's well-deserved reputation, should not blind us to the fact that in important respects Weber's picture of Chinese bureaucracy is a very misleading one.[17]

maintained without belief. Therefore, the retention of religious belief was politically even more important than was the concern for food." This is obviously a reference to *Analects*, 12.7. But the text makes it perfectly clear that the "belief" in question is not religious belief, but confidence in the government or the ruler; this is the interpretation of Legge and, I believe, of all other translators and commentators.

Again Weber writes (ibid., 163): " 'Where we are three I find my master,' Confucius has allegedly said, which meant, I bow to the majority." This must refer to *Analects*, 7.21, which Legge translates, "The Master said, 'When I walk along with two others, they may serve me as my teachers. I will select their good qualities and follow them, and their bad qualities and avoid them.' " Other scholars vary slightly in their interpretations, but none brings in Weber's idea of "bowing to the majority," which is inconceivable on the basis of the text.

These and other distortions of the sense of Chinese materials by Weber cannot be put down to simple ignorance. The fact is that the *Analects*, either in the Chinese original or in Legge's or another translation, does not yield a picture of Confucius that will square with Weber's conception of him. Weber forced it to do so.

17. Talcott Parsons, *Structure and Process in Modern Societies* (Glencoe, Illinois, 1960), 20, points out that "a minimal description of an organization will have to include an outline of the system of values which defines its functions . . ." It is precisely the Chinese system of values of which Weber seems to have had very little understanding or appreciation. Thus (*The Religion of China*, 232) he tells us that in the Chinese character there is "the absence of an inward core, of a unified way of life flowing from some central and autonomous value position." Again Weber tells us (ibid., 235) that the Confucian "way of life could not allow a man an inward aspiration toward a 'unified personality.' " But surely few ways of life, anywhere, have been so characterized as the Confucian by "an inward striving toward a 'unified personality.' " One wonders where Weber could have acquired such ideas. He prefaces these remarks by stating (ibid., 231) that for information concerning the Chinese character "the sociologist essentially depends upon the literature of the missionaries." It would be a little hard on "the missionaries," however, to give them all the credit. It was pointed out in the preceding note that in interpreting some passages in the *Analects* Weber seems to have paid singularly little attention to the judgments of James Legge, a very great missionary scholar. Weber appears to have been unfortunate in selecting which missionaries to believe.

The defects of Weber's treatment of Chinese bureaucracy are those that we should expect when a master of brilliant generalization, possessing inadequate and inaccurate information, attempts to reduce to tidy formulae a range of phenomena that resists comprehension even by the most informed specialists. An example of his uncontrolled generalization is the manner in which he uses the term "literati." He tells us (*The Religion of China*, 42) that the literati were "ritualist advisers" of the princes and (ibid., 108) that "the 'literati' of the feudal period . . . were first of all proficient in ritualism." He also informs us (ibid., 41) that Shang Yang was "a representative of the literati," whereas Shang Yang was very far indeed from being a "ritualist." Again he says (ibid., 111): "If one may trust the Annals, the literati, being adherents of the bureaucratic organization of the state as a compulsory institution, were opponents of feudalism from the very beginning." This is confused and confusing. No matter how we define "literati," whether we limit it to "Confucians" or make it more inclusive, the men it must denote include

Doubt has been expressed that bureaucracy as an institution actually existed in China as early as Weber alleged.[18] On the basis of Weber's account of the Chinese phenomenon, such doubt might be justified. But in fact Chinese bureaucracy was far more similar, as much as two thousand years ago, to that of our own day than even Weber recognized. At one point, for instance, Weber lists three characteristics of bureaucracy which, he says, are "fully developed . . . only in the modern state"; all were in fact fully developed in Han China.[19]

---

individuals and groups whose attitudes on these matters were various and conflicting. This variety and conflict are the stuff of which institutional history is made. Such use of nullifying generalizations reduces history to a meaningless tableau.

18. See Alvin W. Gouldner, "Discussion of Industrial Sociology," in *American Sociological Review*, XIII (1948), 397–398.

19. Weber, *Sociology*, 196, writes: "Modern officialdom functions in the following specific manner: I. There is the principal of fixed and official jurisdictional areas, which are generally ordered by rules, that is, by laws or administrative regulations. I. The regular activities required for the purposes of the bureaucratically governed structure are distributed in a fixed way as official duties. 2. The authority to give the commands required for the discharge of these duties is distributed in a stable way and is strictly delimited by rules concerning the coercive means, physical, sacerdotal, or otherwise, which may be placed at the disposal of officials. 3. Methodical provision is made for the regular and continuous fulfilment of these duties and for the execution of the corresponding rights; only persons who have the generally regulated qualifications to serve are employed.

"In public and lawful government these three elements constitute 'bureaucratic authority.' . . . Bureaucracy, thus understood, is fully developed in political and ecclesiastical communities only in the modern state. . . . "

Weber can hardly be blamed for not realizing that these characteristics were fulfilled as early as Han times; he was no Sinologist, and even Sinologists in his day hardly appreciated the degree to which bureaucratic techniques and regulations were elaborated in early China. Today, when information about them is gradually becoming more available, the facts are sometimes difficult to credit. Karl Bünger, "Die Rechtsidee in der chinesischen Geschichte," in *Saeculum*, III (1952), 211, writes that whereas in the Roman Empire administrative law was little developed, China had already at an early date a body of legal regulations for the administration of the state of "astonishing completeness." See also A. F. P. Hulsewé, *Remnants of Han Law*, I (Leiden, 1955), 5–9. For other criteria of bureaucracy that have been called exclusively "modern," but can be found in China at an early date, see note 51 below.

Weber characterized the Chinese bureaucracy, as distinguished from that of the modern Occident, as "patrimonial" and "prebendal" (Weber, *Sociology*, 207, 243). He explains "patrimonial" recruitment of the administrative staff (Max Weber, *The Theory of Social and Economic Organization*, trans. A. M. Henderson and Talcott Parsons [New York, 1947] [referred to hereafter as: Weber, *Organization*], 342) as recruitment: "From persons who are already related to the chief by ties of personal loyalty. . . . Such persons may be kinsmen, slaves, dependents who are officers of the household, clients, coloni, or freedmen." But long before Han times bureaucratic recruitment in China had come to embrace strangers and even "foreigners," and from the beginning of Han on the bureaucracy was recruited from very diverse sources.

Weber's characterization of the Chinese bureaucracy as "prebendal" is even more curious. He writes (*Sociology*, 207): "We wish to speak of 'prebends' and of a 'prebendal'

Not only the practice but even the theory of bureaucracy in early China shows similarities to that of the present day. In a recent publication I have called attention to the importance of the all-but-forgotten political philosopher Shen Pu-hai 申不害. Shen, who died in 337 B. C., was the highly successful chancellor of a small state in north central China.[20] A book attributed to his authorship[21] had wide circulation in Han times and was studied by emperors and statesmen. It helped to shape the administrative practices of the Ch'in (221–207 B. C.) and Han dynasties. Although it was seldom mentioned in the literature of later periods, there is evidence that it continued to be influential in the small circle of those who controlled the central administration.[22] It was said that the Ming dynasty statesman Chang Chü-cheng, who dominated the imperial government during the decade before his death in 1582,[23] used the

---

organization of office, wherever the lord assigns to the official rent payments for life, payments which are somehow fixed to objects or which are essentially *economic* usufruct from lands or other sources." But the Chinese bureaucracy, from at least as early as Han times, has for the most part been a regularly salaried bureaucracy, paid from the treasury of the state. Indeed, Weber gives another very complicated definition of "prebends" (*Organization*, 351) which would include as such the payment of salary in money to an official by the ruler. Weber even says (*Sociology*, 108) that in the United States of America in the nineteenth century "as the price of victory, the true booty object of the office-prebend was held out precisely at the presidential election." In Weber's lexicon "prebend" appears to have been a term of uncommon flexibility.

It appears impossible to agree that the Chinese bureaucracy was either "patrimonial" or "prebendal" in any meaningful sense.

20. See pp. 79–91 and 92–120. Shen Pu-hai was chancellor of the state of Han 韓, which of course should not be confused with the Han 漢 dynasty.

21. In my opinion most but not all of the quoted materials attributed to this book actually did stem from Shen Pu-hai, though not necessarily in the form in which we have them. I rather doubt that he wrote the book; it was probably put together from sayings attributed to him, somewhat in the manner of the production of the Confucian *Analects*.

22. Liu Pei, the founder of the Shu-Han dynasty, who reigned A. D., 221–223 is quoted as saying in instructions to his son that "the books of Shen [Pu-hai] and Han [Fei-tzu] 韓非子 increase one's sagacity; they should be read and recited." See Yang Shen 楊慎, *Tan-ch'ien Tsung-lu* 丹鉛總錄 (1588), 11.7b. His chancellor, the famous Chu-Ke Liang, is reported to have written out with his own hand several works, including that of Shen Pu-hai, for the use of his ruler's heir; see *Er-shih-ssu Shih* (Shanghai, *T'ung-wen Shu-chü* ed.; 1884), *Shu-chih*, 2.20a. The Sui emperor Wen (reigned A. D. 590–604) is said to have withdrawn his favor from Confucians and given it to "the group advocating *hsing-ming* 刑名 and authoritarian government" (*Er-shih-ssu Shih, Sui-shu,* 75.2b); *hsing-ming* is the method of control of the bureaucracy associated with the name of Shen Pu-hai. Discussions of Shen's doctrines by scholars of Sung and even Ming dynasty date still seem to indicate some familiarity with their actual nature; see Yang, *Tan-ch'ien Tsung-lu,* 11.7a–8a.

23. On the role of Chang Chü-cheng see Charles O. Hucker, "The Tung-lin Movement of the Late Ming Period," in *Chinese Thought and Institutions*, ed. John K. Fairbank (Chicago, 1957), 133–134, 139–140.

methods of Shen Pu-hai in administering the bureaucracy.²⁴ The book of Shen Pu-hai existed as late as the beginning of the eighteenth century, but now seems to be irretrievably lost.²⁵ By means of quotations I have reconstituted and translated a portion of it²⁶ which, though small, provides some insight into the philosophy of Shen Pu-hai.

It is almost purely a philosophy of bureaucratic administration. The truly desperate position of the small state whose destinies Shen Pu-hai guided, not firmly consolidated within and ringed without by powerful and predatory enemies, eliminated all but what are commonly called "rational" considerations.²⁷ No reliance whatever is placed upon religious, traditional, or even familial sanctions. Shen Pu-hai is concerned, with almost mathematical rigor, to describe the way in which a ruler can maintain his position and cause his state to prosper by means of administrative technique and applied psychology. Unlike Shang Yang 商鞅 and Han Fei-tzǔ,²⁸ with whom his name is commonly associated, he does not

24. I am indebted to Professor Robert B. Crawford for bringing to my attention this information concerning Chang Chü-cheng. The doctrines of Shen Pu-hai are twice referred to in the biography of Chang Chü-cheng in Fu Wei-lin 傅維鱗, *Ming-shu* 明書, in *Chi-fu Ts'ung-shu* 畿輔叢書 (1879), 150.13b, 38b. Fu (who died in 1667) wrote: "[Chang] Chü-cheng was by nature severe and illiberal. He was fond of the methods of Shen [Pu-hai] and Han [Fei-tzu], and used clever techniques to control his subordinates." In his appraisal at the end of the biography Fu said, "[Chang] Chü-cheng took as his model the surviving practices of Shen [Pu-hai] and Shang [Yang]." It is interesting that the name of Shen Pu-hai appears in both of these statements. It is rather usual to attribute *Fa-chia* 法家 ideas to every strict official, but the specific reference to techniques of administrative control may indicate that even as late as the seventeenth century there was still some genuine knowledge of the nature of the doctrines of Shen Pu-hai.
25. See pp. 95–96.
26. On p. 97, note 22, I have listed the works in which these quotations occur. It should be noted, however, that they are very cryptic and must be collated and compared with other materials before they are illuminating. I plan to publish my collated texts, with notes, translation, and introduction, in the near future.
27. I place "rational" in quotation marks because I am dubious of the scientific usefulness of this term. It is not easy certainly to distinguish "rational" from "non-rational" conduct within one's own cultural system; to apply the concept unerringly so as to evaluate actions performed in other cultural contexts is difficult indeed.
28. Shang Yang died in 338 B. C., one year before Shen Pu-hai. He was chancellor of Ch'in 秦, which bordered Shen's state of Han on the west. Although the *Shang-chün Shu* 商君書 was not written by him, we can get at least an approximate conception of his ideas from it and other works. Han-fei-tzu, who died in 233 B. C., was a scion of the ruling family of Shen's own state of Han. The work called the *Han-fei-tzu* is very composite, but undoubtedly contains some chapters written by him. Han-fei-tzu tried to combine the doctrines of Shang Yang and Shen Pu-hai, but in the process missed much of what was most important in the philosophy of the latter. It is interesting that when, as very commonly, the name of Shen Pu-hai is mentioned along with that of Shang Yang or of Han-fei-tzu, Shen's seems always to be mentioned first, although the other two figure far more prominently in Chinese literature. Concerning the roles of these three men, see pp. 92–120.

advocate the use of either naked power or harsh punishments. The ruler should not inspire fear, but affection, and should devote himself completely to the common good.[29]

One aspect of the administrative philosophy of Shen Pu-hai is particularly pertinent to the subject of this paper. He points out that it is utterly impossible for a ruler personally to know and deal with all of the particular aspects of his domain; he must make particulars manageable by grouping them in classes, and dealing with them as categories.[30] Similarly he must allow no one minister to gain predominant power, but "cause all of his ministers to go forward together, like the spokes of a wheel."[31] And he must deal with everything and every person by means of completely impersonal technique, with utter objectivity.[32]

I have compared the administrative theory of Shen Pu-hai with that found in a number of writings dealing with statecraft, including texts from ancient Egypt,[33] Babylonia,[34] and Assyria,[35] ancient India,[36] ancient Greece[37] and Rome,[38] tenth-century Byzantium,[39] and the court of the Seljūq Turks in the eleventh century,[40] as well as *The Prince* and *The Discourses* of Machiavelli.[41] There are occasional resemblances, but in

29. *Chʻün-shu Chih-yao* 羣書治要 , ed. Wei Cheng 魏徵 , (*Ssu-pu Tsʻung-kʻan* ed.), 36.266b–27a. (See pp. 81, 98.)

30. *Chʻün-shu Chih-yao*, 36.26a–27a. *Lü-shih Chʻun-chʻiu* (*Ssu-pu Pei-yao* ed.), 17.7a. *Frühling und Herbst des Lü Pu We*, trans. Richard Wilhelm (Jena, 1928), 270.

31. *Chʻün-shu Chih-yao*, 36.25b. *Tʻai-pʻing Yü-lan* (edition of 1879), 638.4b. *Han-fei-tzu* (*Ssu-pu Pei-yao* ed.), 16.6b.

32. *Chʻün-shu Chih-yao*, 36.27a. *Tʻai-pʻing Yü-lan*, 638.4b. *Han-fei-tzu*, 11.11b–12a. Also see pp. 98–105.

33. "The Vizier of Egypt," trans. John A. Wilson, in *Ancient Near Eastern Texts Relating to the Old Testament*, ed. James B. Pritchard (Princeton, 1950), 212–214. "Egyptian Instructions," trans. John A. Wilson, in ibid., 412–424.

34. "Advice to a Prince," in *Babylonian Wisdom Literature*, by W. G. Lambert (Oxford, 1960), 110–115.

35. "The Words of Ahiqar," trans. H. L. Ginsberg, in *Ancient Near Eastern Texts Relating to the Old Testament*, 427–430.

36. Kautilya's *Arthaśāstra*, trans. R. Shamasastry, 5th ed. (Mysore, 1956). *Das altindische Buch vom Welt- und Staatsleben, das Arthaçãstra des Kautilya*, trans. Johann Jakob Meyer (Leipzig, 1926).

37. Plato, "The Republic" and "Laws," in *The Dialogues of Plato*, trans. B. Jowett, Random House ed. (New York, 1937), I, 591–879, II, 407–703. Aristotle, "Politics," trans. Benjamin Jowett, in *The Basic Works of Aristotle*, ed. Richard McKeon (New York, 1941), 1127–1316.

38. Cicero, *De Re Publica, De Legibus, with an English translation by Clinton Walker Keyes* (Cambridge and London, 1928; reprinted 1943).

39. Constantine Porphyrogenitus, *De Administrando Imperio*.

40. Nizām al-Mulk, *The Book of Government or Rules for Kings*, trans. Hubert Darke (London, 1960).

41. Niccolò Machiavelli, *The Prince and The Discourses*, Modern Library ed. (New York, 1940).

general these works seem to be concerned with different problems from those that exercised Shen Pu-hai, and to breathe an altogether different spirit.[42]

I have also compared the ideas of Shen Pu-hai with those of contemporary scholars working in the field of administrative theory, such as Max Weber, Chester I. Barnard, Herbert A. Simon, Talcott Parsons, Robert K. Merton, and Peter M. Blau.[43] The result, which was quite unexpected by me, was to reveal large areas of basic similarity. That there are differences goes without saying, yet in general Shen Pu-hai twenty-three hundred years ago and these scholars working today are dealing with the same kind of problems and sometimes arriving at remarkably similar answers.[44] It was with considerable surprise that I found a cardinal dictum of Shen Pu-hai quoted in almost verbatim translation in the *Political Science Quarterly* as a "Chinese maxim."[45]

42. A part of the reason for this is undoubtedly the fact that the area envisaged for *direct* rule was in general smaller than that contemplated by Shen Pu-hai. This may seem odd, since the Roman dominion of Cicero's day was far larger than Shen's state of Han. But Rome, like most of the Occident until a late date, remained wedded to the city-state conception. Chinese thinkers, however, even when China was split into small units, were aiming at a government that would unite and administer all of China—and for them "China" meant all of the "civilized" world.

43. The works I have read for purposes of this comparison include, among others: *From Max Weber: Essays in Sociology*, trans. Gerth and Mills. Max Weber, *The Theory of Social and Economic Organization*, trans. Talcott Parsons. Max Weber, *The Religion of China*, trans. by Hans H. Gerth. Chester I. Barnard, *The Functions of the Executive* (Cambridge, Mass., 1951). Herbert A. Simon, *Administrative Behavior*, 2d ed. (New York, 1960). Talcott Parsons, *The Structure of Social Action* (New York and London, 1937). Talcott Parsons, *Structure and Process in Modern Societies*. Peter M. Blau, *The Dynamics of Bureaucracy* (Chicago, 1955). Peter M. Blau, *Bureaucracy in Modern Society* (New York, 1956; 7th printing, 1961). *Reader in Bureaucracy*, ed. Robert K. Merton, Ailsa P. Gray, Barbara Hockey, and Hanan G. Selvin (Glencoe, Illinois, 1952; second printing, 1960). *Essays on the Scientific Study of Politics*, ed. Herbert J. Storing (New York, 1962). I have also consulted, but not read in toto, Max Weber, *Gesammelte Aufsätze zur Religionssoziologie* (Tübingen, 1920–1921).

44. These similarities will be described in some detail in my study of Shen Pu-hai. A single example may be cited here. The definition of "authority" given by Chester I. Barnard has been the subject of some discussion in social science literature; see *Essays on the Scientific Study of Politics*, ed. Storing, 132–142. Barnard himself wrote that it was "so contrary to the view widely held by informed persons of many ranks and professions, and so contradictory to legalistic conceptions, and will seem to many so opposed to common experience," that he found it necessary to justify it with some pages of discussion; see Barnard, *The Functions of the Executive*, 163–175. Yet it is quite clear that Barnard's theory of the nature of authority is entirely in consonance with that of Shen Pu-hai; see *Pei-t'ang Shu-ch'ao* 北堂書鈔 , comp. Yü Shih-nan (edition of 1888), 45.9b.

45. Lyman Bryson, "Notes on a Theory of Advice," in *Political Science Quarterly*, LXVI (1951), 322, speaks of "the Chinese maxim of political administration which states that the good administrator does nothing; he does nothing, in order to give his executives the opportunity to do their best." Shen Pu-hai repeatedly says that the skillful ruler "does

If the Chinese developed techniques of bureaucratic government similar to our own, centuries before they appeared in the West, was there any diffusion of them from China, to influence the development of the modern Western state? Clearly there was. The research of Professor S. Y. Teng and Professor Donald F. Lach has shown the influence of Chinese precedent, probably as early as the end of the seventeenth century, on the inauguration of civil service examination in the Occident.[46] For some years I have been working on the question of whether the institution of examination of every kind, academic as well as governmental, was diffused from China to Europe. With the collaboration of my colleagues Professor T. H. Tsien and Professor Muhsin Mahdi it has been possible to determine that the institution of medical examination, for the certification of physicians, was almost certainly diffused from China to Bagdad, and certainly from Bagdad to the court of King Roger II of Sicily about 1140. This appears to be the earliest instance of examination in Europe.

This focused attention on the realm of Roger II which was not only, in the words of the *Cambridge Medieval History*, "the richest and most civilized state in Europe"[47] but also played a crucial role in taking some of the first steps made in Europe toward developing a centralized, bureaucratic state.[48] And there is complete documentary evidence that at Roger's

---

nothing," and various contexts show that the purpose is that his ministers shall not be mere "yes men" but shall rather develop their own ideas and exert themselves. See: *Ch'ün-shu Chih-yao* 36.26b–27a. *Han-fei-tzu* 13.6a. See also pp. 97–99.

46. In a classic paper, Professor Teng examined this whole question and showed conclusively the Chinese influence, in particular, upon the introduction of civil service examinations in Britain in the nineteenth century; see Ssu-yü Teng, "Chinese Influence on the Western Examination System," in *HJAS*, VII (1943), 267–312. My colleague Professor Donald F. Lach has for many years been contributing through his publications to our understanding of Chinese influence on Europe, and studying the question of Chinese influence on the Prussian civil service examinations. He has done a great deal of work on it, but has not as yet published his results. He has most kindly, however, given me access to his unpublished data. He has established that a written examination for legal officials was inaugurated in Berlin in 1693; this appears to be the earliest *written* examination known in Europe (the statement of the article on "Examination" in the current *Encyclopaedia Britannica* to the contrary notwithstanding!). Lach has only gone so far as to say that the Prussian institution of examination "was possibly influenced by the example of China"; see Donald F. Lach, *The Preface to Leibniz' Novissima Sinica* (Honolulu, 1957), 37. But on the basis of his evidence, and of other materials that bear on the problem, I believe that the probability of such influence is very great indeed.

47. *Camb. Med. Hist.*, VI (New York and Cambridge, 1929; reprint of 1936), 131.

48. *Camb. Med. Hist.*, V (New York and Cambridge, 1926; reprint of 1929), 205–206, VI, 148. Charles H. Haskins, "England and Sicily in the Twelfth Century," in *The English Historical Review*, XXVI (1911), 433–447, 641–665.

court there was great interest in and high admiration for the government of China. Furthermore some of the governmental techniques used by Roger show great resemblance to those long known in China. In such matters great caution is of course necessary, to exclude the possibility of convergence. My colleague Professor Robert M. Hartwell, who is versed in both Chinese and European economic history, has made a careful study of the fiscal institutions of Roger II in comparison with those of China. His results show that in this regard at least the evidence for Chinese influence is clear, detailed, and convincing. The practices of Roger II certainly influenced those of his grandson the Holy Roman Emperor Frederick II, and of King Philip VI of France, and probably influenced those of Henry II of England.

In the near future I shall publish detailed evidence concerning this diffusion. It does *not* mean, of course, that the "modern, Western, bureaucratic state" was copied from that of China.[49] But I do believe that, as research progresses, it will come to be recognized that no complete account of the development of Western political institutions can leave the Chinese contribution wholly unconsidered.

And what, it may be asked, has all this to do with the origin of the *hsien* 縣 ? Merely this: The substitution of the *hsien*, as an administrative district governed by an official appointed by and responsible to the central government, for the fief governed by a feudal lord, represented the territorial aspect of the transition from feudalism to centralized bureaucratic government in ancient China. And if what has been said is true, this transition is not of interest only to antiquarians or to Sinologists. It is an event of some importance in world history.

The terms "feudalism" and "bureaucracy" are used and defined, even by some scholars, in ways so various and so complex as to rob them of all usefulness. I propose to employ two minimal, functional definitions. "Feudalism" is a system of government in which a ruler personally delegates limited sovereignty over portions of his domain to vassals.[50] "Bureaucracy" is a system of administration by means of professional

49. [See H. G. Creel, *The Origins of Statecraft in China, I: The Western Chou Empire* (Chicago, 1970), 9–27.] Naturally I am fully aware of such matters as the Norman penchant for organization and centralization, which operated independently of any Chinese influence. But I think it was precisely *because* European states of the twelfth and thirteenth centuries were developing along lines parallel to those taken earlier in China, that they were able to appreciate and utilize certain Chinese techniques. I suspect that diffusion, as distinguished from acculturation, is most likely to occur between cultures that have independently developed culture patterns having a good deal in common.
50. The brevity and simplicity of this definition of "feudalism" will undoubtedly make it unacceptable, if not shocking, to many scholars. I would like to point out that if I am

guilty of error it springs from stupidity rather than from ignorance. I have been studying feudalism as an institution for more than thirty years, and participated in the conference at Princeton which resulted in the volume *Feudalism in History*, edited by Coulborn.

An excellent resumé of the literature debating the nature of feudalism is given in John W. Hall, "Feudalism in Japan—a Reassessment," in *Comparative Studies in Society and History*, V (1962), 15–51. In my opinion there is widespread confusion between the *definition* of feudalism as an institution, and the *description* of institutional complexes designated as feudal that have existed at various times and places. Many scholars give detailed descriptions of the political, social, and economic conditions associated with feudalism in one or more particular situations, and declare that "true" feudalism must include all of these details. It is undoubtedly true that the feudal pattern of government has strong tendencies to produce certain concomitant phenomena: a military aristocracy, a code of "chivalric" honor, a hierarchically organized society, hereditary privilege, etc., etc. But these occur in various guises, they may occur independent of feudalism, and any particular feudal system may at some time lack one or more of such stigmata. A definition, however, should embody only the sine qua non.

"Feudalism" is not, after all, a thing; it is a term, and a term that is perhaps no older than the seventeenth century. It means what it is defined to mean, and in a sense anyone may define it as he wishes if he does so clearly and uses it consistently. My functional definition is designed to make "feudalism" manageable as a concept for the analysis of institutional history. It is intentionally minimal and does not include some factors that are perhaps inseparable from feudalism, but I think that it does imply them.

It may be objected that I am presuming to promulgate a "private definition" of feudalism. In fact, the shoe is on the other foot. I worked out this definition, insofar as I am aware, independently. But having done so, I find that it seems to correspond closely with the sense intended by those who first used the term. Marc Bloch, *Feudal Society*, trans. L. A. Manyon (Chicago, 1961; 2d impression, 1962), xvii–xviii, writes that it appears to have been first employed "to designate a state of society" by the Comte de Boulainvilliers, and that Montesquieu first gave wide currency to the conception. "To Boulainvilliers and Montesquieu, living in an age of absolute monarchy, the most striking characteristic of the Middle Ages was the parcelling out of sovereignty among a host of petty princes, or even lords of villages. It was this characteristic that they meant to denote by the term feudalism ... "

If others wish—and clearly a great many do—to list an array of political, social, and economic phenomena that have occurred in particular situations, and assert that where these phenomena are duplicated, and only there, "feudalism" exists, that is their privilege. But the earlier, simpler, more functional sense of the term seems to me to have much greater usefulness as a conceptual tool. The burden of proof rests upon those who would replace it with more complex and particularized formulae.

There are, no doubt, those who would disagree with the proposition that feudalism should be understood as "a system of government," but this is clearly the position taken by many of the most serious students of the institution. See: Weber, *Organization*, 351, 373–381. Carl Stephenson, *Medieval Feudalism* (Ithaca, New York, 1942), 14, 32, 94. Coulborn, *Feudalism*, 4, 9, 16–18. Bloch, *Feudal Society*, 187, 401, 441.

Concerning the delegation of authority—of what I have called "limited sovereignty"— two authorities in addition to Boulainvilliers and Montesquieu, who were cited above, may be quoted. Stephenson (*Medieval Feudalism*, 32) writes that "seignorial government originated as a delegation of power by the monarchy. . . . " Joseph R. Strayer, in "Feudalism in Western Europe" (in Coulborn, *Feudalism*, 17–18), says: "Effective feudal government is local, and at the local level public authority has become a private possession. Yet . . . kingship survives . . . and by the thirteenth century most lawyers insist that all governmental authority is delegated by the king . . . "

functionaries, whose functions are more or less definitely prescribed.[51] The distinction depends chiefly upon the locus of initiative and decision.

51. This definition is of course much simpler than some scholars would consider necessary, but again I think it includes or implies the essentials. I do *not* propose such a simple definition because this is necessary in order to represent early Chinese government as "bureaucratic." On the contrary, I believe that one can find in the bureaucracy of the Han dynasty nearly all of the many factors that Weber includes in his complex descriptions of *modern* bureaucracy. See: Weber, *Organization*, 329–341. Weber, *Sociology*, 196–204. All three of the characteristics that Weber lists in the latter work, 196, as found fully developed "only in the modern state," were in fact fully present in Han times (see note 19 above). Of the factors listed in his fuller description of modern bureaucracy, those most likely to be called in question are specialized technical competence and pensions.

While it is true that the Chinese civil service (like that of the British Empire) has in theory preferred the "generalist" rather than the "specialist," there was such emphasis on career experience, and such definite sequence of office, that almost any man who attained a high post had survived a rigorous process of practical training and selection. For this process in Han times see Wang, "Han Government," 178–182; for the Sung period see Edward A. Kracke, Jr., *Civil Service in Early Sung China—960–1067* (Cambridge Mass., 1953) (referred to hereafter as: Kracke, *Civil Service*), 87–90, 118–125; for the Ming see Charles O. Hucker, "Governmental Organization of the Ming Dynasty," in *HJAS*, XXI (1958), 30; for the Ch'ing see C. K. Yang, "Some Characteristics of Chinese Bureaucratic Behavior," in *Confucianism in Action*, ed. David S. Nivison and Arthur F. Wright (Stanford, Calif., 1959) (hereafter referred to as: Yang, "Bureaucratic Behavior"), 136–146. The *Yen-t'ieh Lun* 鹽鐵論 gives us what appears to be a reasonably faithful report of a debate at the court of a Han emperor early in the first century B. C. between the high officials—the "ins"—and the scholars criticizing them—the "outs." It is noteworthy that the "ins" lay great emphasis on administrative *expertise*, while the "outs" deprecate it from the Confucian point of view; see *Discourses on Salt and Iron*, trans. Esson M. Gale (Leyden, 1931), 59–61, 86–91, 106–111. It appears probable that technical competence has always played a greater role in Chinese government than Confucian theory would allow. But most of the accounts upon which our knowledge of Chinese government is based were written from the Confucian standpoint.

Pensions for higher members of the bureaucracy existed as early as the Former Han period. At first there were individual grants, but in A. D. 1 the principle was established that officials above a certain grade received one-third of the pay of the office from which they retired, for life. See Hsü T'ien-lin 徐天麟, *Hsi-Han Hui-yao* 西漢會要 (*Kuo-hsüeh Chi-pen Ts'ung-shu* edition), 434–435. Under the Sung dynasty retirement benefits were apparently even more general and liberal; see Kracke, *Civil Service*, 82–83. It is interesting to note that this situation apparently deteriorated later. C. K. Yang, writing primarily of the Ch'ing dynasty situation, says that "there was, of course, no provision for pensions" ("Bureaucratic Behavior," 158). Western scholars have some tendency to take recent practice, for which information is more readily available, as representative of the whole history of bureaucracy in China; this illustrates the fact that such procedure is often misleading.

A number of social scientists have found Weber's complex description of bureaucracy as an "ideal type" to be, however stimulating, insufficiently flexible to be used as a practical norm; instead they propose less rigid criteria. See: Carl J. Friedrich, "Some Observations on Weber's Analysis of Bureaucracy," in *Reader in Bureaucracy*, 27–33. Alvin W. Gouldner, "Discussion of Industrial Sociology," in *American Sociological Review*, XIII (1948), 396–400. Blau, *The Dynamics of Bureaucracy*, 1–3, 202–203. Blau, *Bureaucracy in Modern Society*, 14, 19, 60–66. Yang, "Bureaucratic Behavior," 134–137, 350, n. 4.

A feudal vassal, in governing his domain, *may do* anything that he is not expressly forbidden to do. A bureaucratic official *may not properly do* anything that is not part of his prescribed function.[52]

While it is clear that the Shang dynasty (?1765–1123 B. C.) had a well-developed government, it is difficult to be certain of its exact form.[53] After the Chou conquest, traditionally dated 1122 B. C., the Chou found it both necessary and expedient to rule their extended territories by delegating limited sovereignty to a number of vassals. The feudal system that resulted shows some very detailed similarities to that which grew up in medieval Europe two thousand years later, providing a very interesting case of convergence.[54] But in one respect of fundamental importance the two systems differed sharply. The peoples among whom European feudalism chiefly developed did not have large lineages acknowledging a common ancestry, or unambiguous loyalties based on kinship;[55] it is perhaps for this reason that kinship was less important in European feudalism than in that of China.[56] But in China feudalism, like many other things, was dominated by the kinship system.

What is known as "the Chinese family system" has undergone changes, but through all of Chinese history for which the record is clear and as late as the twentieth century it has been the dominant cultural institution.[57]

52. The tendency of bureaucracy to inhibit initiative has often been noted. See Robert K. Merton, "Bureaucratic Structure and Personality," in *Social Forces*, XVIII (1940), 561–565.

53. A number of Chinese scholars believe that there was clearly a feudal system before Chou, in the Shang dynasty. They may be correct, but in my opinion the evidence is not conclusive.

54. See Ch'i Ssu-ho, "A Comparison between Chinese and European Feudal Institutions," in *Yenching Journal of Social Studies*, IV (Peiping, 1948), 1–13.

55. Weber, *The Religion of China*, p. 86, says, "The sib . . . in the occidental Middle Ages was practically extinct. . . . " See also Bloch, *Feudal Society*, 137–142, 181. A feature of the European system that was lacking in China was the division of loyalty whereby an individual owed loyalty equally to his paternal and maternal relatives, so that in the same lineage the obligations of kinship differed in each generation; see ibid., 137–139.

56. This does not mean that it did not have some importance, for of course it did. But while insisting on this, Bloch also repeatedly points out that in principle blood ties were "foreign to" European feudalism; see Bloch, *Feudal Society*, 123–142, 181, 443. In the Chinese context such an idea would seem very strange.

57. On the political importance of the family in recent times see: Yang, "Bureaucratic Behavior," 157–159. Hsien Chin Hu, *The Common Descent Group in China and Its Functions* (New York, 1948), 53–63, 95–100. Maurice Freedman, *Lineage Organization in Southeastern China* (London, 1958), 73–76, 114–125. During the twentieth century the family has played a diminishing role. Its present status under the Chinese Communists is certainly greatly reduced, but appraisal of the current situation is difficult. At the other end of history we know very little in any detail about the family in the Shang period, but what we do know permits the hypothesis that it was already very important.

The ruler has been called "the Son of Heaven" and "the father and mother of the people"; the people are called"the national family."[58] Max Weber wrote that in China "the sib developed to an extent unknown elsewhere."[59]

Western students often emphasize the negative aspects of the Chinese family system. They are real, but it also has positive values that are sometimes overlooked. It may be recalled that Durkheim diagnosed the great and growing evil of our modern Western civilization as *anomie*, which Talcott Parsons describes as a "state of disorganization where the hold of norms over individual conduct has broken down."[60] And Durkheim found a chief cause of *anomie* to lie in the disappearance, from Western society, of the large solidly integrated kinship group.[61]

In human history two cultures, the Graeco-Roman and the Chinese, have spread their influence more widely than any others.[62] The integration and the drive that have made possible the success of Chinese culture have been derived, more than from any other institution, from the Chinese family system.

We know very little about the kinship organization of Chinese plebeians before the second century B. C. The aristocrats of the Chou period (1122–221 B. C.) belonged to a small number of groups called *hsing* 姓. All the members of a *hsing* were believed to be descended from a common ancestor, often supernatural. The *hsing* was patrilineal and, in theory and usually in fact, exogamous. Collateral branches of the *hsing* were segmented into

---

58. The expression *kuo-chia* 國家 is supposed to derive from the *Mencius*; see *The Chinese Classics*, trans. James Legge, II, *Mencius*, 2d edition (Oxford, 1895), 295. If so, the usual sense of the expression is not that in which it was originally employed, but this is a familiar semantic phenomenon.

59. Weber, *The Religion of China*, 86. On the following page Weber says that "the cohesion of the sib undoubtedly rested wholly upon the ancestor cult." This is surely an exaggeration. The great functional utility of the kinship organization kept the ancestor cult alive, even among agnostic Chinese intellectuals; the two reinforced each other.

60. Émile Durkheim, *Le Suicide* (Paris, 1897), 264–288, 428–451. Parsons, *The Structure of Social Action*, 377.

61. Durkheim, *Le Suicide*, 432–434.

62. The early history of Chinese culture is as yet little known. It is evident, however, that as late as the beginning of the first millennium B. C. "Chinese" culture was completely dominant only over a relatively limited area. Its great extension was the result, in my opinion, primarily of a process of acculturation promoted by the attractive power of the culture (in which kinship solidarity was a major factor), rather than by military conquest or colonization, though both of these latter processes have certainly occurred. It goes without saying that as Chinese culture spread it was modified, and took over elements from other cultures; an instance of this process, involving the culture of Ch'u 楚, will be dealt with in this paper. But the dominant pattern, however modified, remained "Chinese."

groups called *shih* 氏 . All of the members of a *shih* (except, of course, its founder) were descended from a common but relatively recent ancestor. The *shih* usually comprised several generations of kin living together under the leadership of its head. One occasion for the founding of a new *shih* was an enfeoffment; the first holder of a fief became the ancestor of a new *shih*.[63] Because these phenomena disappeared more than two thousand years ago,[64] they have been relatively little studied, and there are no established translations for *hsing* and *shih*.[65] It seems best, therefore, simply to refer to these kinship groups by their Chinese names.[66]

Late in the twelfth century B. C. the Chou conquerors organized the government of their territories by giving fiefs to relatives of their own *hsing* and to allied and conquered chiefs belonging to other *hsing*. The Chou king spoke of all his vassals as "relatives," calling those of his own *hsing* "brothers" and referring to all the others as relatives belonging to other *hsing*. This was not a mere fiction for, since the *hsing* were exogamous, intermarriage between them was inevitable in theory and extensive

63. *Shih* were also started in other ways, but they need not concern us. The whole subject of the *shih* is one on which, considering its importance, we have remarkably little clear information. The difficulty of understanding it may be judged by the fact that Ssu-Ma Ch'ien, writing around 100 B. c., did not distinguish between *hsing* and *shih*, and appears to have confused them. See Takigawa Kametaro 瀧川龜太郎 , *Shih-chi Hui-chu K'ao-cheng* 史記會注考證 (Tokyo, 1932–1934) (referred to hereafter as: *Shih-chi*), 8.2–3.

64. In modern usage both *hsing* and *shih* mean "surname," but to transfer this to antiquity is to compound confusion. In a sense both *were* surnames, but almost every aristocrat had both a *hsing* and a *shih*. But the *hsing* was hardly ever used, anciently, except in connection with women (it is demonstrably for this reason, and not as is sometimes alleged as a relic of matriliny, that many *hsing* had the element meaning "woman" as a part of the character).

65. Max Weber (*Gesammelte Aufsätze zur Religionssoziologie*, I, 314–316, 373–379) did not distinguish *hsing* and *shih*, but called both *Sippe*. Gustav Haloun, "Contributions to the History of Clan Settlement in Ancient China, I," in *Asia Major*, I (1924), 76–111, used "clan" as a general term for kinship groupings, and referred to the *hsing* and *shih* by the Chinese characters. Marcel Granet, *La Polygynie Sororale et le sororat dans la Chine féodale* (Paris, 1920), 50, spoke of the "familles seigneuriales," some of which shared the same *hsing*, and apparently distinguished the *shih* (although he did not cite the term) as "branches d'un même tronc." In another work, Granet, *La Religion des Chinois* (Paris, 1922), 40, he referred to the designation of the *shih* as "un *cognomen* et non pas un nom de famille"; the groups thus designated he called "les rameaux d'une même tronc." See also Granet, *La Féodalité chinoise* (Oslo, 1952), 99, 125, 173–174. Henri Maspero, *La Chine antique*, rev. ed. (Paris, 1955), 100, 103, translated *hsing* as "clan" and *shih* as "famille." Wolfram Eberhard, *A History of China*, trans. E. W. Dickes (London, 1950), 26, 50–51, uses "family" to denote both *hsing* and *shih*. Hu, *The Common Descent Group in China and Its Functions*, 11–12, briefly describes this historical phenomenon but employs the romanizations *hsing* and *shih*.

66. There is some variation in the terminology used by anthropologists to denote such kinship groups, in this and other countries.

in fact.[67] Vassals practiced subinfeudation on the same pattern. Thus China became covered by a vast network of relationship ties, of blood and of marriage, linking all of the aristocrats who ruled it, both high and low. The political pattern was almost wholly assimilated to that of the kinship system. Questions of the civic duty of the individual, and of peace and war between feudal domains, were commonly in theory and often in fact judged by criteria of kinship.[68] China was, as Max Weber has said, a "familistic state."[69]

It would be small exaggeration to say that in the eighth century B. C. almost every institution, whether religious, political, social, or economic, could be regarded as a function of the kinship system. The *sine qua non* of a political capital, at whatever level, was the ancestral temple of its ruler, and this temple was normally the *locus* of most of the most important activities, whether religious, familial, political (including the enfeoffment of vassals), diplomatic, or even military.[70] A comprehensive code, based primarily upon the kinship system,[71] made it possible for an individual

---

67. *The Ch'un Ts'ew, with the Tso Chuen*, trans. James Legge, in *The Chinese Classics*, V (London, 1872), 343 (Duke Ch'eng, year 2), 714 (Duke Chao, year 26) (hereafter this work will be referred to as "Legge, *Tso-chuan*": in every case the reference will not be to Legge's translation, but to the Chinese text, and the page number will be followed by the name of the reigning duke of Lu and the number of the year of his reign).

The characters used to refer to vassals belonging to other *hsing* are *sheng chiu* 甥舅 . These are sometimes translated as "sororal nephews and maternal uncles," but in fact each character has a number of meanings, more than one of which may apply here. For a discussion of these rather complex phenomena, see Han-yi Fêng, *The Chinese Kinship System* (Cambridge, Mass., 1948), 45–50.

Not only the king but also lesser rulers spoke of vassals belonging to other *hsing* in this way. As used by the king this may have been in part a fiction, since the Chou house may not have intermarried with all of its vassals. Yet there was certainly some such intermarriage. The third century A. D. commentator Tu Yü said that the rulers of the state of Ch'i intermarried with the Chou house for generations; see *Ch'un-ch'iu Tso-chuan Chu-su*, in *Shih-san-ching Chu-su* (Nanchang, 1815), 25.25a.

68. *Kuo-yü* (*Ssu-pu Pei-yao* ed.), 2.6a, says that a subordinate cannot appeal over the head of his overlord, for if that were permitted "there would be litigation between father and son, and all hierarchy would be subverted." On the importance of kinship in political affairs, see Legge, *Tso-chuan*, 143 (Hsi 5), 354 (Ch'eng 4), 545 (Hsiang 29).

69. Weber, *Organization*, 368.

70. Legge, *Tso-chuan*, 31 (Yin 11), 38 (Huan 2), 81 (Chuang 8), 127 (Min 2), 292 (Hsüan 3), 438 (Hsiang 9), 454 (Hsiang 12), 510 (Hsiang 25), 666 (Chao 17), 858 (Ai 26).

71. This code was, of course, *li* 禮 . This is commonly translated as "ritual," but this is most inadequate. The concept was redefined by Confucius, but as we find it in the *Tso-chuan* it often epitomizes the whole Chinese tradition, and civilized as distinguished from "barbarian" usage. It also prescribed the obligations, religious, social, and political, of everyone from plebeians to rulers; see Legge, *Tso-chuan* 715 (Chao 26) (the attribution of this speech is no doubt apocryphal, but this does not nullify its importance). *Li* included ritual, but a great deal more.

to determine his duty with a minimum of conflict between the demands of religion, of kinship, and of the state. One's moral duty might be difficult to carry out, but it was relatively easy to see where one's duty lay. Some Chinese of much later periods have looked back to this time with nostalgia.[72] They have perhaps been attracted quite as much by this absence of moral complication, and the fact that the demands of the family and the state were as one, as by any liking for feudalism as such.

Yet if moral conflicts were minimized for the individual, conflicts between groups were commonplace. This was made almost inevitable by a difference between the organization of the *hsing* and that of the *shih*, the importance of which has often been overlooked.[73] The *hsing* was a large and rather loose "common descent group," sharing an attitude of solidarity which in a specific situation might or might not produce united action. But the much smaller *shih* was, in the fullest sense of Max Weber's terminology, a "corporate group."[74] It had a head, who ruled the group and its members. It held property in common. Its members fought together in war, and often fought against other *shih*. If it attempted a coup d'état and won, every member of the *shih* gained in prestige, power, and wealth. If it failed, the whole *shih* might be exterminated, and this often happened.

72. Ma Tuan-lin, *Wen-hsien T'ung-k'ao* (Ming Chia-ching edition), Preface, 9. W. T. de Bary, "Chinese Despotism and the Confucian Ideal: A Seventeenth Century View," in *Chinese Thought and Institutions*, ed. John K. Fairbank (Chicago, 1957), 169, 196–197.

73. Maspero, *La Chine antique*, 103, distinguished them but in my opinion did not characterize them well. He wrote that the *hsing* "n'avait qu'une importance religieuse." Of the *shih* he wrote that "elle était essentiellement civile et même administrative." Both descriptions are inadequate. Granet, *La Polygynie Sororale et le sororat dans la Chine féodale*, 48–51, describes the aristocratic kinship organization in a highly theoretical manner. Thus he writes that "les seigneuries de même nom [i.e., *hsing*] ne doivent point se faire la guerre." No doubt they ought not, but they did it frequently. Again he says that "le lien qui attache le vassal au suzerain étant absolu, les familles ne pouvaient se lier entre elles par des liens d'interdépendance compléte, pas plus qu'un fils de famille, dès qu'existe une autorité domestique, n'est laisseé libre de contracter des amitiés qui l'engagent jusqu'a la mort." But in this case how can we explain the fact that in state after state the authority of suzerains *was* undermined by strong alliances between their vassals? These conflicts between the theory and historic fact tend to become clarified if we understand the difference between the organization of the *hsing* and that of the *shih*.

74. Weber, *Organization*, 145–146. Weber's term was *Verband*; "corporate group" is the felicitous translation of Talcott Parsons. Weber wrote that "it is sufficient for there to be a person or persons in authority—the head of a family [etc.] . . . whose action is concerned with carrying into effect the order governing the corporate group. . . . Whether or not a corporate group exists is entirely a matter of the presence of a person in authority, with or without an administrative staff." The *shih* also fulfilled the requirements of some other definitions of a "corporate group," since it held property in common and persisted for generations.

Almost every sanction of religion, of public morality, and of self-interest impelled the individual to act with his *shih*.

When the king enfeoffed his relatives and other loyal retainers, he did so in order to create powerful supporters of his rule. He also appointed functionaries, whom we might call proto-bureaucrats (since they were not professionals, but military aristocrats), and awarded them fiefs as compensation.[75] The result was probably to strengthen the overlord in the beginning, but the situation altered rapidly. In Chou China as in medieval Europe fiefs were originally, in theory, not hereditary.[76] But every vassal thus enfeoffed automatically became the founder of a new *shih*, and the object of a cult carried on by his descendants. The conservation and acquisition of prestige, power, and wealth for the *shih* became

75. Our knowledge of Western Chou government is so slight as to be almost nonexistent. From the fragmentary evidence it appears quite possible that there was, in its early portion, a more effective and centralized administration than critical scholars have usually been willing to suppose. This was first called to my attention by my wife, Dr. Lorraine Creel, on the basis of her study of Western Chou bronze inscriptions. More recently Professor Hsü Cho-yün has pointed out to me further evidence of this kind. That there were functionaries, who may be called "proto-bureaucrats," is clear; but it is difficult to determine to what extent they may have functioned in the domains of vassals as well as of the king. For a few of many pertinent references, see: Kuo Mo-jo 郭沫若 , *Liang-Chou Chin-wen-tz'u Ta-hsi K'ao-shih* 兩周金文辭大系考釋 (Tokyo, 1935) (referred to hereafter as: Kuo, *Chin-wen K'ao-shih*), 5b–10a, 35a–39b, 133a–139a. *The Chinese Classics*, trans. James Legge, vol. III, *The Shoo-king*, 381, 399, 410–411, 414.

In this connection there always arises the question of the relation of the *Chou-li* 周禮 to actual Western Chou government. It is restudied in a recent paper: Sven Broman, "Studies on the Chou Li," in *Bulletin of the Museum of Far Eastern Antiquities, Stockholm*, XXXIII (1961), 1–89. Broman concludes: "Thus the Chou Li depicts a governing system which, in all its essentials, prevailed in middle and late feudal Chou in the various states and has its roots in the system pertaining to late Yin and early Chou" (ibid., 73). For my own part, I should agree that the "roots" of the *Chou-li* system undoubtedly do lie in Western Chou, to a degree that scholars have often been unwilling to credit. But that the system itself, in anything like the fullness and complexity that we find in the *Chou-li*, existed at any time in the Chou period does not seem to me to be proved even by the voluminous and interesting evidence that Broman has assembled. My own hypothesis is that the *Chou-li* is probably a late Chan-kuo elaboration upon governmental institutions that did exist, and thus is no mere figment of imagination. But to determine what the actual substratum was will require much future research, and may be impossible. For such research, Broman's paper provides material of great value.

76. Ch'i Ssu-ho 齊思和 , *Chou-tai Hsi-ming Li K'ao* 周代錫命禮考 , in *Yenching Hsüeh-pao*, XXXII (1947), 221–223. Stephenson, *Medieval Feudalism*, 23–24. Bloch, *Feudal Society*, 190–210. There is a widespread misconception that the hereditary transmission of fiefs is an essential property of feudalism. Thus Chang Yin-lin 張蔭麟 , *Chou-tai ti Feng-chien She-hui* 周代的封建社會 , in *Ch'ing-hua Hsüeh-pao*, X (1935), 803, makes it a part of his definition of feudalism. But hereditary transmission nullifies one of the principal objectives of feudalism: the appointment of vassals of known loyalty and capacity. Circumstances usually bring about hereditary transmission of fiefs, but where it is firmly established feudalism as an effective method of government is usually moribund if not in fact dead.

the sacred duty of its every member and retainer. As compared with this loyalty binding the *shih* together, the ties linking the *shih* with the overlord were tenuous. Even a ruler of a feudal state denounced as a criminal a retainer who opposed his *shih* to support its overlord the ruler of his state.[77]

Once a fief or even an office was held by a *shih*, it was difficult and often impossible for the ruler to transfer it to another. Not all *shih* were belligerent and grasping, but the tendency was for those that were to expand their power and their territory at the expense of their overlords and their less bellicose neighbors. First the kingdom and then the feudal states were torn apart. Only the fear of warlike "barbarians" on the borders compelled united action, but it was sporadic and uncertain. The situation became one, essentially, of anarchy. The very principle of kinship solidarity, which united China as a nation, became so dominant in its particular manifestation as loyalty to the *shih* that it threatened disaster. Pareto has discussed the possibility that the underlying beliefs of a society may come to conflict with conditions to such an extent that the society may be destroyed.[78]

This might have happened in ancient China, but it did not. The power of the *shih* was curbed, and the authority of central government was reestablished, yet the principle of kinship solidarity was able to continue as a dominant force. How was this accomplished?

Confucius attacked the problem around the end of the sixth century B. C. He stressed kinship, but his emphasis was significantly new. His injunctions to kinship loyalty were concerned exclusively with the nuclear family; on the subject of loyalty to either the *hsing* or the *shih* he was completely silent. While reaffirming the primacy of kinship, Confucius identified the highest good of each kinship group with that of society as a whole.[79]

---

77. Legge, *Tso-chuan*, 654 (Chao 14).

78. Vilfredo Pareto, *Traité de sociologie générale*, French translation by Pierre Boven, revised by the author (Paris, 1917–1919),1112–1113.

79. Confucius and his disciples, as reported in the *Analects*, treat kinship as the archetype of the social and political order. But it is significant that the only kinship ties mentioned in the *Analects* are those between parents and children, and those between brothers; see *Analects*, 1.2, 1.6–7, 1.11, 2.5–8, 2.20–21, 4.18–19, 4.21, 8.2, 9.15, 11.4, 11.21, 11.23, 12.5, 12.11, 13.7, 13.18, 13.20, 13.28, 17.9, 17.21, 19.18. Kinship ties beyond the nuclear family, and the question of the duty of loyalty to *hsing* or *shih*, simply go unmentioned in the *Analects*. Certainly Confucius enjoins family solidarity in *Analects*, 13.18, but again this relates only to the nuclear family. Questions of getting and keeping office and wealth, and of loyalty to one's superiors beyond the nuclear family, were deeply involved, according to the traditional morality, with the interests of the *shih*, yet Confucius argues that they should be determined on the ground of moral imperatives aiming at the good of the whole society; see *Analects*, 4.5, 4.16, 7.15, 8.13.3, 11.16, 11.23, 12.9, 14.1, 14.13, 14.17–18, 15.6.2, 15.8, 15.31.

This moral principle played an important role in subsequent history, but Confucians always tended to the belief that moral principle is sufficient in itself, and that it is unnecessary to be much concerned with the machinery of government. Yet it was a major reform of this machinery that had the more immediate effect in dealing with the danger, and this reform was under way long before Confucius was born.

Shen Pu-hai in antiquity and social scientists in our own day have emphasized the indispensability, for centralized administration, of impersonality and categorization.[80] A ruler could not really rule if his nominal subordinates were an assortment of fierce and temperamental vassals, some of whom might be richer and more powerful than himself. What was needed was to divide the state, as the kings of France began to do in the eleventh century A. D., into small and approximately equal administrative districts, each governed by an official appointed by and obedient to the ruler.[81]

This was done, in China, by instituting the small districts known as *hsien*, each under the control of a centrally appointed bureaucrat. This system was applied to the whole country by the Ch'in 秦 dynasty in 221 B. C.[82] It has continued in force to the present day. Since the *hsien* had existed in the state of Ch'in 秦 before Ch'in conquered the rest of China, and is alleged to have existed there earlier than elsewhere, a number of scholars both Chinese and Western have ascribed its origin to the state of Ch'in. Since the western state of Ch'in was regarded as at least semibarbarian, it is considered natural that this annulment of the political privilege of the Chinese kinship group known as the *shih* should have had such an origin.[83]

The role of Ch'in in connection with the institution of the *hsien* was clearly an important one. In Ch'in the *hsien* was made the basis, in 350

80. *Ch'ün-shu Chih-yao*, 36.25b–27a. *Lü-shih Ch'un-ch'iu* 17.7a. *Frühling und Herbst des Lü Pu We*, trans. Wilhelm, 270. *T'ai-p'ing Yü-lan*, 638.4b. *Han-fei-tzu*, 11.11b–12a, 16.6b. Merton, "Bureaucratic Structure and Personality," 561, 565–566.

81. Bloch, *Feudal Society*, 424–425. The failure of heirs was a principal cause of the reversion of European fiefs to the crown, but in China a failure of male offspring was rare because of aristocratic polygyny. Furthermore, not only sons but also brothers could inherit the leadership of a *shih*, and therefore could inherit the fief. See also: James W. Fesler, "French Field Administration: The Beginnings," in *Comparative Studies in History and Society*, V (1962), 76–111.

82. Se-ma Tsien, *Les Mémoires historiques*, trans. Édouard Chavannes (Paris, 1895–1905) (referred to hereafter as *Mem.Hist.*), II, 132, 530–532.

83. Chao I 趙翼 , *Kai-yü Ts'ung-k'ao* 陔餘叢考 , in *Ou-pei Ch'üan-chi* 甌北全集 (1877), 16.8b–10a. Yao Nai 姚鼐 , *Hsi-pao Hsüan Wen-chi* 惜抱軒文集 (*Ssu-pu Pei-yao* ed.) 2.1a. Ch'i Ssu-ho 齊思和 , *Chan-kuo Chih-tu K'ao* 戰國制度攷 , in *Yenching Hsüeh-pao*, XXIV (1938), 214, n. 369. Derk Bodde, *China's First Unifier* (Leiden, 1938), 135–139, 238–243.

B. C., of a centralized control of the state that may well have been more systematic and effective than any that had previously existed elsewhere.[84] And it was a ruler of Ch'in, who completed the conquest of China and styled himself "First Emperor," who extended this institution to all of China. Nevertheless, the evidence that the *hsien* as an instrument of centralized control was *originated* in Ch'in is decidedly weak.

The character *hsien* 縣 appears to be composed of a pictograph of a severed human head and the cord with which such grisly objects were suspended in public places. Thus it has the meaning of "to suspend."[85] It is probably from this basic idea that it came to be used to designate areas that were "attached" to a town, as "suburbs" are,[86] and possibly areas that were "annexed" after conquest.[87] The term *hsien* was also used to mean an administrative district under direct control of the central government, perhaps because it was administratively "attached." Scholars have rather commonly assumed that this last sense, that of a directly controlled administrative district, is intended wherever the character *hsien* is used to denote an area, but this is demonstrably erroneous.[88] Although it has been alleged that areas called *hsien* existed in much earlier periods, no firm evidence seems to attest them before the Ch'un-ch'iu period (722–464 B. C.).[89]

84. *Mem.Hist.* II, 65–66.

85. Ting Fu-pao 丁福保 , *Shuo-wen Chieh-tzu Ku-lin* 說文解字詁林 (1928), 3970a–3971b. Legge, *Tso-chuan*, 181 (Hsi 22), 443 (Hsiang 10). Forms of this character appearing in pre-Ch'in bronze inscriptions also contain the element *mu* 木 meaning "tree," probably representing the post from which heads were sometimes supended. But if we may judge from the *Shuo-wen*, this component of the character had been dropped by Han times.

86. Kuo, *Chin-wen K'ao-shih*, 203a.

87. Chang Yin-lin, *Chou-tai ti Feng-chien She-hui*, 826, and Ku Chieh-kang 顧頡剛 , *Ch'un-ch'iu Shih-tai ti Hsien* 春秋時代的縣 , in *Yü-kung* 禹貢 VII, nos. 6–7 (referred to hereafter as: Ku, *Ch'un-ch'iu Hsien*), 179, seem to consider this to be the original sense in which the character was used to denote territory. In my opinion, however, our evidence is not adequate to warrant a firm conclusion on this point.

88. A bronze vessel ascribed to the reign of Duke Ling of Ch'i 齊 (581–554) records that the duke gave to a retainer a city and two towns and "their three hundred *hsien*" (Kuo, *Chin-wen K'ao-shih*, 202b–205b). Bodde, *China's First Unifier*, 238–241, says that "it is impossible, however, to suppose that such an enormous number as three hundred *hsien* could have been given to anyone in Ch'i as this time, when a little later, as we know from the *Tso-chuan*, the total number of *hsien*, in the equally large state of Chin, amounted to only forty-nine." Bodde appears to question the authenticity of the inscription, on this ground alone. But surely it is clear that the term *hsien*, as used here, does not refer to administrative districts but only to small "suburban" areas associated with towns.

Various cases of the use of the term *hsien* where it denotes territory, but not the directly controlled administrative district, are cited in Ku, *Ch'un-ch'iu Hsien*, 180–184.

89. See Ku, *Ch'un-ch'iu Hsien*, 169–170, 180–181, 184–187.

The theory that the institution of the *hsien* originated in the state of
Ch'in rests entirely upon a single passage in the *Shih-chi*. It states that in
688 and 687 B. C. Ch'in captured four pieces of territory and *hsien chih*
縣之 , which may mean either that it made *hsien* of them or merely that
it annexed them.[90] There is nothing to indicate that *hsien* as used here
denoted an administrative district, and indeed the text of the *Shih-chi*
itself yields evidence against the view that such districts were in general
use in Ch'in.[91] Neither in the *Shih-chi* nor in any other work, except for
one very dubious case, is the term *hsien* used again in connection with the
state of Ch'in, during the entire Ch'un-ch'iu period.[92] Neither is there
any indication at all that the *hsien* existed in Ch'in *as an administrative
district* at any early date. Such evidence as we have makes it appear that
Ch'in was slow in developing governmental institutions, a borrower rather
than an innovator.[93] And if Ch'in had originated the institution of the
hsien it would have been unlikely to have been copied by other states, for
in the Ch'un-ch'iu period Ch'in was not admired nor was it even greatly
feared.

90. *Shih-chi*, 5.16–17. Even if Ssu-Ma Ch'ien, writing this passage around 100 B. C.,
intended it to mean that Ch'in made these areas into districts that were called *hsien*,
this would not necessarily prove that districts so called existed in Ch'in in the seventh
century B. C. The *Huai-nan-tzu*, written by contemporaries of Ssu-Ma Ch'ien, at one point
says that the whole world was possessed by two kings who are traditional exemplars of
wickedness, Chieh (whose reign is doubtfully dated 1818–1766 B. c.) and Chou (1154–1123
B. C.). The text says that every region "was [included in their] *chün* 郡 and *hsien*"; see
Huai-nan-tzu (*Ssu-pu Pei-yao* ed.), 13.9b. In fact, however, the territorial division known
as the *chün* appears in the literature even later than the *hsien*; see Bodde, *China's First
Unifier*, 139–140, 243–246. And there is no evidence to indicate that *chün* and *hsien* existed
at the early date to which the passage in the *Huai-nan-tzu* refers. Furthermore, it is
improbable that its author had any special intention to indicate that they did; he was
merely using terminology current in his day. The same may well be true of this *Shih-chi*
passage; the expression *hsien chih* may simply mean that Ch'in incorporated these areas
in its territory. The *Shih-chi* is a valuable history, but on such points of detail it does not
have as much specifically evidential force as the *Tso-chuan*.
91. A later passage in the same chapter (*Shih-chi*, 5.36) tells us that in 623 B. c. Ch'in
"attacked the king of the Jung and added [to its territory] twelve states, [thus] opening
up territory of a thousand *li* [in extent]." Yet in connection with this major annexation
the character *hsien* is not used at all; this would seem to cast grave doubt on the interpretation of *Shih-chi*, 5.16–17, as proof that as early as 688 B. C. Ch'in used the *hsien*
as a political institution.
92. The *Tso-chuan* makes no reference to *hsien* in Ch'in. A passage in the *Kuo-yü* 國語
(*Ssu-pu Pei-yao* ed.), 8.10b, records a conversation implying that Ch'in had *hsien* in 651
B. c. But Bodde, *China's First Unifier*, 243–244, states the evidence which shows that this
mention of *hsien* is probably a later addition to the text.
93. While the *Tso-chuan* has little information on Ch'in, it appears that Ssu-Ma Ch'ien
had a history of the state and used it in writing his chapter on Ch'in in the *Shih-chi*;
see: *Shih-chi*, 5.2 (commentary, cols. 1–4). Ch'i, *Chan-kuo Chih-tu K'ao*, 214, n. 369. This

In the *Tso-chuan*, our best source for the Ch'un-ch'iu period, *hsien* are mentioned most frequently in connection with the state of Chin 晉 . Chin, bordering Ch'in to the east, included much of the modern provinces of Shansi and Hopei and parts of others. It was a major power and its political institutions were destined to exercise important influence upon the shaping of China's governmental system. The first mention of a *hsien* in Chin occurs under the year 627 B. C.[94] By 543 the whole state appears to have been divided into *hsien* under administrative officials.[95] Yet in spite of this fact Chin became less and less centralized. *Hsien* were inherited, and a single *shih* expanded its holdings to as many as eight *hsien*.[96] In the light of all the evidence, it looks as if the institution of the *hsien* had been adopted in Chin in an effort to establish centralized government,

chapter gives no evidence that Ch'in had any special type of organization to assure control by the central government. Compare its late establishment of taxation, in 348 B. C. (*Shih-chi* 5.54), with the development in Ch'u two centuries earlier, described in Legge, *Tso-chuan*, 512 (Hsiang 25). The great advances in government in Ch'in are ascribed to two men, Pai Li Hsi 百里奚 and Shang Yang; neither was a native of Ch'in and both presumably took administrative techniques with them to Ch'in when they went there.

94. Legge, *Tso-chuan*, 223 (Hsi 33).

95. See Legge, *Tso-chuan*, 552 (Hsiang 30), where the chancellor asks the old man who is his *hsien tai-fu* 縣大夫 , evidently assuming that no matter where he comes from in the state of Chin he must have one. The idea that a whole state might, in the Ch'un-ch'iu period, have been divided into *hsien* seems to be contrary to that of most scholars, who view the *hsien* as comprehending only peripheral territories at that time. On this and various other grounds Ku Chieh-kang, *Ch'un-ch'iu Hsien*, 190–193, denounces this passage in the *Tso-chuan* as a forgery inserted by Liu Hsin (died A. D. 23). However correct that theory may be, some of his criticisms undoubtedly tell against the passage, and may possibly invalidate it as evidence that all of Chin was divided into *hsien*. But there is other evidence of this. Only six years later, in 537 B. C., we are told that Chin had forty-nine *hsien* which could furnish four thousand nine hundred chariots of war (Legge, *Tso-chuan*, 602 [Choa 5]). By implication, this must mean that these *hsien* included virtually the whole state, for this is a very large number of chariots; it may be the largest attributed to any state in the Ch'un-ch'iu period. The *Tso-chuan* (ibid., 645 [Chao 13]) reports that eight years later, in 529, when Chin held a review of its military might to overawe the other states, it assembled only four thousand chariots.

96. From studying everything that is said about *hsien* in Chin in the *Tso-chuan*, I am inclined to think that hereditary transmission was normal. The evidence on specific cases is sometimes complex. In Legge, *Tso-chuan*, 586 (Chao 3), Chao Wen-tzu is quoted as saying, "Wen is my *hsien*." This claim is apparently based on heredity. Ibid., 574 (Chao 1), implies that the ancestral temple of the Chao *shih* was at Wen. Chao Wen-tzu died in 541, but as late as 493 we find that the *tai-fu* of Wen is named Chao Lo; see ibid., 797 (Ai 2). It would appear therefore that the Wen *hsien* was hereditary in the Chao *shih*. Ibid., 602 (Chao 5), says that "the Han [*shih*] draws its revenues from seven towns which [with their attached territories] all amount to *hsien*"; this would clearly seem to indicate hereditary tenure. Two years later the Han holdings were enlarged with yet another *hsien*; see ibid., 613 (Chao 7).

but had been quickly subverted by powerful *shih* which transformed the *hsien* into hereditary holdings of the usual type. But if adopted, adopted from where?

The only other state in which the *hsien* seems to have functioned as an administrative institution, in Ch'un-ch'iu times, is the great Yangtze valley state of Ch'u 楚 . [97] And Ch'u seems to be the obvious place of origin, although this fact has been overlooked by most scholars for a variety of reasons.[98] One reason is probably the tone of depreciation (alternating with admiration) with which Ch'u is mentioned in the literature. In fact, the northern states regarded this great southern power with both envy and fear.

97. References to *hsien* in states other than Ch'in, Chin, and Ch'u are either of dubious authenticity, or do not appear to refer to the administrative institution. In Legge, *Tso-chuan*, 592 (Chao 4), a speech attributed to an officer of Lu in the year 538 b. c. uses the character *hsien*, but the speech is fanciful and dubious and in any case does not indicate that the *hsien* was a political institution in Lu. A conversation recorded in *Kuo-yü*, 2.8b–9b, supposed to have taken place in the period 606–586 b. c. and relating to the state of Ch'en, twice uses the character *hsien*, but again the conversation is of dubious authenticity and there is no indication that it refers to a political institution. Note 88, above, discusses the bronze inscription of the state of Ch'i which has the character *hsien*, but clearly not as a governmental institution. Legge, *Tso-chuan*, 679 (Chao 20), gives the only occurrence of *hsien* in that work as relating to Ch'i, but again not as a governmental institution. It is so mentioned as occurring in Ch'i in the Ch'un-ch'iu period in: *Kuo-yü*, 6.1a–8a. *Kuan-tzu* 管子 (*Ssu-pu Pei-yao* ed.), 22.8b–9a. *Yen-tzu Ch'un-ch'iu* 晏子春秋 (*Ssu-pu Pei-yao* ed.), 7.11a. *Shuo-yüan* 說苑 (*Ssu-pu Ts'ung-k'an* ed.), 2.15a. For reasons that would require a great deal of space to detail, each of these references is highly questionable. Bodde, *China's First Unifier*, 240–243, has summarized evidence against them; I would cite evidence additional to his, and I agree with his conclusion that it is doubtful that the *hsien* existed as an administrative institution in Ch'i, insofar as the Ch'un-ch'iu period is concerned. In Bodde's compilation of data on *hsien* (ibid., 238–240) he notes references to *hsien* during the Ch'un-ch'iu period only for Ch'i (which he questions), Chin, Ch'in, Ch'u, and Wu 吳 . Ku Chieh-kang, *Ch'un-ch'iu Hsien*, 170–179, also cites only the same five states. The single reference for Wu, for the year 545 b. c., occurs in *Shih-chi* 10–11 (*Mem.Hist.*, IV, 7). But this same incident is related in Legge, *Tso-chuan*, 538 (Hsiang 28), where the same place is not called a *hsien*; this raises the possibility that the author of the *Shih-chi* simply added the term *hsien* as an ordinary term for such a place. Together with the fact that neither the *Tso-chuan* nor, insofar as I am aware, any other work says that the *hsien* existed as a governmental institution in Wu during the Ch'un-ch'iu period, this would seem to make it impossible to give much weight to this reference in the *Shih-chi*.

98. A principal reason is certainly the rather cryptic nature of the reference in the *Tso-chuan* to the earliest recorded establishments of *hsien* in Ch'u; see note 115, below. This early date has not been entirely overlooked, however. Both Ku Chieh-kang, *Ch'un-ch'iu Hsien*, 170–173, and T'ung Shu-yeh 童書業 , *Ch'un-ch'iu Shih* 春秋史 (1946), 84, take note of it and say that *hsien* appeared in Ch'in and Ch'u at around the same time. Chang Yin-lin, *Chou-tai ti Feng-chien She-hui*, 826, appears to have considered *hsien* to be earlier in Ch'in, but he says that the administration through *hsien* in Ch'u constituted "the

Whether or not Ch'u should be said to have been a part of "China" before, or even at the beginning of, the Ch'un-ch'iu period is a debated point. Traditional Chinese history represents the rulers of Ch'u as vassals of the Chou royal house, from early in the Chou dynasty, but this is most improbable.[99] The rulers of Ch'u called themselves *wang* 王 , "king," and the men of the northern states called them by this title even though it was supposed to be reserved for the Chou king.[100] For most of the time from its first emergence into the clear light of history in the eighth century B. C. until it was destroyed in 223 B. C. Ch'u was larger, and perhaps richer and more powerful, than any of the northern states.[101] It was predicted that Ch'u would conquer all of them, and it very nearly did so.[102] The original culture of Ch'u was probably a variant of what we call "Chinese" culture, and may have been derived in part from· earlier

---

beginnings of the institution of government through *hsien and chün*."

In the course of making final revisions of this paper for publication I encountered an essay by Hung Liang-chi (1746–1809) in which he states that "in the Ch'un-ch'iu period the tendency toward the conversion of fiefs into *chün* and *hsien* was already under way; it was initiated in Ch'u and continued in Ch'in and Chin": Hung Liang-chi 洪亮吉 , *Ch'un-ch'iu Shih I Ta-i Wei Hsien Shih yü Ch'u Lun* 春秋時以大邑爲縣始于楚論 , in *Keng-sheng-chai Wen Chia Chi* 更生齋文甲集 (1802), 2.1–2. This little essay, less than seven hundred characters in length, naturally does not marshal all the evidence or deal with all the problems, but Hung's incisive mind saw through to the point which most others have missed.

99. The evidence for the traditional view that the ruler of Ch'u was enfeoffed in recognition of loyal service by the Chou King Ch'eng (ruled 1115–1079 B. C.), as stated in *Shih-chi*, 40.5–6, seems very inadequate. The *Shih-chi* (40.5–8) gives the impression that the rulers of Ch'u were loyal vassals until the reign of Hsiung Ch'ü (887–878 B. C.). But a bronze inscription dated to the reign of King Ch'eng himself speaks of a military expedition by the king against the ruler of Ch'u; see Kuo, *Chin-wen K'ao-shih*, 3. And the original text of the *Bamboo Books*, as reconstituted by Wang Kuo-wei 王國維 , says that in 1037 B. C. the Chou king Chao made an expedition against Ch'u; see Wang, *Ku-pen Chu-shu Chi-nien Chi-chiao* 古本竹書紀年輯校 , in *Wang Chung-ch'io Kung I-shu* 王忠慤公遺書 III (1928), 7a. In this work the state of Ch'u is named in fourteen passages, of which ten concern military actions and not one indicates that Ch'u was a vassal state of the Chou house, or subordinate to it (ibid., 7a, 9b, 11b, 12b, 15a, 16a, 17b–19a). Such evidence as we have seems to accord best with the hypothesis that Ch'u was an independent state from the earliest time we know until it was conquered by Ch'in in 223 B. C.

100. The Ch'u ruler is called *wang* as early as an entry for 706 B. C.: Legge *Tso-chuan*, 46 (Huan 6). I have not made a statistical study on this point, but it is my impression that while rulers of other states are sometimes called by this title in the *Tso-chuan*, it is applied earlier and much more commonly to the ruler of Ch'u.

101. Ch'i, *Chan-kuo Chih-tu K'ao*, 213. Hu Hou-hsüan 胡厚宣 , *Ch'u Min-tsu Yüan yü Tung-fang K'ao* 楚民族源於東方考 , in *Shih-hsüeh Lun-ts'ung* 史學論叢, I (1934), 2–4. Legge, *Tso-chuan*, 185 (Hsi 23). *Kuo-yü*, 18.8a.

102. *Kuo-yü*, 18.3b. Legge, *Tso-chuan*, 292 (Hsüan 3). Fu Ssu-nien 傅斯年 , *Hsin-huo Pu-tz'u Hsieh-pen Hou-chi Pa* 新獲卜辭寫本後記跋, in *An-yang Fa-chüeh Pao-kao* 安陽發掘報告, II (Peiping, 1930), 351–352.

contacts with the Shang kingdom.[103] Ch'u underwent a very rapid and thorough acculturation from the northern states,[104] but this may well have been a two-way process. Both architecture and art were highly developed in Ch'u, and it has been suggested that Han dynasty painting may have derived from Ch'u. In literature also the culture of Ch'u was

103. The origins of the people of Ch'u are difficult to determine with certainty. Some Chinese scholars have considered them to derive from the eastern people known as *I* 夷 . See: Hu, *Ch'u Min-tsu Yüan yü Tung-fang K'ao.* Kuo Mo-jo 郭沫若 , *Yin-Chou Ching-t'ung-ch'i Ming-wen Yen-chiu* 殷周青銅器銘文研究 (Shanghai, 1931), I, 51–52. Yang K'uan, 楊寬 , *Chung-kuo Shang-ku-shih Tao-lun* 中國上古史導論 , in *Ku-shih Pien* 古史辨 , 7A (Shanghai, 1941), 93, 119, n. 4. A southwestern origin, on the other hand, is posited by Wolfram Eberhard, who writes: "Der Staat Ch'u entstand im Gebiet der Pa-Kultur und verlagerte sich im Lauf der Chou-zeit immer weiter nach Osten''; Eberhard, *Lokal-kulturen im alten China,* II (Peking, 1942), 371. See also: Eberhard, *Kultur und Siedlung der Randvölker Chinas* (Leiden, 1942), 331–332. Eberhard, *Lokalkulturen im alten China,* I (Leiden, 1942), 321, 357–359, 363.

Considerable geographical barriers separated the people of Ch'u from those of the north; these alone might have been expected to produce some cultural differences. In the *Tso-chuan* the many passages telling of events in Ch'u give the impression of a people whose culture, on the whole, differs only in certain respects from that of the Chinese and they are never stigmatized as utterly different, or nonhuman, as "barbarian" peoples, often are in that work. Arthur Waley, *An Introduction to the Study of Chinese Painting* (New York, 1923), 21, wrote that the people of Ch'u "were not wholly different from the Chinese either in speech or race; the relation may be compared with that of Rome to the Italic tribes."

Various scholars have pointed to similarities or connections between the people of Ch'u and those of the Shang dynasty. See: Kuo, *Chin-wen K'ao-shih,* Preface, 4b. Hu, *Ch'u Min-tsu Yüan yü Tung-fang K'ao,* 32–38. Fu, *Hsin-huo Pu-tz'u Hsieh-pen Hou-chi Pa,* 349–370. Wolfram Eberhard, "Early Chinese Cultures and Their Development: A New Working-Hypothesis," in *Annual Report of the Board of Regents of the Smithsonian Institution, 1937* (Washington, 1938), 524. The discovery of bronzes of Shang type in Hupei may lend some corroboration to the theory of such connection; see Cheng Te-k'un, *Archeology in China,* II (Toronto, 1960), 160.

104. Whatever their connections with Shang culture may have been, the people of Ch'u clearly admired and took over much of that of Chou China. The *Shih-ching* and the *Shu-ching* were quoted by nobles and even by rulers of Ch'u; see Legge, *Tso-chuan,* 255 (Wen 10), 315 (Hsüan 12), 341 (Ch'eng 2), 342 (Ch'eng 2), 751 (Ting 4), and *Kuo-yü,* 17.7, 17.10a, 17.10b, 18.1a. *Kuo-yü,* 17.1a–2a gives a curriculum proposed by a Ch'u officer for the education of the heir of King Chuang of Ch'u (reigned 613–591 B.C.). It includes various historical works, poetry, ceremonial, and music, and is indistinguishable from the curriculum that might have been used in a northern state (unless by the emphasis that is also given to statecraft, which may reflect the development of that art in Ch'u). An important avenue of acculturation is indicated by the anecdotes concerning the wife of King Wu of Ch'u (reigned 740–690), a woman of a small state to the north of Ch'u. She is quoted as moralizing to the king in a highly "Chinese" manner, while he treats her words with great respect; see Legge, *Tso-chuan,* 60 (Huan 13), 76 (Chuang 5). Many other indications give the same impression, so that Ch'i Ssu-ho goes so far as to assert that by the Ch'un-ch'iu period Ch'u had already been entirely assimilated to Chou culture; see Ch'i 齊思和 , *Feng-chien Chih-tu yü Ju-chia Ssu-hsiang* 封建制度與儒家思想 , in *Yenching Hsüeh-pao,* XXII (1937), 189.

by no means negligible.[105] While men of the northern states occasionally sneered at Ch'u as "barbarian," they more often spoke of it with grudging and fearful admiration.[106] They particularly envied its government,[107] and with reason.

Throughout the Ch'un-ch'iu and Chan-kuo (463–222 B. C.) periods a single ruling house maintained a remarkably centralized rule over Ch'u, unique in China.[108] This was no accident. The rulers appointed their chief ministers, usually from among men related to the dynasty but selected on the basis of ability and experience, and they changed them,

105. It seems impossible to say whether architecture was more highly developed in Ch'u than in the northern states, but certainly there was great interest in it. Duke Hsiang of Lu (reigned 572–542 B. C.) visited Ch'u in 545 B. C. and remained for half a year. Duke Hsiang was then in the twenty-eighth year of his reign over what was considered the most "Chinese" of the feudal states, and through his travels must have been very familiar with the architecture of the northern region. But he was apparently quite captivated with that of Ch'u, and on his return to Lu erected what was called a "Ch'u palace." No doubt this provoked criticism in Lu. One of his officers is recorded as saying, "The ruler desires [to live in the manner of] Ch'u, and therefore has built this palace; if he does not return to Ch'u, he will die in this palace." And in fact, he did! See: Legge, *Tso-chuan*, 539 (Hsiang 28), 544 (Hsiang 29), 559 (Hsiang 31).

King Ling of Ch'u (reigned 540–529 B. C.) built a tower of which he was so proud that he took extraordinary measures to persuade other rulers to attend the celebration of its completion (Legge, *Tso-chuan*, 612, 613 [Chao 7]). Its size and elaborate ornament are described in *Kuo-yü*, 17.6a. King P'ing of Ch'u (reigned 528–516 B. C.) was criticized for toiling the people by building palaces "without measure"; Legge, *Tso-chuan*, 674 (Chao 19).

The well-known discoveries in the region of Changsha have shown that Ch'u had an art of extraordinary delicacy and vivacity. Lawrence Sickman writes: "The recent finds of magnificently decorated lacquer at Ch'ang-sha are added evidence to support the suggestion of Arthur Waley that painting in the Han Dynasty may have been derived from the State of Ch'u"; Lawrence Sickman and Alexander Soper, *The Art and Architecture of China* (Penguin Books, 1956), 31. See also Waley, *An Introduction to the Study of Chinese Painting*, 21–23.

On the literary culture of the state of Ch'u, see Hung Liang-chi, *Keng-sheng-chai Wen Chia Chi*, in 2.11–12b. Hung considered it to have been the most cultivated state, in regard to literature.

106. In fact references to the men of Ch'u as "barbarians," by those of other states, are quite rare; for such an instance (by a claimant to the Chou throne who has fled to safety in Ch'u), see Legge, *Tso-chuan*, 714 (Chao 26). Those of Ch'u sometimes speak of themselves as "barbarians," ironically, as in *Kuo-yü*, 18.8b. There is a good deal of praise of Ch'u rulers and officials in the *Tso-chuan*, in one case by Confucius; see for instance Legge, *Tso-chuan*, 808 (Ai 6), 851 (Ai 18).

107. Legge, *Tso-chuan*, 309 (Hsüan 11), 312–313 (Hsüan 12), 468 (Hsiang 15).

108. This is, I think, the conclusion that must be drawn from a careful study of the materials, but it is difficult to prove by citation of evidence. Ku Tung-kao (1679–1759) made what may well be the most thorough study ever undertaken of the Ch'un-ch'iu period. He discusses the troubles that beset the administration of the various states and says, "But although Ch'u was a barbarian state, from the Ch'un-ch'iu through the Chan-kuo

and sometimes executed them, almost at will.[109] Hereditary office was almost nonexistent.[110] There was at least a rudimentary concept of progression by seniority from lower to higher office.[111] Whether or not

period, for four or five centuries, its power remained strong among the feudal lords. To the end it was free from the tendency for superiors to tyrannize or for subordinates to usurp their places. It attained the highest excellence of administrative institutions." Ku Tung-kao 顧棟高 , *Ch'un-ch'iu Ta-shih Piao* 春秋大事表 , in *Huang-ch'ing Ching-chieh Hsü-pien* 皇清經解續編 (1886–1888), 102.15b–16a. Ch'i Ssu-ho, *Feng-chien Chih-tu yü Ju-chia Ssu-hsiang*, 192, points out that the southern states of Ch'u, Wu, and Yüeh 越 were more centralized than those of the north, but that Wu and Yüeh were destroyed by war. He also characterizes Ch'in as maintaining centralized control. This is undoubtedly correct. Nevertheless, the territory of Ch'in was smaller than that of Ch'u during most of the period in question. And while we have little knowledge of the government of Ch'in, what we have would seem to show that its administration was much less complex and developed than that of Ch'u; see note 93, above.

109. Legge, *Tso-chuan*, 223 (Hsi 33), 312 (Hsüan 12), 425 (Hsiang 5), 493–494 (Hsiang 22), 654 (Chao 14), 848–849 (Ai 17).

110. The only office in Ch'u that seems clearly to have been hereditary is that of Mo-ao 莫敖 , which seems wherever it is mentioned in the *Tso-chuan* to be occupied by a member of the Ch'ü 屈 family (to which the poet Ch'ü Yüan, 343–277 B. C., belonged). The history of this office is quite interesting. At the beginning of the Ch'un-ch'iu period, in records of events in 701, 700, and 699 B. C., the Mo-ao appears to have been the principal minister of Ch'u; Legge, *Tso-chuan*, 55 (Huan 11), 58 (Huan 12), 60 (Huan 13). In an entry for 690 B. C. the Mo-ao is named immediately after the Ling-yin 令尹 , which may mean that the Ling-yin, who was appointed by the ruler without primary regard to heredity, had already become the chief minister as he was to remain throughout Ch'u history; Legge, *Tso-chuan*, 76 (Chuang 5). Significantly the office of Mo-ao is not even mentioned again for one hundred and thirty-two years, and while the office is occasionally named thereafter there is nothing to show that any great importance attaches to it; Legge, *Tso-chuan*, 468 (Hsiang 15), 494 (Hsiang 22), 497 (Hsiang 23), 512 (Hsiang 25), 601 (Chao 5). One would seem justified in inferring that while the office of Mo-ao continued to be transmitted in the same family, it became a more or less empty honor.

111. Men appear to have been appointed to the higher offices in Ch'u on the basis of proven merit, which would seem to require that they demonstrate their worth in a lower office first. It can be shown that in some cases at least they did move from lower to higher office, but a full demonstration of this would require detailed study which has not yet, insofar as I know, been made. Sometimes they were demoted on the basis of demonstrated incompetence, as in the case of Tzu-hsi who was twice moved from a higher to a lower office, and so resented these successive demotions that he plotted rebellion and was killed; Legge, *Tso-chuan*, 205 (Hsi 28), 255 (Wen 10).

Clearly there was no *definite* progression from one office to another in Ch'u, but there are indications that the concept of an official career, in which one rose by achievement from one office to another, existed in Ch'u from an early date. After the great battle of Ch'eng-p'u in which Chin defeated Ch'u, in 632 B. C., the ruler of Ch'u reproached his chief minister who thereupon committed suicide. Duke Wen of Chin exulted at the news, asserting that a certain Wei Lü-ch'en would now be made chief minister and that he would be less devoted to the public welfare; Legge, *Tso-chuan*, 205 (Hsi 28). There is no evidence that in fact this Wei Lü-ch'en did become chief minister. But five years earlier, when the chief minister who later committed suicide was appointed, Wei Lü-ch'en (here called Shu-po) was sufficiently important to be able to question

there was any feudalism in Ch'u is difficult to determine, but if there was it appears to have been unimportant.[112] Although the salaried official is considered a phenomenon of the Chan-kuo period, the chancellor of Ch'u is said to have been paid a salary in kind from the middle of the

whether the appointment was for the good of the state; Legge, *Tso-chuan*, 184 (Hsi 23). At around the same time as this event the future Duke Wen of Chin, then an exile, spent some time in Ch'u; see Legge, *Tso-chuan*, 185 (Hsi 23), and *Shih-chi*, 39.43–45. Apparently he formed a high opinion of the qualifications of Wei Lü-ch'en, and also believed that such qualifications would assure succession to the office of chief minister.

Somewhat similar evidence is furnished by a statement recorded as having been made by the occupant of the office of chief minister of Ch'u in 479 B. C. He was warned against his protégé, named Sheng, and he replied, "After my death, [in accordance with] the order [of succession] of the state of Ch'u, if Sheng does not become Ling-yin [chief minister] or Minister of War, who will?"; Legge, *Tso-chuan*, 844 (Ai 16). The character *tz'u* 次, which in Ch'un-ch'iu and Chan-kuo literature commonly denotes the order of succession to office, occurs as part of the name of certain books said to have been essential to the functioning of the government of Ch'u; see *Chan-kuo Ts'e*, 14.10b.

112. Mei Ssu-p'ing 梅思平, *Ch'un-ch'iu Shih-tai ti Cheng-chih he K'ung-tzu ti Cheng-chih Ssu-hsiang* 春秋時代的政治和孔子的政治思想, in *Ku-shih Pien*, II (Peking, 1930), 165–168, says that in Ch'u, from the beginning of the Ch'un-ch'iu period, feudalism was of a different sort from that of the other states. In Ch'u, he says, officials were given fiefs but they merely received the revenues from them, while other officials were sent by the ruler to administer them. According to my definition of "feudalism," this is not feudalism at all. But I am not sure that in fact we have enough evidence to say that this was definitely the situation in Ch'u. Certainly however the men who held titles that are translated as those of "administrators" of certain territories were used by the central government to perform functions outside of those territories, in many cases.

In a "pure" feudal situation the ruler who delegates limited sovereignty is able to take it back, and replace one feudatory with another. In some feudal situations this is done. But the delegation of sovereignty over a piece of territory, even though there is some limitation of the sovereignty, commonly permits the vassal and his family to entrench themselves strongly, so that it becomes increasingly difficult for the overlord to dislodge him, or even to prevent his heirs from enjoying the fief. Thus the condition in which sons succeed their fathers as vassals, while not at all an essential property of feudalism as such, is one that by the logic of circumstances tends to develop in feudal states that persist for very long. In Ch'u, while there does seem to have been some inheritance of lands, we find the ruler taking lands away from aristocrats and moving them around with a freedom that seems much greater than that enjoyed by rulers of other states. Clearly the Ch'u aristocrats were on the whole less firmly entrenched than those of other states, which may indicate that they did not enjoy limited sovereignty, i.e., that they were not feudatories. In 529 B. C. King Ling of Ch'u lost his life as a result of a revolt by a number of families which, it is said, had lost their lands and their offices; Legge, *Tso-chuan*, 642–643 (Ai 13). But Ling was a particularly oppressive king who gained the throne by murdering his predecessor, and it is not clear whether it was because his deprivations were considered contrary to the royal prerogative, or because they were so extensive, that they were so violently resented.

In my opinion it is impossible to say, at least without a more careful study than any that has been made to my knowledge, whether or not Ch'u actually had feudalism. But if there was feudalism, the vassals were normally held in such tight control by the central authority that it did not limit the power of the ruler as feudal institutions commonly do.

seventh century B. C.[113] Ch'u collected statistics on both its resources and its population, and appears to have had a written corpus of governmental procedures.[114]

The *hsien* is mentioned as existing in Ch'u approximately as early as in Ch'in, and there are indirect indications that Ch'u may have had the *hsien* even earlier.[115] Furthermore, unlike the case for Ch'in at any early date, there is evidence that the *hsien* in Ch'u was an institution by which the central government controlled the state. Whether or not *hsien* in Ch'u were sometimes transmitted hereditarily is not entirely clear, but it is clear that the central government moved *hsien* administrators about

113. Ch'i Ssu-ho, *Chan-kuo Chih-tu K'ao*, 198, says that in the Ch'un-ch'iu period ministers were paid only by being given the revenues from estates, while the payment of salaries in grain began in the Chan-kuo period. For the "Chinese" states this seems to be correct, but the chief minister of Ch'u is said to have received a daily allowance of grain and meat from the ruler beginning around the middle of the seventh century B. C.; see *Kuo-yü*, 18.5b. This anecdote might be dismissed as fanciful, but it is supported by another passage in the same chapter of the *Kuo-yü* (18.5a) which, presumably speaking of the ruler of Ch'u, says that "the king takes constant revenues with which to feed the myriad officers." Further corroboration is the elaborate survey of lands of the state of Ch'u, for purposes of taxation, made in 548 B. C.; Legge, *Tso-chuan*, 512 (Hsiang 25). In contrast, *Kuo-yü*, 10.14a, says that in the state of Chin under Duke Wen (reigned 635–628 B. C.) the duke's officers lived upon the produce of their estates.
114. Legge, *Tso-chuan*, 312 (Hsüan 12), 342 (Cheng 2), 512 (Hsiang 25). *Chan-kuo Ts'e*, 14.10b.
115. The evidence for the first appearance of the *hsien* in Ch'u is rather concealed in the *Tso-chuan*, which is undoubtedly the reason that most scholars have overlooked it. Thus Bodde, *China's First Unifier*, 239, lists 598 B. C. as the date of the earliest mention. But the *Tso-chuan* entry for the year 478, Legge, *Tso-chuan*, 848 (Ai 17), records the statement by a Ch'u official that under the Ch'u king Wen (reigned 689–675) the states of Shen 申 and Hsi 息 were made *hsien* by Ch'u. Both Legge, *Tso-chuan*, 78 (Chuang 6), and the *Shih-chi* (*Mem. Hist.*, IV, 345) say that King Wen attacked Shen in 688. Shen does not figure again in the *Tso-chuan* as an independent state. In 664 we encounter the name of a Shen Kung 申公 ; Legge, *Tso-chuan*, 117 (Chuang 30). This evidently means Shen had been made a *hsien*, since *kung* was one of the two titles used for *hsien* administrators in Ch'u. Further corroboration is the fact that in 635 we find a Shen army fighting for Ch'u, under command of a Ch'u officer; Legge, *Tso-chuan*, 194 (Hsi 25). Chavannes thought that this indicated that Ch'u annexed Shen in 688: see *Mem.Hist.*, II, 50, n. 3, and IV, 345, n. 2. The extinction (implying annexation) of Hsi by Ch'u is reported in the *Tso-chuan* under the year 680, but this is a retrospective reference and the event must have happened some time previously; see Legge, *Tso-chuan*, p. 91 (Chuang 14).

Furthermore, the Tso-chuan tells of two men who were caused to *yin* 尹 districts under King Wu of Ch'u, who reigned 740–690; Legge, *Tso-chuan*, 97 (Chuang 18). While the term *hsien* is not used here, *yin* as a title of *hsien* administrators was regularly used in Ch'u; this looks very much as if the institution of the *hsien* may have existed in Ch'u even before 690 B. C. In the light of all this evidence, it appears that the *hsien* can be documented as having existed in Ch'u approximately as early as, and perhaps much earlier than, 688 B. C., which is the date for which the *Shih-chi* first uses the term *hsien* in connection with Ch'in.

and used them as its functionaries.[116] From a very early date Ch'u appears to have had at least a proto-bureaucratic government.

Why was there this difference in centralization between Ch'u and the northern states? I suggest that a part of the reason was a difference in the kinship structure in Ch'u, before it became completely assimilated to Chinese culture. *Analects*, 13.18, says: "The Duke of She said to Confucius, 'Among us there are those who are upright; if the father steals a sheep, the son will testify against him.' Confucius replied, 'Among us the upright act differently; the son shields the father and the father shields the son.'" The Duke of She was an outstanding figure in Ch'u.[117] Many small indications augment the impression this gives, that there was less kinship solidarity in Ch'u.

In fact there is evidence which justifies the hypothesis that the institution of the *shih* 氏 may originally not have existed in Ch'u at all, but may have been taken over in the course of the Ch'un-ch'iu period, as a part of the process of the acculturation of Ch'u from the north; it is only rarely, and quite late in the Ch'un-ch'iu period, that we find reference to kinship groups called *shih* in Ch'u.[118] Furthermore aristocratic kinship

116. Legge, *Tso-chuan*, 194 (Hsi 25), 255 (Wen 10), 359 (Ch'eng 6), 362 (Ch'eng 7), 477 (Hsiang 18), 520 (Hsiang 26), 594 (Chao 4), 719 (Chao 27), 721 (Chao 27), 751 (Ting 4), 844 (Ai 16). *Kuo-yü*, 17.8b–9b, 18.11a.

117. Legge, *Tso-chuan*, 844–845 (Ai 16). The title "Duke" as used here has caused much unnecessary confusion. Ch'u lay outside the political system of the Chinese states. Its ruler called himself *wang*, "King," and called certain of his administrators of *hsien*, *kung*, "dukes." The Chinese commentators, and some Western scholars after them, have called these "usurped" titles.

118. In the northern states we constantly find references to these groups. They are called by the surname used by their members, plus the character *shih*. The Chi-shih 季氏 of Lu is a well-known example. The *Ch'un-ch'iu Ching-chuan Yin-te* 春秋經傳引得 (Peiping, 1937), 1176–1177, lists no less than fifty-six occurrences of the expression *Chi-shih*. Other surnames followed by *shih* are numerous in other northern states. Ku Tung-kao, *Ch'un-ch'iu Ta-shih Piao*, 89.25a–31b, lists nine surnames used by important kinship groups that are mentioned in the *Tso-chuan* as holding office in Ch'u. Sun Yao 孫曜 , *Ch'un-ch'iu Shih-tai chih Shih-tsu* 春秋時代之世族 (Shanghai, 1936), 185–188, adds eighteen more surnames of Ch'u individuals mentioned in the *Tso-chuan*, making a total of twenty-seven. I have checked all twenty-seven with the *Ch'un-ch'iu Ching-chuan Yin-te*. They occur in the *Tso-chuan*, followed by the character *shih*, a total of only fifteen times, as follows (the citations are preceded by letters to facilitate later reference; all are to Legge, *Tso-chuan*): A, 531 (Hsiang 27); B, 632 (Chao 11); C, 632 (2d time, Chao 11); D, 642 (Chao 13); E, 654 (Chao 14); F, 654 (2d time, Chao 14); G, 720 (Chao 27); H, 720 (2d time, Chao 27); I, 720 (3d time, Chao 27); J, 720 (4th time, Chao 27); K, 720 (5th time, Chao 27); L, 720 (6th time, Chao 27); M, 751 (Ting 4); N, 758 (Ting 5); O, 845 (Ai 16). Since Ch'u sometimes used different terminology from that of the northern states, it might be supposed that in this sense *shih* was simply replaced in Ch'u by another term denoting a group equivalent to the *shih*, but in fact this does not seem to be the case. To check this I have examined all occurrences of the nine important surnames listed by Ku Tung-kao;

groups in Ch'u do not appear to have been "corporations"; they do not seem to have had any regularly recognized heads. Aristocratic kinship groups in Ch'u did sometimes act together, even in revolt. But they were less solidly organized and thus posed less of a threat to the central government than did those of the northern states.[119] This fact undoubtedly facilitated the development of a system of centralized control, of which an important organ was the *hsien*, in Ch'u.

---

with them I have found only one case of use of such a character. This is *tsu* 族 which is used together with *shih* in the passage lettered D.

It is clear, then, that according to the testimony of the *Tso-chuan* (much our best source for the period) the concept of the *shih* did not play a great role in Ch'u. Even more significant is the fact that of the nine surnames listed by Ku Tung-kao as those of the kinship groups holding important offices in Ch'u, *only a single one* is found among this list linked with *shih*. Thus the political role of the *shih* in Ch'u was apparently negligible. Furthermore, the earliest of the instances listed above dates from 546 B. C., so that every one of them falls in the final third of the Ch'un-ch'iu period. This certainly permits the hypothesis that the concept and the institution of the *shih* were taken over by Ch'u from the northern states.

The term *shih* does occur at an earlier date in connection with the Ch'u kinship group known as the Jo-Ao 若敖 . But this group was very different from the *shih* of the northern states. "Jo-Ao" was the name of a ruler of Ch'u who reigned from 790 to 764 B. C. From his sons (aside from his heir who of course continued the ruling line) there descended two kinship groups which used, respectively, the surnames Tou 鬥 and Ch'eng 成 . Although they used two surnames, these descendants of Jo-Ao maintained a strong sense of group unity. They composed what was probably the strongest kinship group in Ch'u, until 605 B. C. when they rebelled and were exterminated (except for one man in Ch'u and such fugitives as may have fled the state). Clearly, however, the Jo-Ao group was not a *shih* in the sense in which this term was used in the northern states. Not only did its members not have a single common surname, but the group apparently had no recognized head (see note 119, below). Significantly the *Tso-chuan* does not refer to either a *Tou shih* or a *Ch'eng shih*. Yet in two passages, under the years 618 and 605 B. C., the *Tso-chuan* refers to the "*Jo-Ao shih*"; Legge, *Tso-chuan*, 253 (Wen 9), 295 (Hsüan 4). Apparently the author of the *Tso-chuan* used the term *shih* here analogically, because while this group was not a *shih* in the northern sense, the northern vocabulary had no term that would precisely fit this Ch'u phenomenon.

119. There are, I think, clear indications that the aristocratic family in Ch'u was, at an early date, organized differently from that of the northern states. We cannot expect a great deal of evidence for this, however, for the reason that Ch'u was undergoing rapid acculturation from the north during the Ch'un-ch'iu period. Our information about Ch'u becomes more abundant as communication with the northern states becomes more common, but this same communication tended, *pari passu*, to wipe out differences. Thus the record inevitably minimizes differences, and magnifies similarities, between Ch'u and the north.

Nevertheless there are significant indications of difference. Legge, *Tso-chuan*, 228 (Wen 1), reports a conversation of 626 B. C. in which the chief minister of Ch'u, discussing the succession to the throne, says: "The constant rule concerning the succession in Ch'u is that a younger son is chosen." This contrasts sharply with the northern norm according to which the eldest son of the principal wife was supposed to have the chief claim (though it was not always honored). Legge, *Tso-chuan*, 644 (Chao 13), reports a conversation of

What is the evidence that Chin took the institution of the *hsien* from Ch'u? It is circumstantial but considerable. At the beginning of the Ch'un-ch'iu period great power was held in Chin by clans related to the ducal house. Between 671 and 669 B. C. Duke Hsien massacred them all;

---

529 B. C., a century later, between two officers of the state of Chin in which one of them says, "When there is trouble in the Mi *hsing* 芈姓 [i.e., in the ruling house of Ch'u] they always establish the youngest scion as ruler; this is the constant rule of Ch'u." This qualification may merely be the northerner's explanation for this "queer" custom; alternatively it may indicate that in Ch'u, because of acculturation, the practice was beginning to be modified.

Another small indication that the kinship organization was different in Ch'u appears in *Kuo-yü*, 18.2b. King P'ing of Ch'u (reigned 528–516 B. C.) was sacrificed to by one of his sons who was not his heir. In the northern system only the heir (who was also ipso facto the head of the *hsing* or *shih*) was supposed to sacrifice to the deceased father, so that this would have been a usurpation of the ruler's function. Yet although the ruler of Ch'u knew of this sacrifice, the text seems clearly to indicate that he did not resent it.

The crucial question regarding the organization of the kinship group in Ch'u is whether it had a head. In the *Tso-chuan* we find it constantly indicated, in unmistakable terms, that a certain individual is the head of a certain *shih* in one of the northern states, but there are few cases of any such clear indication that any individual in Ch'u is the recognized head of a kinship group. And if such leadership over the group did exist in Ch'u it does not appear to have descended, as it normally did in the north, from eldest son to eldest son.

This appears, for instance, from the tale of the complicated viscissitudes of the Jo-Ao kinship group (see note 118, above), which was perhaps the most important in Ch'u. One of its members, Tzu-wen, held the office of chief minister from 664 to 637 B. C. In a northern state, a man holding such an office would normally have been the head of his *shih*. The younger brother of Tzu-wen, named Tzu-liang, held the office of second importance in the state, that of Minister of War; in a northern state it would have been almost impossible for two brothers to have held the two highest offices unless they had also been brothers of the ruler of the state. After the death of Tzu-wen his son Tzu-yang became chief minister, and Tzu-yüeh (son of Tzu-liang) became Minister of War. A plot was formed by another minister, as a result of which Tzu-yang was killed and Tzu-yüeh succeeded him as chief minister. Tzu-yüeh thereupon got the members of the Jo-Ao group to rise and kill the minister responsible for the death of Tzu-yang, and they prepared to attack the ruler of Ch'u. In a battle the ruler defeated the Jo-Ao and wiped out the group. While these events were occurring there was also living a son of Tzu-yang, who would seem as a descendant of the line of elder sons to have had (according to the *shih* system of the north) best claim to be the head of the Jo-Ao group. But he was away on a mission to the state of Ch'i, and apparently had nothing whatever to do with the rebellion. When he heard of it he returned to Ch'u and proclaimed his loyalty to the ruler. He was not put to death with the other members of his group. See: Legge, *Tso-chuan*, 117 (Chuang 30), 184 (Hsi 23), 295–296 (Hsüan 4). *Ch'un-ch'iu Tso-chuan Chu-su*, 21.23a. Ku, *Ch'un-ch'iu Ta-shih Piao*, 89.25. All this is rather complicated, but it would seem to show with some clarity that the kinship group in Ch'u did not have the same kind of organization and definite leadership that was the norm for the *shih* of the northern states.

There is further evidence of this. In the "corporate" *shih* of the northern states, the head of the *shih* was regarded as its virtual embodiment. Thus the surname plus *shih* was not only used to designate the *shih* but also to designate its head. It is often impossible

he also exiled all of his sons except the heir.[120] In 635 one of these sons returned to become Duke Wen. During his exile Wen had spent some time in Ch'u, and appears to have learned a good deal about its government.[121] It was evident that, if the northern states were to be saved from conquest by Ch'u, Chin would have to save them. In 632, in a great battle that exhausted both states, Chin thwarted the expansive ambitions of Ch'u.[122]

During the reign of Duke Wen and his successors the government of Chin was drastically reformed. And it is in precisely this period that a number of able officials of Ch'u, fleeing from the severe control of its government, were welcomed in Chin and given office there.[123] It is reasonable to suppose that this may not be unconnected with the fact that the new governmental machinery of Chin came to resemble that of Ch'u.

The *hsien* is first mentioned as existing in Chin in 627 B. C., at least sixty years later than our first reference for *hsien* in Ch'u. Evidence of a *system* of government by means of *hsien* is also much earlier for Ch'u than for Chin.[124] Furthermore, in Ch'u the *hsien* actually functioned as an

---

to determine, for instance, whether *Chi-shih* means "the Chi *shih*" or "the head of the Chi *shih*." For some cases in which it is fairly clear that a surname plus *shih* denotes the head of the *shih* as an individual, see: Legge, *Tso-chuan*, 497 (Hsiang 23), 498 (Hsiang 23), 707 (Chao 25), 783 (Ting 13), 806 (Ai 6), 827 (Ai 12). In the fifteen passages listed in note 118, above, in which a Ch'u surname is followed by *shih*, it seems clear that an individual is not designated in those lettered B, C, I, K, and N. An individual may be designated, but this is not certain, in passages D, F, J, M, and O. An individual probably is designated in A, E, G, H, and L. But of all these latter passages, only A concerns a member of one of the nine principal kinship groups of Ch'u listed by Ku Tung-kao. Thus in the entire *Tso-chuan* the manner of reference often used of *shih* heads in the northern states occurs only once as designating a member of a Ch'u kinship group of great consequence. This is additional evidence, negative but not negligible, against the existence of the *shih* as a "corporation" in Ch'u.

120. Legge, *Tso-chuan*, 105 (Chuang 23), 107 (Chuang 24), 109 (Chuang 25), 289 (Hsüan 2). *Kuo-yü* 8.4a.

121. Legge, *Tso-chuan*, 185 (Hsi 23), 204–205 (Hsi 28). For knowledge of the Ch'u system of official careers, by Duke Wen of Chin, see note 111, above.

122. Legge, *Tso-chuan*, 205 (Hsi 28).

123. Legge, *Tso-chuan*, 331 (Hsüan 17), 342 (Ch'eng 2), 362 (Ch'eng 7), 365 (Ch'eng 8), 391 (Ch'eng 16), 521–522 (Hsiang 26). *Kuo-yü* 17.3b–5b. Legge, *Tso-chuan*, p. 521 (Hsiang 26), quotes a statement to the effect that many of the ablest officials of Chin were fugitives from Ch'u.

124. It was pointed out in note 115, above, that there is evidence that the *hsien* as an administrative district *may* have existed in Ch'u even in the period 740–690 B. C., and that the first clearly datable establishment of a *hsien* by Ch'u probably took place in 688 B. C. In 598 B. C. we find the ruler of Ch'u saying, "The feudal lords and *hsien-kung* 縣公 have all congratulated me"; Legge, *Tso-chuan*, 309 (Hsüan 11). *Hsien-kung* is the title of one of the two classes of *hsien* administrators used by Ch'u. Since the ruler here speaks of "all" of them, this appears to imply that they compose a numerous group. And in 597 B. C. we find reference to the "nine *hsien*" of Ch'u; Legge, *Tso-chuan*, 311 (Hsüan 12).

instrument for centralized control, while in Chin if it ever did so this was only for a brief period, after which it became subverted. This looks as if Chin had not invented the device, but instead had tried unsuccessfully to adopt it.

Another parallel is the way in which the principal offices of Chin were filled. As in Ch'u, they were held by aristocrats but were not hereditary. These officers were selected on the basis of ability, character, and experience. There was a definite hierarchy of office and a recognized order of seniority. Although individual careers varied, they almost always involved movement from lower to progressively higher office.[125] After

---

It is possible, however, that "nine" is used here in the sense of "many," and that Ch'u had more than nine *hsien* at this time; see Ku, *Ch'un-ch'iu Hsien*, 172. These and other indications make it quite clear that Ch'u had a system of government in which the *hsien* played an important role, which was thoroughly established well before the beginning of the sixth century B. C.

For Chin, on the other hand, the earliest reference of any kind to a *hsien* is from 627 B. C.; Legge, *Tso-chuan*, 223 (Hsi 33). But this merely says that Duke Hsiang gave a *hsien* as a reward to one of his officers. There is nothing to show that the *hsien* was at that time an administrative unit in Chin, and the context makes this at least uncertain. References in 594 and 578 B. C. are similarly equivocal; ibid., 327 (Hsüan 15), 380 (Ch'eng 13). But in a conversation of 547 B. C. it is said that Chin plans to give a *hsien* to a refugee from Ch'u, with the evident meaning that Chin intends to make him one of its officials; ibid., 522 (Hsiang 26). Here, then, in 547 B. C., we have rather definite evidence that the *hsien* as an administrative unit existed in Chin.

125. There was an established hierarchy of office. Probably no official passed through all the stages, but the normal practice was to move from lower to higher office. It was very rare for a man to be appointed chief minister without having served an apprenticeship in at least one lower office. All of the higher offices in Chin were, in title, those of commander or lieutenant commander of one of the various armies, but in fact their functions included civil as well as military administration. This also is a parallel to the Ch'u administration, where the two highest officials performed both civil and military functions.

It is possible to reconstruct individual careers on the basis of the data given in Ku Tung-kao, *Ch'un-ch'iu Ta-shih Piao*, 86, though this sometimes needs to be supplemented. Two examples of careers may be cited. Han Chüeh is mentioned as holding the post of Ssu-ma (at this time an unimportant office in Chin), in 597 and again in 589 B. C. In 588 he is said to have been promoted to be commander of the *hsin-chung-chün*. In 578 he was commander of the *hsia-chün*, and by 573 he had been promoted to be chief minister of Chin. For this career see: Legge, *Tso-chuan*, 312 (Hsüan 12), 339 (Ch'eng 2), 381 (Ch'eng 13). *Ch'un-ch'iu Tso-chuan Chu-su*, 26.5a. Fan Yang appears in 557 as a mere *kung-tsu-tai-fu*. By 537 he was apparently commander of the *hsia-chün*. He is said to have become lieutenant commander of the *chung-chün*, but the date at which he assumed this office is uncertain. When the commander of the *chung-chün* (i.e., the chief minister of Chin) died in 509, Fan Yang apparently succeeded to this office. The difficulty of determining these careers is well illustrated by the case of Fan Yang, for whom the evidence seems reasonably solid but is for the most part inferential. See: Legge, *Tso-chuan*, 471 (Hsiang 16), 602 (Chao 5), 742 (Ting 1). *Ch'un-ch'iu Tso-chuan Chu-su*, 54.3a, 4a. I am deeply indebted to Professor C. Y. Hsü for his invaluable assistance in working out the careers of these and other Chin officials.

the power in Chin passed out of the hands of the dukes, these offices continued to be filled in the same way. The principal *shih* of Chin seem in effect to have constituted themselves an informal collegial body. Recognizing the dangers of anarchy within and enemies without, they voluntarily abated the claims of *shih* acquisitiveness. It was an uneasy and temporary truce, and in the end Chin was torn into three parts. But there can be no doubt that some of the foundations for China's bureaucratic government of later times were then laid in Chin.

It appears probable, then, that Ch'u showed the way out of China's danger posed by the development of the very kinship solidarity, which had earlier united Chinese society, to such an extreme that it threatened to destroy it. Ch'u was different enough to provide an alternative, yet sufficiently cultured to be admired or at least envied and sufficiently strong to be feared—two powerful stimuli to diffusion. It is not surprising that the native state of Shen Pu-hai adjoined Ch'u, while the state whose destinies he guided was one of the three into which Chin was divided.[126]

The basic motifs underlying this early history never wholly disappeared from China's traditional government. Ever since the third century B. C. it has been predominantly bureaucratic, characterized by the impersonal controls that bureaucracy invokes to maintain centralized control. At the same time the Confucian insistence upon decentralization of initiative and decision, upon the right of the individual official to follow his conscience, has been a powerful force.[127] And personal relationships between officials, based in part upon the familial pattern, have mitigated the rigor of official relations, and established patterns of "informal organization" within the governmental hierarchy.[128]

The existence of such cliques has been officially frowned upon, and these phenomena have sometimes been criticized as "Oriental inefficiency."

The official career, with an orderly progression from lower to higher office based upon experience and achievement, was not merely a fact in Chin; it was a recognized concept. See: Legge, *Tso-chuan*, 350 (Ch'eng 3), 437 (Hsiang 11). *Kuo-yü*, 10.17a–18a, 13.3b. The *Kuo-yü*, 2.14, records a conversation in which a Chin officer boasts to an officer of the Chou court that his merit is such that he will surely become chief minister of Chin. The Chou officer replies, "You are certainly worthy, but the state of Chin in promoting [officers] does not violate the order [of seniority]; I am afraid that [command of] the government will not come to you." Another Chou officer comments that no less than seven Chin officials have prior seniority over the man in question.

126. Shen Pu-hai was a native of Cheng, which adjoined Ch'u. During his lifetime Cheng was conquered by Han, one of the three states into which Chin was divided, of which he became chancellor.

127. See for instance de Bary, "Chinese Despotism and the Confucian Ideal: A Seventeenth-century View," 178–179, 195–197.

128. Yang, "Bureaucratic Behavior," 156–164.

It is only recently that students of administration have come to recognize that, as Chester I. Barnard says, "formal organizations . . . create and require informal organizations." [129] Peter M. Blau reports that "many studies have found that the existence of cohesive bonds between coworkers is a prerequisite for high morale and optimum performance of duties." [130] Naturally this does not mean that such crosscurrents did not at times produce inefficiency, but only that there are two sides to the coin.

China's traditional government is surely among the more remarkable of human institutions. Its structure was formed, more than two thousand years ago, on the basis of an administrative philosophy that emphasized impartiality and impersonality. It has been staffed by men to whom, for the most part, the cultivation of personal relationships has been almost a religion. The predictable tensions have always been present, and at times acute. A theorist might have expected that it would collapse in a generation. In fact it outlasted every contemporary government. To the beginning of the twentieth century its record of longevity, and of adaptation to radically changed situations with a minimum of disruption of basic structure, was unmatched by that of any other governmental system.

129. Barnard, *The Functions of the Executive*, 120.
130. Blau, *Bureaucracy in Modern Society*, 56.

8

The Role of the Horse in Chinese History

The term "chivalry" has come to stand for so much that is so important, in so many aspects of European history, that we may tend to forget that its original sense was "cavalry." The connotations with which the word "chivalry" has become charged underline the fact that the horse, as a cavalry mount, has been by no means a negligible factor. Undoubtedly many of the same phenomena would have occurred in somewhat different form, but European history would not have been entirely the same if the cavalry horse had not been invented.

We may not be accustomed to thinking of the cavalry horse as an invention. But it was one, and not the simplest: like most important inventions it was a combination and culmination of a number of other inventions. It appears to have first been developed in Western Asia or Southeastern Europe. Spreading early to various parts of Europe it became of some importance there. But the cavalry horse had its most extensive and most deadly development among the nomadic peoples of Asia. Its impact was felt by China somewhat later than by Europe, but its influence upon many aspects of Chinese history has been tremendous. For some two thousand years China's foreign relations, military policy, economic well-being, and indeed its very existence as an independent state were importantly conditioned by the horse.

The steppes of Central Asia and Southeastern Europe are the regions in which much of the history of the cavalry horse unfolded. But these arid lands have not always been peopled by fierce, horse-riding, nomadic warriors. Their earliest known inhabitants seem to have been men who were not even pastoral, but at least chiefly agricultural; such agriculture must have been carried on in particularly favorable areas, such as oases. The rearing of domestic animals appears to have been a subsequent

Reprinted from the *American Historical Review*, LXX (1965), 647–672 (© 1965 by Herrlee G. Creel).

development.[1] Both Karl Jettmar and James F. Downs conclude that the technique of the domestication of the horse was developed in the Near East and spread eastward through Asia. If this is correct, it must have reached China quite early, for it appears likely that the horse was domesticated in eastern China in late Neolithic times.[2] But even after the horse was kept as a domestic animal, this did not mean that its keepers were at once riders, much less mounted warriors.

Downs distinguishes three phases in the employment of the horse for transportation. One (no doubt the earliest) is its use for traction, including the pulling of chariots. The second is the use of the horse as a "moving seat," ridden simply as a means of transportation. The third is the development of the horse into a charger of war.

The transition from the second to the third step is not so simple as it might seem. Downs, who speaks from an extensive practical experience with horses unusual in a scholar,[3] points out that training the horse for war is no easy matter. It is a highly temperamental "animal of 'flight' rather than 'fight.' " Yet it must be taught to "face loud noises, leap fences, charge into crowds, and gallop at man's command, often to its own destruction."

Furthermore, Downs argues, the development of really effective mounts for war required the breeding of horses larger than those found in the wild state. "The only wild breed of horses known in recent history, Przevalsky's horse *(E. przewalskii poliakoff)* of the Central Asian Steppe, averages about 13 hands" (a hand equals four inches). Such a horse, he says, is so small that its value "in war or hunting would have been negligible." The modern domestic horse, averaging fifteen hands, is a product of selective breeding and feeding.[4]

In our information concerning the characteristics of the horses that were early used as cavalry mounts in East Asia, the factor of size is rarely mentioned.[5] But it is perfectly clear that horses preferred for war were

---

1. Karl Jettmar, "Les Plus Anciennes Civilisations d'éleveurs des steppes d'Asie Centrale," *Cahiers d'histoire mondiale*, I (no. 4, 1954), 760–783; James F. Downs, "The Origin and Spread of Riding in the Near East and Central Asia," *American Anthropologist*, LXIII (Dec. 1961), 1199; Owen Lattimore, *Inner Asian Frontiers of China* (New York, 1940), 157–163, 328.
2. Downs, "Origin and Spread of Riding," 1201; Jettmar, "Éleveurs des Steppes," 775; H. G. Creel, *Studies in Early Chinese Culture, First Series* (Baltimore, 1937), 189–90.
3. Downs, "Origin and Spread of Riding," 1202, says: "The observations on the nature of the horse are drawn mainly from my own experience as an amateur and professional horseman in the show ring, hunt field, racing, and occasionally as a cowboy."
4. Ibid.
5. Though there seem to be no specific statements in the early Chinese materials that

greatly superior to ordinary horses in speed, agility, and stamina. It seems evident, then, that the successful use of cavalry in war required three things: the mastery of the technique of riding and using the paraphernalia of cavalry warfare; the technique of training horses for war; and the breeding of, or acquisition of, horses suitable for mounted warfare, which must possess qualities not found in the ordinary horse.

In China the horse, which may have been domesticated in late Neolithic times, was driven to chariots in the Shang (?1765–1123 B. C.) and Chou (1122–256 B. C.) periods. There seems to be no clear evidence that horses were ridden in China until very shortly before 300 B. C.[6] Two well-known books, which are commonly dated as having been written around this time, fail to mention riding in contexts where we would certainly expect such reference if riding had been at all common.[7] And a very clear

---

horses used for cavalry mounts needed to be larger than other horses, there is much ground for inference that they were. Thus the proposal made in 146 B. C. that horses taller than thirteen hands, whose teeth were not yet smooth, be forbidden to be exported from the imperial domain, was almost certainly designed to conserve large horses for cavalry use. (See *History of the Former Han Dynasty*, trans. Homer H. Dubs [3 vols., Baltimore, 1938–1955], I, 321.) Much later, in A. D. 1061, we find the superintendent of imperial pastures complaining that careless practices in breeding produced horses so small that they were not equal to the demands of war. (Sung Ch'i 宋祁 , *Ching-wen Chi* 景文集 , *Kuo-hsüeh Chi-pen Ts'ung-shu* ed. [Shanghai, 1937], 368).

6. Eduard Erkes, "Das Pferd im alten China," *T'oung Pao*, XXXVI (pt. 1, 1942), 50–52, cites a number of passages that have been held to prove that riding took place earlier, but shows that they do not. A single Shang burial in which one man accompanies one horse has been argued to indicate horseback riding in the Shang period, but the evidence seems quite inadequate. (See Shih Chang-ju 石璋如 , *Yin-hsü Tsui-chin chih Chung-yao Fa-hsien, Fu Lun Hsiao-t'un Ti-ts'eng* 殷墟最近之重要發現附論小屯地層, in *Chung-kuo K'ao-ku Hsüeh-pao* 中國考古學報 , II [1947], 21–24; Franz Hančar, *Das Pferd in prähistorischer und früher historischer Zeit* [Vienna and Munich, 1956], 275–276.) Homer H. Dubs, "The Great Fire in the State of Lu3TU in 492 B. C.," *Journal of the American Oriental Society*, LXXXIV (no. 1, 1964), 15–16, finds in the *Tso-chuan* a reference to cavalry at this early date. But neither James Legge nor Séraphin Couvreur, in translating this passage, supposes there to be any reference to cavalry, and in my opinion both the text and the commentary indicate that the horses mentioned here were to be used to draw vehicles.

7. The *Sun-tzu* 孫子 is said to be the earliest extant Chinese work on the art of war. Its date and authorship are uncertain, but it is generally considered to date from the Warring States period. (See Chang Hsin-ch'eng 張心澂 , *Wei-shu T'ung-k'ao* 偽書通考 [Changsha, 1939], 797–801; Samuel B. Griffith, *Sun Tzu, The Art of War* [Oxford, 1963], 1–12.) This text includes no mention of cavalry, though it does refer to the use of horse-drawn chariots in war. (See: *Sun-tzu* [*Ssu-pu Pei-yao* ed.], 2.1a, 9.14b, 16b, 18a. Griffith, *Sun Tzu, The Art of War*, 72, 119, 120.) Griffith says: "It is significant that Sun Tzu does not refer to cavalry. Cavalry was not made an integral branch in any Chinese army until 320 B. C. when King Wu Ling of Chao State introduced it—and trousers. It is reasonable to assume that if cavalry had been familiar to Sun Tzu he would have mentioned it." (Ibid., 11.) The *Chuang-tzu* is commonly dated from around 300 B. C. Its ninth section, called "Horses' Hoofs," denouncing the restraints that government lays on men, decries the

account tells us that King Wu-ling of the northern Chinese state of Chao, who reigned from 325 to 299 B. C., took over the technique of riding and cavalry warfare in openly avowed imitation of the practice of the nomads.[8]

The time and place of "the invention of riding" might well be impossible to determine. There is reason to believe that other animals may have been ridden long before the horse.[9] But our concern is with a more complex and specific technique: that of the mounted archer. The mounted nomads of Asia, who took the cavalry horse to the borders of China and compelled the Chinese to deal with it as a problem, were bowmen, and it is the technique of archery from horseback that the Chinese adopted. It seems to be generally agreed that this technique first comes to our knowledge, and was probably first developed, among nomadic peoples living in Western Asia and Southeastern Europe. Although mounted archers may have existed much earlier, the typical mounted nomadic bowman seems first to have been pictured in an Assyrian relief of the ninth century B. C.[10]

The technique of riding diffused through Eastern Europe rapidly, from about 800 B. C. onward.[11] It would seem logical to suppose that the technique of the mounted bowman would have spread across Asia, through nomadic peoples, quite rapidly, but in fact it seems to have been remarkably slow in penetrating to the borders of China. The excavation of the "Pazyryk kurgans"—five splendid subterranean tombs of nomadic chiefs, located near Pazyryk in the Altai Mountains not far from the western tip of Outer Mongolia—has made it clear that fine saddle horses were being bred and ridden in that area not later than the fifth century B. C. The men buried in them had many Chinese objects and were apparently influenced

---

unnatural treatment to which horses used by men are subjected. And while it refers to the harnessing and yoking of horses, nothing in the chapter seems to make any reference to riding or the paraphernalia of riding. (See: *Chuang-tzu* [*Ssu-pu Pei-yao* ed.], 4.6a–8b. *The Writings of Kwang-zze*, trans. James Legge, *Sacred Books of the East*, XXXIX and XL [2 vols. reprinted in 1, London, 1927], I, 276–280.)

8. *Chan-kuo Ts'e* 戰國策 (*Ssu-pu Pei-yao* ed.), 19.5b–9b; Takigawa Kametaro 瀧川龜太郎, *Shih-Chi Hui-chu K'ao-cheng* 史記會注考證 [referred to hereafter as *Shih-chi*] (10 vols., Tokyo, 1932–1934), 43.50–69; Se-ma Ts'ien, *Les Mémoires historiques*, trans. Édouard Chavannes (5 vols., Paris, 1895–1905), V, 71–94.

9. Downs, "Origin and Spread of Riding," 1196–1197.

10. Hančar, *Das Pferd*, 551–563; T. Sulimirski, "Scythian Antiquities in Western Asia," *Artibus Asiae*, XVII (pts. 3–4, 1954), 282–318; Downs, "Origin and Spread of Riding," 1200–1202.

11. *A History of Technology*, ed. Charles Singer et al. (5 vols., Oxford, Eng., 1954–1958), II, 555.

by Chinese art.[12] Nevertheless, there seems to be no indication in Chinese literature that the nomadic peoples with whom the Chinese were in contact fought from horseback at an early date. Accounts of battles in 714 B. C. and again as late as 541 B. C. state specifically that the nomadic tribes of the northern border regions with whom the Chinese fought were foot soldiers.[13]

It may be, in fact, that mounted men are not clearly mentioned in Chinese literature until the account of the manner in which King Wu-ling of Chao adopted the technique of the mounted nomadic bowmen.[14] It is very detailed and circumstantial. Even though the danger from the mounted warrior was pressing, the Chinese resisted riding because, among other things, it required the wearing of a short jacket rather than the long gown which, in Chinese eyes, was obligatory for a man of status. The King succeeded, by a combination of persuasion and force, in forming a corps of mounted archers, which was very successful in defending the state and even extending its borders.[15]

---

12. A. P. Okladnikov, *Ancient Population of Siberia and Its Cultures* (Cambridge, Mass., 1959), 36–39. Ellis H. Minns, "The Art of the Northern Nomads," *Proceedings of the British Academy, 1942*, XXVIII (London, 1942), 47–99. M. P. Griaznov and Eugene A. Golomshtok, "The Pazirik Burial of Altai," *American Journal of Archaeology*, XXXVII (no. 1, 1933), 30–45. Franz Hančar, "The Eurasian Animal Style and the Altai Complex (Cultural Historical Interpretation with a Consideration of the Newest Pazyryk Discoveries of 1946–1949)," *Artibus Asiae*, XV (pts. 1–2, 1952), 171–194. Karl Jettmar, "The Altai before the Turks," *Bulletin of the Museum of Far Eastern Antiquities, Stockholm*, XXIII (1951), 135–223. Otto Maenchen-Helfen, "A Chinese Bronze with Central-Asiatic Motives," ibid., XXX (1958), 168–169. John F. Haskins, "The Pazyryk Felt Screen and the Barbarian Captivity of Ts'ai Wên-chi," ibid., XXXV (1963), 141–160; M. P. Griaznov, *L'Art ancien de l'Altaï* (Leningrad, 1958). Chester S. Chard, "First Radiocarbon Dates from the U. S. S. R.," *Arctic Anthropology*, I (1962), 84–86, publishes data indicating that Pazyryk Kurgan 5 has been dated to 530–430 B. C., and Kurgan 2 to 530–250 B. C. Haskins, "Pazyryk Felt Screen," 157, n. 91, gives a different radiocarbon dating from Soviet sources for Kurgan 5, indicating a mean date of 390 B. C.
13. *The Ch'un Ts'ew [Ch'un-ch'iu] with the Tso Chuen [Tso-chuan]* [referred to hereafter as *Tso-chuan*], trans. James Legge (2 vols., London, 1872), 27 (translation, 28), 572 (translation, 579).
14. There may be such references, but I know of none, and none of those who have studied the matter, whose works I have read, seems to mention them. (See Erkes, "Das Pferd," 54–55; Lattimore, *Inner Asian Frontiers of China*, 60–61; William Montgomery McGovern, *The Early Empires of Central Asia* [Chapel Hill, N. C., 1939], 100–101.)
15. *Chan-kuo Ts'e*, 19.5b–9b; *Shih-chi*, 43.50–69; Se-ma Ts'ien, *Mémoires historiques*, V, 71–94. There is no assurance, however, that the discussion of this problem actually took place in the precise form in which it is set down. The language of the debate, with some variations, is used in a quite different context in *Shang-chün Shu (Ssu-pu Pei-yao* ed.), 1.1a–3b; *The Book of Lord Shang*, trans. J. J. L. Duyvendak (London, 1928), 167–175. The detailed resemblance of these texts is discussed in Ch'i Ssu-ho 齊思和 , *Shang Yang Pien-fa K'ao* 商鞅變法考 , *Yen-ching Hsüeh-pao* 燕京學報 , XXXIII (1947), 172–176.

Even though there seems to be no earlier reference to them, we may be perfectly sure that mounted nomads had been encountered by Chinese well before that time. The first Chinese who saw them may have laughed at such "barbarian antics"; certainly they could not possibly have understood the gravity of this portent for China's future. It is also clear that, while we have such an explicit record only for Chao, other Chinese states must have taken over the technique of riding at about the same time if not even earlier.[16] Many historical events of the greatest moment must necessarily go unrecorded simply because historians would have to be prophets to recognize their importance.

The unobtrusive manner in which the phenomenon of the mounted archer appears in Chinese history would seem to corroborate Owen Lattimore's contention, which archaeological data subsequently discovered seem to support, that "horse nomadism" was not brought to the borders of China by any sudden migration, or conquest by a particular people.[17] Instead there would seem to have been a movement across Asia, from west to east, of the technique of mounted warfare. And if this required superior horses, there must have gone with it either superior breeding stock, a superior technique of breeding and rearing horses, or both.[18]

Many scholars have held, on the basis of considerable evidence, that the technique of cavalry warfare that the Chinese adopted from their nomadic neighbors was transmitted across Asia from a place of origin in Iran or among nomads living in areas bordering on Iran.[19] And Iran and the lands adjacent to it have been, from very early times, an almost legendary reservoir of superior horses. P. N. Tretiakov and A. L. Mongait

Ch'i appears to think that the version concerned with King Wu-ling is the original, and this may be true. It seems likely, however, that the text as we have it is a literarily elaborated version of a discussion and an incident that did, nevertheless, actually take place.

16. Erkes, "Das Pferd," 52–54, cites evidence that riding was well known in some other states at around this same time, or very shortly thereafter.

17. Lattimore, *Inner Asian Frontiers of China*, 162–163.

18. This thesis of the eastward movement of horse culture has been vigorously denied by a recent Chinese writer. He finds the domestication of the horse to have begun in China as early as anywhere else, and the chariot and the technique of riding to have been invented in China. (See Hsieh Ch'eng-chia 謝成俠 , *Chung-kuo Yang-ma Shih* 中國養馬史 [Peking, 1959], 26–27, 74–75, 79, 89.) Concerning the first two, it would seem that in fact our evidence does not really permit a certain conclusion either way; as for riding, the evidence cited by Hsieh is distinctly weak. Since so many Western writers have tended to insist that almost everything important must have gone from the West to China, it is not surprising to find a Chinese reversing the thesis.

19. Berthold Laufer, *Chinese Clay Figures*, Pt. I, *Prolegomena on the History of Defensive Armor* (Chicago, 1914), 222–232; McGovern, *Central Asia*, 99–104; Minns, "Art of the Northern Nomads," 76–77.

point out that "the thoroughbred horses raised on Armenian pastures were so famous that they ranked first on the list of tributes due the Achaemeneans. . . . the Armenians had to contribute 20,000 foals to the king on Mithra's holiday."[20] Darius I, the Achaemenian ruler who reigned from 521 to 486 B. C., and whose conquests gave Persia an extent "greater than that of any earlier empire west of China,"[21] called Persia a land "beautiful, possessing good horses, possessing good men," and therefore fearing no enemy.[22] Herodotus relates that Darius and his allies agreed that the rule should go to him "whose steed first neighed after the sun was up," and that Darius gained the throne by a trick that caused his horse to neigh first.[23] This is doubtless legend, but significant in the importance it gives to the horse.

Franz Hančar, in his extensive study of the early history of the horse, concludes that the art of breeding fine horses arose in the great area of Western Asia lying just north of Iran, including the regions now known as Kazakhstan, Turkmenistan, Uzbekistan, Tadzhikistan, and Kirghizistan; he calls this area "Turan." It is here, he believes, that the type of the riding horse, as a goal for breeding, was established during the first millennium B. C.[24]

In the Altai Mountains, on the eastern edge of this area, lie the Pazyryk kurgans. Here, frozen in solid ice since as early as the fifth century B. C., were excavated the remains of what are doubtless the best - preserved early horses known. From them, Hančar believes, we can know what the early horses of Turan were like. Sixty-nine complete horses, and partial skeletons of eighteen more, were exhaustively studied by V. O. Vitt. He found that their size ranged from only 128 centimeters (12.59 hands) to 150 centimeters (14.76 hands). Thus while the smallest of these horses were even smaller than the average wild Przhevalski's horse, the largest were taller than the minimal height attained by the highly prized Arab horse today.[25]

"Quite contrary to all expectations," Eugene A. Golomshtok writes, "the Pazirik horse is not the well known type of wild horse found in Siberia (Equus Przevalskii), or the short sturdy Kirghizian type, but

20. P. N. Tretiakov and A. L. Mongait, *Contributions to the Ancient History of the U. S. S. R., with Special Reference to Transcaucasia*, trans. Vladimir M. Maurin, ed. Henry Field and Paul Tolstoy (Cambridge, Mass., 1961), 62.

21. *Cambridge Ancient History* (12 vols., Cambridge, 1923–1939), IV, 2.

22. Ibid., 4; Laufer, *Chinese Clay Figures*, 210.

23. *The History of Herodotus*, trans. George Rawlinson (New York, 1932), 179–180.

24. Hančar, *Das Pferd*, 355–372.

25. Ibid., 362–363; Brian Seymour Vesey-FitzGerald, *The Book of the Horse* (Los Angeles, 1947), 147.

shows evidence of long domestication and breeding, reminding one of the racing type found among the Arabs." A. P. Okladnikov says that the Pazyryk horses "were excellent riding horses of the best breeds of the East, of noble blood, stately and lively jumpers of gold-brown color. They were not fed green fodder but selected grain, and were kept in well-attended stalls."[26]

These statements presumably refer to the larger Pazyryk horses, which differ so much from the smallest that they have sometimes been supposed to be a different breed, imported from the famous horse-raising lands to the west of the Altai. But Vitt, on the basis of his study, believes that the variation is due not to difference of breed but rather to the use of such techniques as better feeding, selective breeding, and castration.[27] It would seem entirely likely that as the interest in superior horses grew there occurred both a diffusion of techniques of breeding and some movement of superior breeding stock across Asia.

Concerning the horses of the nomads who lived farther east, on the borders of China, we are dependent for information on Chinese sources. Regarding the horse in China itself, our information is by no means so complete as could be wished.[28] There seems to be general agreement, however, that the basic stock of early Chinese horses was the wild Przhevalski's horse.[29] It was undoubtedly improved somewhat in breeding by the Chinese and may early have been crossed with some imported stock. A recent archaeological find indicates that at least some Chinese horses of the tenth century B. C. had a configuration remarkably similar to that of the typical "Mongol pony" of the present day.[30] As early as the

26. Griaznov, "The Pazirik Burial of Altai," 45, n. f (by Eugene A. Golomshtok); Okladnikov, *Ancient Population of Siberia*, 37.

27. Hančar, *Das Pferd*, 363–364.

28. While many skeletons of horses, dating from late Neolithic times onward, have been excavated in China, I have been able to find no published data giving the results of expert examination and measurement of these materials.

29. Hančar, *Das Pferd*, 265–266; W. Perceval Yetts, "The Horse: A Factor in Early Chinese History," *Eurasia Septentrionalis Antiqua*, IX (1934), 242; Arthur de Carle Sowerby, "The Horse and Other Beasts of Burden in China," *China Journal*, XXVI (Dec. 1937), 282; Edward H. Schafer, *The Golden Peaches of Samarkand: A Study of T'ang Exotics* (Berkeley and Los Angeles, 1963), 61–62. Many fossils of the Przhevalski's horse have been excavated in China, showing that it was present from an early time. (Hsieh, *Yang-ma Shih*, 21–25.)

30. A bronze statuette of a horse, nearly thirteen inches high, was dug up in 1956. Its inscription, deciphered by Kuo Mo-jo, indicates that it was cast in the tenth century B. C. to commemorate a gift of two horses from the king. (See Kuo Mo-jo 郭沫若, *Li Ch'i-ming K'ao-shih* 盉器銘考釋, in *K'ao-ku Hsüeh-pao* 考古學報 [no. 2, 1957], 1–6; on the "Mongol pony," see Sowerby, "Beasts of Burden in China," 284 and facing illustration.) Interestingly enough, the "Mongol pony" is also believed to be the Przhevalski's horse altered by an undetermined amount of interbreeding with imported stock.

fourteenth century B. C. matched teams of various kinds of horses, distinguished both as to color and to size, were available in the stables of the Shang kings.[31] Clearly, some skill in breeding had already been developed. Poems and documents dating from early in the first millennium B. C. refer frequently to prized horses of special colors and characteristics.[32] The judging of horses was early recognized as a special art; a work written in the middle of the third century B. C. lists ten men who were "skilled at judging horses in antiquity."[33]

We have little evidence from which to deduce, with certainty, the size of early Chinese horses, but there is reason to believe that they were ordinarily rather small.[34] As late as 146 B. C. the Chinese Imperial

31. Kuo Mo-jo, *Pu-tz'u T'ung-tsuan* 卜辭通纂 (Tokyo, 1933); *K'ao-shih*, 155b–157a.
32. *The Shoo King* [*Shu-ching*], trans. James Legge (2 vols., London, 1865), II, 562; *The She King* [*Shih-ching*], trans. id. (2 vols., London, 1871), I, 131, 193–194, II, 260, 291, 532; *The Book of Songs* [*Shih-ching*], trans. Arthur Waley (Boston and New York, 1937), 110, 111, 123, 134, 289; Erkes, "Das Pferd," 41–43.
33. *Lü-shih Ch'un-ch'iu* 呂氏春秋 (*Ssu-pu Pei-yao* ed.), 20.19a; *Frühling und Herbst des Lü Bu We*, trans. Richard Wilhelm (Jena, 1928), 372.
34. They were not so small, however, as a passage in W. Eberhard, *Lokalkulturen im Alten China*, I (Suppl. to Vol. XXXVII, *T'oung Pao* [1942]), 14, would indicate. He writes: "Die Pferde sind 3½ Fuss (rund 81 cm) hoch und 4,4 Fuss (rund 102 cm) lang (Hou-Han-shu 54, 5a)." It seems clear that he has misinterpreted the text. The passage is discussing a bronze model of a horse that the Han general Ma Yüan caused to be cast. The text (*Hou-Han-shu*, in *Er-shih-ssu Shih* [Shanghai, 1884], 54.11b) says that this bronze "horse was three ch'ih five ts'un high, and four ch'ih four ts'un in circumference." There were, to be sure, horses even smaller than this in Latter Han times. (See ibid., 115.10b.) But these were curiosities. It is clear that the usual horse at this time was not 81 centimeters in height. The work known as the *Chou-li* 周禮 cannot be dated with certainty, but must have come to its present form during one of the late centuries B. C. It classifies horses as those six, seven, and eight ch'ih 尺 ("Chinese feet") tall. (See *Chou-li Chu-su*, in *Shih-san Ching Chu-su* [Nanchang, 1815], 33.8a; *Le Tcheou-li* [*Chou-li*], *ou Rites des Tcheou*, trans. Édouard Biot [2 vols., Paris, 1851; photographic reprint, Peking, 1940], II, 261–262.) But it is impossible to tell what is the actual height referred to, since we cannot date the *Chou-li*, and the length of the ch'ih in Chou times probably varied with the time and place. Wu Ch'eng-lo 吳承洛 , *Chung-kuo Tu-liang Heng Shih* 中國度量衡史 (Shanghai, 1937), 130–131, calculates that the early Chou ch'ih measured only .1991 meter, which would make the 6-ch'ih horse stand only 11.76 hands high, much shorter than the wild horse. Nancy Lee Swann, *Food and Money in Ancient China* (Princeton, N. J., 1950), 362, gives the length of the Han ch'ih as 9.094 inches. By this longer measure the 8-ch'ih horse would have exceeded 18 hands, which is hardly conceivable. The largest modern draft horse, the Shire, only exceeds 17. (See George Gaylord Simpson, *Horses* [New York, 1951], 44–45.) And even by this improbably large measure, the 6-ch'ih horse would have measured only a little more than 13½ hands, only slightly larger than the wild horse. Significantly, the *Chou-li* calls only the 6-ch'ih animals "horses," giving special names to the larger equines. It seems likely, then, that the ordinary horse in early China was not much larger than the wild horse. Hsieh, *Yang-ma Shih*, 29, publishes photographs of excavated skeletons of Shang horses and says: "If we calculate on the basis of the horse bones in Plates 8 and 9, the height of Yin [Shang] horses may be estimated at about 145

Secretary memorialized the throne proposing a ban on the export, from the imperial domain, of horses more than thirteen hands high whose teeth were not yet smooth.[35] This implies that horses larger than the wild horse were still somewhat rare and were considered so valuable that they must not be permitted to be lost to the imperial domain until they had reached an advanced age. The purpose was probably to conserve horses fit for war, of which China has usually had a shortage.

Like many other peoples the Chinese have commonly had a strong tendency toward ethnocentrism. When, in order to strengthen his army, King Wu-ling of Chao wished to adopt the "barbarian" practice of riding, one of his critics asserted that China itself was the place "where all things of value and utility are assembled."[36] Yet the Chinese seem never to have had this attitude with regard to horses. The horses of distant lands, usually to the west or the north, and even of their nomadic enemies near at hand have commonly been acknowledged quite frankly to be superior.

Even though mounted nomads in East Asia do not seem to be mentioned until the fourth century B. C., the nomads living on China's borders had horses long before this time.[37] Erkes, in his study of the horse in ancient China, finds that it is impossible to point to any particular region of China as outstanding in the breeding of horses, from which he concludes that they were raised in all parts of the country.[38] Undoubtedly they were, but evidently no region was producing especially fine horses. Even in antiquity, it appears, the best horses were commonly obtained from the nomads.

Early in the ninth century B. C., we are told, an attack by the Chinese on certain northern nomads resulted in the capture of a thousand horses.[39] In 538 B. C. the ruler of a northern Chinese state boasted that it feared no enemy because, among other assets, it had many horses. But one of his

---

centimeters" (p. 33). This is equal to more than 14 hands. But it seems impossible to be certain on what basis this estimate was made. If it was from inspection of photographs, it is hard to know what reliance to place on it.

35. Dubs, *History of the Former Han Dynasty*, I, 321. It appears that in ancient China, as today, the height of horses was normally calculated to the withers. (See Hsieh, *Yang-ma Shih*, 35.)

36. *Chan-kuo Ts'e*, 19.7a; *Shih-chi*, 43.54; Se-ma Ts'ien, *Mémoires historiques*, V, 77.

37. We know that the nomads of Western Asia used wagons as early as the eighth century B. C., and those near China probably had them early although specific evidence for them seems to be lacking until about the second century B. C. (See: Ellis H. Minns, *Scythians and Greeks* [Cambridge, 1913], 50–52. McGovern, *Central Asia*, 52–53; *Chou-li*, 39.4ab. *Shih-chi*, 110.30, 44, 52. Burton Watson, *Records of the Grand Historian of China, Translated from the Shih-chi of Ssu-ma Ch'ien* [2 vols., New York and London, 1961], II, 168, 177, 182.)

38. Erkes, "Das Pferd," 36.

39. Wang Kuo-wei 王國維 , *Ku-pen Chu-shu Chi-nien Chi-chiao* 古本竹書紀年輯校 , in *Wang Chung-ch'io Kung I-shu* 王忠慤公遺書 (42 vols., n.p., 1927–1928), III, 8a.

ministers rebuked his complacency and asserted that horses, apparently meaning the best horses, came from "northern Chi 冀 ."[40] The exact location of this area is debated, but it was approximately in the northern tip of the modern Shansi Province, then a border area inhabited by nomads who may have been partly Sinicized.[41] In connection with the fierce struggles between the contending Chinese states in the fourth century B. C., emphasis was laid upon the strategic importance of controlling the horses of this region and importing horses from the northern nomads known as Hu 胡 .[42] In the third century B. C., the philosopher Hsün-tzu named fast horses as the special product of the "north sea," that is, of the vaguely defined region north of China.[43]

Emperor Wu of the Former Han dynasty, who reigned from 140 to 87 B. C., had an ability to focus attention upon himself that might be envied by a publicity agent of the twentieth century. His extensive and flamboyant efforts to secure "heavenly, blood-sweating horses" from Fergana, which were crowned with success around 100 B. C., have probably been studied and written about more than all the other importations of horses to China combined. The incident was important, but not, insofar as the acquisition of horses was concerned, that important. The number secured was small as compared with some later importations. And this was by no means the first acquisition of superior horses from abroad.

For some time the Chinese had been engaged in grim struggles with the nomads known as the Hsiung-nu 匈奴 (probably the people who, when they appeared in the West, were known as Huns). The superiority

---

40. *Tso-chuan*, 592 (translation, 596). The name of this area was combined with the signific for "horse" to make the character *chi* 驥 which was used to denote especially fine horses. Confucius (*Analects*, 14.35) and others used this term frequently. A *chi* was said to be able to run 1,000 li (about 258 miles) in a day. This is clearly fable. The messenger service of Darius I, around 500 B. C., and the American pony express in 1860 and 1861, using relays of fresh horses, covered only about 180 and 244 miles per day respectively. (See *History of Technology*, ed. Singer et al., II, 495–496; *Encyclopaedia Britannica* [11th ed., 29 vols., New York, 1910–1911], VI, 637, X, 85.)

41. Almost certainly this reference is to Chi-chou 冀州 ; the reference to the "nine chou" just preceding (*Tso-chuan*, 592) indicates this. This is presumably the idea of the commentator Tu Yü (*Ch'un-ch'iu Tso-chuan Chu-su*, in *Shih-san Ching Chu-su*, 42.20a) who says that these northern regions comprise Yen 燕 and Tai 代 . I think that Erkes ("Das Pferd," 38) misunderstood this when he translated it as "das Tai von Yen." For the boundaries of Chi-chou, and the location of Tai and Yen, see Albert Herrmann, *Historical and Commercial Atlas of China* (Cambridge, Mass., 1935), 10–11, 15; a similar location is indicated in Hsieh, *Yang-ma Shih*, 25.

42. *Chan-kuo Ts'e*, 3.1b, 18.8a.

43. *Hsün-tzu* (*Ssu-pu Pei-yao* ed.), 5.6a; *The Works of Hsüntze*, trans. Homer H. Dubs (London, 1928), 133.

of their horses had long been recognized. Some two decades before Emperor Wu ascended the throne, a Chinese official, Ch'ao Ts'o, had pointed out that "the territory of the Hsiung-nu and the skills it demands are different from those of China. In climbing up and down mountains, and crossing ravines and mountain torrents, the horses of China cannot compare with those of the Hsiung-nu."[44] And there are clear indications that the Chinese had long been securing some superior horses from such peoples as the Hsiung-nu.

Ssu-ma Ch'ien, writing around 100 B. C., said that the Hsiung-nu, in addition to rearing numerous sheep, cattle, and horses, kept a number of rare animals, of which at least two seem to be special types of horses.[45] Both were present in considerable numbers in the stables of Emperor Wu.[46] One of them, the k'uai-t'i,[47] is particularly interesting. It is said to have been an excellent horse of the northern nomads, able on the third day after its birth to jump over its mother; this legend was no doubt based upon the ability to jump for which the mounts of the nomads were renowned. A poet of the Latter Han period wrote that k'uai-t'i were used, along with horses from Fergana, as war horses in expeditions against the nomads.[48]

These facts lend particular interest to a statement made by the minister Li Ssu to the ruler of the state of Ch'in in 237 B. C. An edict had been issued calling for the expulsion of all ministers who were not natives of Ch'in, which would have meant the dismissal of Li Ssu. In order to

44. Wang Hsien-ch'ien, *Ch'ien-Han-shu Pu-chu* [referred to hereafter as *Han-shu*], (1900), 49.10b.

45. I.e., the *k'uai-t'i* 駃騠 and the *t'ao-t'u* 駒騊 ; *Shih-chi*, 110.2–3. The translation given in Watson, *Records*, II, 155, differs at some points from my understanding of the terms. Namio Egami, "The *K'uai-t'i*, the *T'ao-yü*, and the *Tan-hsi*, the Strange Domestic Animals of the Hsiung-nu," *Memoirs of the Research Department of the Toyo Bunko*, XIII (1951), 103–111, explains the *t'ao-t'u* to be the wild Przhevalski's horse. But if so, and if the Przhevalski's horse was the commonest horse of the Mongolian area and of China, it is hard to understand why Ssu-ma Ch'ien should have called the *t'ao-t'u* a "rare" animal of the Hsiung-nu (*Shih-chi*, 110.2–3); still less is it clear why *t'ao-t'u* should have been numbered among the rare and valuable importations found in the palace stables of Emperor Wu. (*Yen-t'ieh Lun* [*Ssu-pu Pei-yao* ed.], 3.4b; Huan K'uan, *Discourses on Salt and Iron*, trans. Esson M. Gale [Leiden, 1931], 92.) This identification seems improbable. Egami also ("Strange Domestic Animals," 111–123) identifies the *t'an-hsi* 驒騱 as "the wild ass, probably the *kulan*"; his argument does not seem very convincing, but there appears to be little basis for a firm identification of this animal.

46. *Yen-t'ieh Lun*, 3.4b; *Discourses on Salt and Iron*, 92.

47. An exact translation of *k'uai-t'i* seems difficult, but both characters appear to denote a swift horse. (See: Wang Nien-sun 王念孫 , *Kuang-ya Su-cheng* 廣雅疏証 [1796], 10B.64b. Egami, "Strange Domestic Animals," 98.)

48. *Shih-chi*, 83.22, 87.9; *Hou-Han-shu*, 110A.4b.

counteract it he pointed out that Ch'in imported a great many things that were desirable and even essential. Thus "if only those things produced in Ch'in were to be permitted, then . . . the women of Cheng and Wei would not occupy the rear palaces, and fine horses and *k'uai-t'i* would not fill the outer stables."[49] From this it is evident that *k'uai-t'i* were being imported to Ch'in in considerable numbers at least a century and a half before Emperor Wu of Han secured horses from Fergana. It is quite clear, in fact, that Ch'in was buying horses from the northern nomads at this time. We have information about one merchant who, at about this time, made a practice of acquiring unusual silks which he presented to a ruler of the northern nomads, who in return gave him cattle and horses in large numbers. This pleased the ruler of Ch'in so much that he treated the merchant with great honor.[50] This may help to explain the way in which Chinese silks found their way to the Pazyryk kurgans.

Namio Egami has argued that the *k'uai-t'i* is "the Aryan horse originally bred on the shores of the Aral and Caspian Seas," and even that it was "blood-sweating" like those obtained from Fergana by Emperor Wu.[51] His conclusions do not seem convincing in all respects, but it is entirely probable that the best horses of the nomads of Eastern Asia came from stock imported from Western Asia. We have seen that in the middle of the second century B. C. Ch'ao Ts'o said that the horses of China could not compare with those of the Hsiung-nu "in climbing up and down mountains, and crossing raviness and mountain torrents." Fourteen centuries later Marco Polo used remarkably similar language in describing the horses of Bactria, which lies just southwest of Fergana.[52] He said:

And again you may know that very good horses are bred there and they are great runners and have such hard hoofs that they need to wear no irons on their feet. And they go in the mountains always, and the men gallop with them over the mountain slopes where other animals could not gallop, nor would they dare to gallop there.[53]

One of the most famous generals of the Han period, Ma Yüan (14 B. C.– A. D. 49), was renowned as a connoisseur of horses. His surname, Ma,

49. *Shih-chi*, 87.9; for the date of this memorial, see ibid., 6.11.
50. Ibid., 129.15–16; *Han-shu*, 91.5b–6a; Swann, *Food and Money*, 430.
51. Egami, "Strange Domestic Animals," 90–103.
52. Arthur Waley, "The Heavenly Horses of Ferghana: A New View," *History Today*, V (Feb. 1955), 96, says: "The belief of some historians that Ferghana was once part of the Greek kingdom of Bactria is based upon misunderstanding of the Chinese texts."
53. Yetts, "The Horse," 246–247. This is a translation of a composite version of the text of Marco Polo, based in part upon a recently discovered text.

means horse, which was not accidental. The founder of his family was a general, in the third century B. C., in the service of the state of Chao (the northern state, it will be recalled, which is the first Chinese state on record as having used cavalry). After a brilliant victory his ruler conferred upon Ma Yüan's ancestor the title of *Ma-fu chün* 馬服君 , "Horse-taming Lord"; his descendants thereafter took Ma as their surname.[54]

Although he grew up in the capital, Ma Yüan, after some vicissitudes, became a wealthy stockman in the northern border area, raising cattle, horses, and sheep. He was involved in the fighting that attended the rise of the Latter Han dynasty and became an honored general under its first emperor; his daughter was married to the heir apparent and became a famous empress. He was fond of shooting the bow from horseback and was a connoisseur of horses.

Ma Yüan melted down a bronze drum he had captured in Indochina and cast a bronze model of a horse, which was designed to make clear the points to be observed in judging horses. In the inscription cast on it he gave the derivation of his connoisseurship of horses, naming his teacher, his teacher's teacher, and so forth, going back for four generations. In this inscription he said, "Horses are the foundation of military might, the great resource of the state."[55]

They were, indeed. The militant nomads, on their swift and strong horses, were China's greatest danger and would continue to be for almost two thousand years. From being a serious annoyance earlier, they had become a dire menace when, just at the beginning of the Han dynasty, their formerly scattered bands were consolidated under an able leader. The Chinese themselves were not firmly united, and only a combination of warfare, diplomacy, and costly bribery staved off disaster. Serious raids were frequent, and in 166 B. C. the Hsiung-nu pushed deep into Chinese territory, carrying off large numbers of animals and people and sending their scouts to a point within sight of the capital. Despite the most strenuous efforts against him, the Hsiung-nu leader remained within China for more than a month, and when he retired the pursuing Chinese could not kill one of the enemy.[56]

The Chinese needed horses desperately. At the beginning of Han, around 200 B. C., they were extremely scarce, probably as a result of the preceding years of civil war. As Nancy Lee Swann points out, "the supply of horses for the armed forces was a great strain on Han resources." The

54. *Shih-chi*, 81.15; *Hou-Han-shu*, 54.1a.
55. Ibid., 54.
56. *Shih-chi*, 110.37–38; Watson, *Records*, II, 172–173.

government used many devices to stimulate breeding, and in time horses became more numerous.[57] By 119 B. C. Wu, the "Martial Emperor," was able to send an army of 100,000 cavalry followed by several hundred thousand infantry into the northern wilds. They surrounded the ruler of the Hsiung-nu, but he escaped; the Chinese army nevertheless is said to have killed or captured some 80,000 nomads. It was a great victory, but it cost the Chinese dearly. The treasury was so depleted that the armies got hardly any pay. The Chinese are said to have lost, in addition to "several tens of thousands" of men killed, more than 100,000 military horses; presumably this included some of those used for transport as well as cavalry horses. One can only speculate on the reasons for such a toll; probably the fact that the Chinese horses were not accustomed to the Hsiung-nu country, or adequate to the exertions it demanded, had much to do with it. The result was that the Chinese, for lack of horses, were unable to attack the Hsiung-nu effectively for some time.[58]

Emperor Wu had many plans (and indeed he needed them) for withstanding and if possible crushing the Hsiung-nu. Soon after he came to the throne, at the age of fifteen, he heard that a nomadic people known as the Yüeh-chih月氏, who had been driven west from their former homeland and settled in Bactria (approximately modern Afghanistan), were thirsting for revenge against the Hsiung-nu who had dispossessed them. Wu called for volunteers to pass through the lands of the Hsiung-nu and establish relations with the Yüeh-chih. A young "Court Gentleman," a member of the palace guard, Chang Ch'ien, was among those who responded. He was appointed envoy and set off with a party of some hundred men about 139 B. C.[59] Thus one of the great voyages of exploration of all history was rather directly caused by the rise of the mounted warrior in Asia. As was predictable, Chang Ch'ien was captured by the Hsiung-nu, but eventually managed to escape and to reach the Yüeh-chih. He found them comfortable and prosperous, not disposed to seek revenge and still less to help China. After further adventures he returned to China around 126 B. C., having lost all but one of his companions on the way.

Although Chang Ch'ien had failed to secure an alliance with the Yüeh-chih he brought back invaluable information. His geographical knowledge

57. *Han-shu*, 24A.9b, 15b, 24B.4a, 9b–10a, 17b, 18ab; Swann, *Food and Money*, 37–39, 149, 175, 231, 262, 304, 308–309.

58. *Han-shu*, 6.16ab, 24B.12b; Dubs, *History of the Former Han Dynasty*, II, 65–66; Swann, *Food and Money*, 274–275; *Shih-chi*, 110.52–54; Watson, *Records*, II, 182–183.

59. *Han-shu*, 61.1a–2b; *Shih-chi*, 123.2–3; Watson, *Records*, II, 264. The dates of Chang Ch'ien's journey are variously given. Both *Shih-chi*, 123.6 (Watson, *Records*, II, 266), and *Han-shu*, 61.2b, say that he was gone for thirteen years, and Wang Hsien-ch'ien (*Han-shu*, 61.2b, commentary) says that he returned in 126 B. C.

helped the Chinese armies fighting the Hsiung-nu, and the Emperor questioned him eagerly about the lands he had seen. Chang suggested an alliance with another nomadic people, the Wu-sun 烏孫 , who were disaffected with the Hsiung-nu. This diplomatic effort was partially successful, and in return for the Emperor's gifts the Wu-sun sent him "several tens" of horses. Before this the Emperor had divined, using the *Book of Changes*, and had been told that he would obtain "spirit horses" from the northwest. When he received those from the Wu-sun he was delighted and called them "heavenly horses." But by this time China was in communication with Fergana, and Emperor Wu heard that there were still finer horses there.[60]

This is not surprising since that fertile region lies within the southeastern portion of what Hančar calls Turan, which he believes to be the original home of fine riding horses. At the beginning of the twentieth century it still produced large numbers of horses, and according to W. Perceval Yetts, "Scythians, bringing horses from Ferghāna, are among the tribute-bearers represented at Persepolis."[61] The Chinese of the Han period found the horses of Fergana to be "even more robust" than those they obtained from the Wu-sun.[62] In size they must have towered above the horses then common in China. A court official writing in the first century A. D. said that the "blood-sweating" Fergana horses were "all seven ch'ih in height" (63.66 inches,[63] almost exactly 16 hands). This is $4\frac{1}{2}$ inches taller than the tallest horses found in the Pazyryk kurgans, and almost as tall as the minimum standard for a modern Percheron draft mare.[64] In the eleventh century A. D., war horses purchased by the Chinese government ranged only up to 57.73 inches, 6 inches shorter than the Fergana horses of a thousand years earlier.[65] And a text of the tenth century said that the "official horses" of that day (perhaps those ridden or driven by officials of high prestige) were still of the stock of Fergana, which was "extremely large."[66]

60. Ibid., 61.1a–6a; *Shih-chi*, 123.1–32; Watson, *Records*, II, 264–280.
61. *Encyclopaedia Britannica*, X, 270; Yetts, "The Horse," 247.
62. *Shih-chi*, 123.24; Watson, *Records*, II, 274; *Han-shu*, 61.6a.
63. Wei Hung 衛宏 , *Han-kuan Chiu-i* 漢官舊儀 , in *Jung-yüan Ts'ung-shu* 榕園叢書 (Kuang-tung, 1874), *hsia* 4b. The Han ch'ih measured .231 meter, according to Dubs, *History of the Former Han Dynasty*, I, 279. For the Latter Han ch'ih, Yang K'uan 楊寬 , *Chung-kuo Li-tai Ch'ih-tu K'ao* 中國歷代尺度考 (Changsha, 1938), 75, gives .232 meter, a negligible difference.
64. Hančar, *Das Pferd*, 363; Vesey-FitzGerald, *Book of the Horse*, 628.
65. *Sung-shih* (in *Er-shih-ssu Shih*), 198.7a. For the conversion value of 4 ch'ih 7 ts'un of Sung times, see Hsieh, *Yang-ma Shih*, 34.
66. *T'ang Hui-yao* 唐會要 , comp. Wang P'u 王溥 , ed. Yang Chia-lo 楊家駱 (Taipei,

Some of his numerous envoys told Emperor Wu that the people of
Fergana had some particularly splendid horses, but that they kept them
hidden and refused to give any to the Chinese. He therefore sent a party
with much gold to secure some of them. But the men of Fergana reflected
that China was far away and that the road lay through uninhabited desert
areas without food or water. The Chinese came in parties of only a few
hundreds, but even so they ran out of food, and over half died on the way.
How could a great army reach Fergana? And their finest horses were their
treasure; they refused to part with any. The Chinese envoys, enraged,
cursed them and left. The people of Fergana responded to these insults
by murdering the Chinese.

The Emperor's rage may be imagined. Assured that three thousand
Chinese soldiers could crush Fergana, he sent out "several tens of
thousands" in 104 B. C. The march took a terrible toll, and only a few
thousand reached their destination. They were beaten, and the survivors
returned to the Chinese border after two years. The Emperor, still more
furious, ordered that any of these soldiers who dared to enter China
should be beheaded on the spot. The Hsiung-nu were making trouble
again, and his advisers pleaded with the Emperor to give up the Fergana
project. He answered by putting the protesters in prison and then pressed
huge plans for a new expedition. "The whole empire was thrown into
turmoil" with the preparations. Sixty thousand more soldiers were
provided, in addition to whom there were many porters and personal
attendants. The animals mustered included a hundred thousand cattle,
more than thirty thousand horses, and tens of thousands of donkeys,

<hr>

1950), 1036. Waley, "Heavenly Horses of Ferghana," 102, takes the position that the horses
of Fergana were sought by the Han Emperor Wu "in order to secure Heavenly Horses
which would carry him to Heaven." He says that "there is no evidence that Heavenly
Horses were used in battle either in Ferghana or in China." (Ibid., 102.) But in fact, as
we have seen, the use of Fergana horses in fighting is mentioned in *Hou-Han-shu*, 110A.4b.
By speaking here of "Heavenly Horses" Waley is evading the real question: were horses
obtained from Fergana used in battle in Han times? The answer is that they were. Waley
also says: "Nowhere, I think, is it said that they [i.e., "Heavenly Horses"] were larger
than Chinese horses, though this has constantly been assumed by Western writers." (Ibid.)
The evidence cited above certainly indicates that the Fergana horses were extremely
large and that there is every reason to feel assured that they were much larger than most
of the horses in China both in Han times and later. Further evidence against Waley's view
is the nature of the titles of the two men sent by the Emperor to Fergana "to select good
horses." (*Shih-chi*, 123.37.) These would appear to be ordinary official titles and refer to
"managing horses" and "driving horses." If the purpose had been primarily to select
horses having special religious virtues, why did the Emperor not send men with religious
qualifications? Certainly there was some religious aspect to this curious affair, and Waley
has performed a service by emphasizing it. But in doing so he has given undue attention to
a part of the evidence and neglected other parts of it entirely.

mules, and camels. Great stores of crossbows and other weapons were laid up, and so much food that even the grueling desert marches did not exhaust it. Engineers skilled in water control were provided to divert the water supplies of besieged cities. And two men versed in judging horses were sent to select the finest of the Fergana steeds.

An army of thirty thousand Chinese actually reached Fergana. After a siege of more than forty days, the people of Fergana killed their king and agreed to surrender some of their horses. The Chinese set up a new king favorable to themselves and withdrew with the horses; they selected "several tens of the best horses" and more than three thousand stallions and mares of lesser quality. Emperor Wu was delighted with them; they were called "blood-sweating heavenly horses." Presumably this name was applied only to the finest horses. The adjective "heavenly" was probably connected with Wu's religious or magical ideas about them; the most plausible theory to account for "blood-sweating" is that it refers to small lesions caused by parasites.[67]

The total military effort to secure horses from Fergana had taken four years.[68] If this had been its only purpose these might well rank as the most expensive horses in history. The reign of Wu left the country bankrupt; his military ventures were among the principal reasons for this, and the expedition to Fergana was one of the most costly.[69] The economic drain is impossible to calculate. Of all the men and horses that set out for Fergana, it is recorded that only something over ten thousand men and one thousand horses returned alive to China.[70]

Various motivations have been put forward for this grandiose expedition. It has been alleged that this was "to a large extent a religious quest."[71] Undoubtedly this played a role; Emperor Wu also established new sacrifices, patronized magicians, and sent out expeditions to look for islands in the Eastern Sea that were supposedly inhabited by immortals.[72] It has also been argued that the Emperor's chief incentive was to secure larger and fleeter mounts for his troops, and in the light of all the evidence

67. Waley, "Heavenly Horses of Ferghana"; Richard Edwards, "The Cave Reliefs at Ma Hao," *Artibus Asiae*, XVII (pt. 1, 1954), 13–28; Dubs, *History of the Former Han Dynasty*, II, 134–135.

68. The account of the Fergana expedition is contained in *Shih-chi*, 123.32–42; Watson, *Records*, II, 280–288; *Han-shu*, 61.

69. Dubs, *History of the Former Han Dynasty*, II, 12–13, 17.

70. *Shih-chi*, 123.41; Watson, *Records*, II, 287.

71. Waley, "Heavenly Horses of Ferghana"; see note 66, above.

72. Dubs, *History of the Former Han Dynasty*, II, 19–20; *Shih-chi*, 28.24–86; Se-ma Ts'ien, *Mémoires historiques*, III, 436–516; Watson, *Records*, II, 26–67.

it seems clear that this did play a role.[73] But Emperor Wu was a complex character. In addition to these motives, he also acted from the desire to extend the influence of his empire and the fame of his name.

After the return of Chang Ch'ien from his trail-blazing journey, the Emperor questioned him eagerly about the lands he had visited.

> Thus the emperor learned of such countries as Fergana, Bactria, and Parthia, all large states having many unusual products, cultivating the soil in a manner similar to that of the Chinese, militarily weak, and prizing China's valuable goods. To their north there were such peoples as the Yüeh-chih and the K'ang-chü; these were militarily strong, but by means of gifts and the lure of profit they could be induced to accept Chinese sovereignty. If their allegiance could only be achieved by fair dealing, the empire could be extended for ten thousand *li* to embrace men of strange customs whose languages would have to be repeatedly retranslated through nine interpreters—thus the awe-inspiring virtue of the emperor would be extended to all lands within the four seas. The emperor, overjoyed, agreed with Chang Ch'ien's words.[74]

Emperor Wu was not noted for "fair dealing" within China, but the remoteness of Central Asia initially constrained him. As we have seen, he sent envoys with much gold to buy some of the fine horses of Fergana. But when his offer was not only refused but his envoys killed, more than his pride was at stake. After his first army had returned from Fergana, beaten, the situation was even graver. "The emperor had undertaken to punish Fergana. Fergana was a small state; if he could not even subdue it, then such states as Bactria would despise China, and he would certainly never get the fine horses of Fergana . . . . China would be a laughingstock among the nations."[75]

This first great Chinese military thrust deep into Central Asia, of such historic moment, was only in part occasioned by the need for horses. But it was a factor. Once the Chinese had set up regular communications with Central Asia, and established a protectorate over a portion of it, the importation of superior equine stock must have been relatively easy. A number of scholars have pointed out that the representations of the horse in Han dynasty art show two types. One of these is believed to be the smaller horse common in China before the advent of Central Asian

73. Yetts, "The Horse."
74. *Shih-chi*, 123.16–17; Watson, *Records*, II, 269–270; *Han-shu*, 61.3ab.
75. *Shih-chi*, 123.35–36; Watson, *Records*, II, 283; *Han-shu*, 61.10a.

horses in quantity; the other is plausibly held to depict the larger and more highly bred horses from Central Asia. And certainly the typical larger horses shown in Han dynasty reliefs show striking resemblance to horses depicted on Bactrian coins of the second century B. C.[76]

The cavalry horse, which seems to have been unknown in China early in the fourth century B. C., had become firmly established in the role it was to play in subsequent Chinese history even before the beginning of the Christian era. By virtue of it the nomads had become a deadly threat and were able at times to invade Chinese territory almost at will. The Chinese had to develop cavalry to counter the nomads, and even though they made great economic sacrifices to breed cavalry horses they still had to secure additional mounts from outside their borders. Both to secure horses and to outflank the Hsiung-nu they pushed far into Central Asia, opening a new chapter in China's political and military history and in its foreign relations.

Although the menace of the mounted nomad was seldom wholly absent, it subsided greatly during most of the latter portion of the Han period. But at the beginning of the fourth century A. D. the long-pending threat of nomadic conquest became a reality. For nearly two centuries north China was ruled chiefly by invaders of nomadic origin, who at times divided the area into a number of small states. After China was again unified, and shortly after the T'ang dynasty (618–906) was established, the nomadic danger was emphasized by a Turkish raid that reached the walls of the capital. The T'ang built up a strong force of cavalry, but for this they needed horses.

At the beginning of T'ang its army is said to have had only 5,000 horses, but a vigorous breeding program increased these to 700,000 in a few decades. But there was nevertheless a constant demand for foreign horses. Those they received from Samarkand were believed by the men of T'ang to be of the same blood as the "heavenly horses" of Fergana, and it is said that six true "blood-sweating horses" were sent from Fergana to the Chinese emperor in the middle of the eighth century. Even some Arab horses were brought by Moslem envoys. But most of the T'ang horses came from the Turkish tribes to the north. We read of one gift from a Turkish tribe of 50,000 "grizzled black-maned horses," but for the most part they had to be bought, and at high prices. "In 773," Edward H.

---

76. Salomon Reinach, "La Représentation du galop dans l'art ancien et moderne," *Revue archéologique*, 3d ser., XXXVIII (1901), 225–227; Berthold Laufer, *Chinese Pottery of the Han Dynasty* (Leiden, 1909), 161–162; C. W. Bishop, "The Horses of T'ang T'ai-tsung," *Museum Journal*, IX (pts. 3, 4; 1918), 250–251, 260–261; Yetts, "The Horse," 240–245; Dubs, *History of the Former Han Dynasty*, II, 135.

Schafer writes, "the Uighurs [a Turkish people] sent a special agent with ten thousand horses for sale. Their cost was more than the annual income of the government from taxes."[77]

Horses played a very important role in the silk trade. We have seen that as early as the third century B. C. a merchant in the state of Ch'in made a practice of seeking out unusual silks to present to a ruler of the northern nomads, who gave him large numbers of horses and cattle in return. The animals he received, the Chinese text tells us, were of ten times the value of the goods he gave.[78] And in the first century B. C. we find a high Chinese official gloating over the buying power of Chinese silks, which could be exchanged with the Hsiung-nu for fine horses and other commodities necessary to China, thus "using the non-essential to trade for the fundamental." Thus, he said, "a single length of plain silk secures from the Hsiung-nu goods worth many pieces of gold, thus draining away the resources of our enemy."[79] In fact, of course, this situation reflected supply and demand. Among the Hsiung-nu fine riding horses were plentiful and silk was a rarity, while in China the reverse was true. But horses were essential to the Chinese, as silk was not to the nomads, and in time this came, inevitably, to be reflected in the terms of exchange.

At the beginning of the ninth century, Arthur Waley writes,

> Fifty pieces of silk, in theory fifty Chinese feet long, were paid for each horse, and as the horses arrived sometimes ten thousand at a time, the production of so much silk was a severe strain on the silk industries of the Yangtze and Huai valleys, and even by using a coarse weave and cutting down the length of the strip to "thirty-odd feet" (supposed still to be charitably counted as forty) the women workers could not meet the demand. The Uighurs were dissatisfied with the silk they were getting, and complained . . . [80]

The financial impact on China was grave. "In the early part of the ninth century," Schafer says, "it was not unusual for the shattered nation to pay out a million bolts of taffeta in a year in exchange for a hundred thousand decrepit nags, the dregs of the northern marches."[81] Although our information about the actual operations of the silk trade across Central Asia is regrettably slight, it seems probable that much of the silk that was

77. *T'ang-shu* (in *Er-shih-ssu Shih*), 50; Schafer, *Golden Peaches*, 58–64.
78. *Shih-chi*, 129.15–16; *Han-shu*, 91.5b–6a; Swann, *Food and Money*, 430.
79. *Yen-t'ieh Lun*, 1.5ab; *Discourses on Salt and Iron*, 14.
80. Arthur Waley, *The Life and Times of Po Chü-i, 772–846* A. D. (London, 1949), 55.
81. Schafer, *Golden Peaches*, 64.

traded to nomads, from an early day, for horses, was in turn traded by them still farther to the west, where its rarity, increasing with the distance from China, would give it greater and greater value.

Control of military horses played a role in the rebellion of An Lu-shan, which, although it was put down, decisively weakened the T'ang dynasty. An Lu-shan, an able general of Turkish and Sogdian ancestry, became a favorite of Emperor Hsüan-tsung, who reigned from 712 to 756, and his famous consort Yang Kuei-fei.[82] Among the responsibilities given to him was extensive jurisdiction over the cavalry horses of the empire. An quietly selected the best war horses and sent them to the territory under his personal control in the northeast, thus giving him a considerable advantage when he was ready to revolt and proclaim himself emperor in 755.[83] An captured the T'ang capital, and his rebellion was only quelled with the help of numerous foreign troops, including even some Moslems from far to the west.[84]

Sung Ch'i (998–1061) was a famous scholar and an eminent official who had extensive practical experience with the effort to bolster the defenses of China's borders. He wrote:

> The reason why our enemies to the north and west are able to withstand China is precisely because they have many horses and their men are adept at riding; this is their strength. China has few horses, and its men are not accustomed to riding; this is China's weakness. . . . The court constantly tries, with our weakness, to oppose our enemies' strength, so that we lose every battle. . . . Those who propose remedies for this situation merely wish to increase our armed forces in order to overwhelm the enemy. They do not realize that, without horses, we can never create an effective military force.

In another memorial Sung pointed out that, while China had a large number of cavalrymen, only one or two out of ten had a horse to ride.[85]

Many of China's most able men devoted their attention to the perennial problem of securing enough good horses. These included Po Chü-i (whom we tend to think of as a poet, forgetting his very active political career), Ssu-Ma Kuang, Wang An-shih, Ou-Yang Hsiu, and a great many others

82. Edwin G. Pulleyblank, *The Background of the Rebellion of An Lu-shan* (Cambridge, 1955), 7–23.

83. *T'ang-shu*, 50.17b.

84. F. S. Drake, "Mohammedanism in the T'ang Dynasty," *Monumenta Serica*, VIII (1943), 7–11; H.A.R. Gibb, "Chinese Records of the Arabs in Central Asia," *Bulletin of the School of Oriental Studies, London Institution*, II (1921–1923), 618–619.

85. Sung, *Ching-wen Chi*, 366, 369.

less famous but scarcely less important.[86] But the difficulty was never permanently eliminated. The *History of the Ch'ing Dynasty* comments that "when we read over the various discussions of the problem of the procurement and management of the government's horses, advanced during the Sung and Ming periods, not one proposes a workable solution." The concern of the Sung dynasty (960–1279) was fully justified, in view of the fact that it was terminated by the Mongol conquest. "The Yüan [Mongol] house took the empire," the *History of the Yüan Dynasty* tells us, "by virtue of the bow and the horse."[87]

Whereas silk seems to have been the principal commodity exchanged for horses in early times, it appears to have been replaced in first position by tea. This does not mean, of course, that money also was not paid out; it was, and in 1077 the Finance Commissioner, in a communication to the emperor, named war horses as one of the chief commodities for which funds were needed.[88] But since tea came to be in great demand by the nomads, the Chinese made use of this fact to procure horses. Official "Tea and Horse Offices" were established by the Sung government in border areas, to control the sale of tea to the nomads and the purchase of horses from them. Similar "Tea and Horse Offices" were set up under the Ming and Ch'ing dynasties. The Chinese government tried to maintain the price of tea, beyond China's borders, at an artificially high price in order to enhance its buying power in terms of horses. This naturally led to smuggling, and the death penalty was at times imposed for the unauthorized sale of tea to the nomads.[89]

Under the Yüan dynasty (1280–1367) large numbers of Mongols came to live in China, and one might suppose that the technique of breeding cavalry mounts would have become well established in China. But there seems to be no evidence that it did. From the beginning of the Ming dynasty (1368–1643) the need for horses was critical, and great efforts were made to import them. When the Ming had been established for more than a century they were still importing ten thousand head a year, and importation at almost this rate was still going on near the end of the

86. Waley, *Po Chü-i*, 55–56; Ssu-ma Kuang 司馬光 , *Wen-kuo Wen-cheng Ssu-ma Kung Wen-chi* 溫國文正司馬公文集 (*Ssu-pu Ts'ung-k'an* ed.), 50.2b–8a; Ou-yang Hsiu 歐陽修 , *Wen-chung Kung Wen-chi* 文忠公文集 (*Ssu-pu Ts'ung-k'an* ed.), 112.7b–10b, 113.3a–4a; Sung, *Ching-wen Chi*, 366–70, 372–73.

87. *Ch'ing-shih* (8 vols., Taipei, 1961), III, 1730; *Yüan-shih* (in *Er-shih-ssu Shih*), 100.1a.

88. Li Tao 李燾 , *Hsü Tzu-chih T'ung-chien Ch'ang Pien* 續資治通鑑長編 (Chekiang Shuchü, 1881), 283.8a.

89. *Sung-shih*, 167.17b–18b, 198.24b–25a; *Ming-shih* (in *Er-shih-ssu Shih*), 80.19b–22b, 92.24a; *Ch'ing-shih*, III, 1731.

dynasty.[90] Even the Manchus, who themselves had been horsemen, when they controlled China during the Ch'ing dynasty (1644–1911), continued to import horses to China Proper (as distinct from such areas as Mongolia, Manchuria, Chinese Turkestan, and Tibet, which the Ch'ing rulers also controlled). They did not try to supply all of their need for horses by breeding them within China Proper.[91] Sowerby writes:

> The Chinese do not seem to have gone in much for horse-breeding since the Mongol conquest, depending for their supplies of these animals upon Mongolia. . . . China is the chief market for gelded Mongol ponies of from four to eight years. The Mongols seem disinclined to part with their mares, requiring them for breeding purposes. Such mares as do happen to reach China are usually crossed with donkeys to produce mules, which are considered superior to horses, both as draft and pack animals.[92]

The reasons behind China's failure to solve the horse problem are complex. The economic situation was undoubtedly important. Intensive agriculture in China has not left much room for pasture. Although pasture lands were set aside within China Proper, on the basis of military necessity, this practice was attacked on the ground that it removed land from farming and interfered with the livelihood of the people.[93] The Mongol conquest, in which a large proportion of the inhabitants of north China were slaughtered, had been a terrible lesson, and the succeeding Ming dynasty at first established extensive pastures for raising military horses in the center of China. But the demand for agricultural land gradually reduced them, until the principal pastures were again in the border areas where they had usually been.[94] The border areas were suited for the purpose, but they were also vulnerable to raids by nomads, who sometimes made off with the horses.

The Chinese failure to solve the problem of breeding horses was not caused by the lack of a serious and systematic approach to it. We have seen that selective breeding was being practiced in China even before the first millennium B. C. and that a methodical discipline for judging the qualities

90. *Ming-shih*, 80.25b–26a, 92.25a; *Ming Hui-yao* 明會要 , comp. Lung Wen-pin 龍文彬 (Taipei, 1950), 1205. The last reference indicates that the number of horses sometimes fell below this figure, but apparently only because the Chinese were unable to obtain as many horses as they wanted.

91. *Ch'ing-shih*, III, 1730–1731.

92. Sowerby, "Beasts of Burden in China," 284.

93. Sung, *Ching-wen Chi*, 368–369, 372–373.

94. *Ming-shih*, 92.22b–23b.

of horses was developed well before the Christian era. Veterinary medicine, for the treatment of horses, was being practiced as early as the fifth century B. C.[95] From early in the first millennium B. C. we have evidence that there were government officials in charge of the procurement and rearing of horses, both at the royal court and in various states; in some cases their rank was high.[96] The Ch'in (221–207 B. C.) and Han dynasties had special bureaucratic structures to supervise governmental activities concerned with horses; under the Han it was quite elaborate, and the official in charge of it ranked eighth among the highest ministers of the empire. Subsequent dynasties had comparable governmental organs, revised and at times greatly elaborated.[97] At least as early as the T'ang dynasty careful records were kept in which each horse belonging to the government was individually registered and graded as to quality. The horses themselves were branded to show their origin and qualitative ranking.[98]

Yet with all this care to distinguish the best horses, it is not clear that there was equal attention to breeding from them. In 1061 Sung Ch'i, in his capacity as superintendent of government pastures, complained that it had long been the practice to permit the various equine strains to mix indiscriminately. "Sometimes the sire is large and the dam small, sometimes the sire is small and the dam large. At the time of breeding there is no selection or discrimination; thus there is no means of obtaining large and excellent horses." The resulting horses could not measure up, he said, to the demands of warfare.[99]

The riding horse was forced upon the Chinese. It was first thrust upon their attention as a new and deadly weapon that their nomadic enemies had acquired, and it seems always to have been regarded primarily as an instrument for fighting the nomads. King Wu-ling of Chao, around

95. *Mo-tzu* (*Ssu-pu Pei-yao* ed.), 2.10a; *The Ethical and Political Works of Motse*, trans. Yi-pao Mei (London, 1929), 49. A state establishment for veterinary medicine is described in the *Chou-li*; while this work cannot be definitely dated, or entirely credited, it dates from before the Christian era, and there may well have existed (though not, as tradition holds, at the beginning of the Chou dynasty) something corresponding to the institutions it describes. (See *Chou-li*, 1.11a, 5.8b–9a, 33.6b; *Tcheou-li*, I, 9, 98–99, II, 259–260.)

96. *The She King*, 322; *Tso-chuan*, 407, 801. Seven Broman, "Studies on the Chou Li," *Bulletin of the Museum of Far Eastern Antiquities, Stockholm*, XXXIII (1961), 44–45, lists references concerning officials in charge of horses in a number of works; a few of these references are of doubtful date, but most of them are valid for the Chou period.

97. Sun K'ai 孫楷, *Ch'in Hui-yao* 秦會要, supplemented by Shih Chih-mien 施之勉 and Hsü Fu 徐復, in *Chung-hua Ts'ung-shu* (Taipei, 1956), 214; *Han-shu*, 19A.12a–13a, 19B.1a; Hsieh, *Yang-ma Shih*, 68–71.

98. Ibid., 126–129.

99. Sung, *Ching-wen Chi*, 368.

300 B. C., encountered strong prejudice when he compelled his subjects to take up riding as a matter of military necessity. A century and a half later, when cavalry had long been important in the Chinese armies, Ch'ao Ts'o stated as a matter of course that the Chinese could not compare with the nomads as riders—and he appears to have assumed that they never could.[100] As late as the eleventh century A. D., after northern China had gone through the experience of being conquered and ruled by wave after wave of nomadic horsemen, Sung Ch'i could still write that the Chinese were "unaccustomed to riding."[101]

Some Chinese, certainly, became outstanding horsemen. But it is hard to avoid the impression that to Chinese in general the riding horse remained something strange, almost foreign in nature. Horses, and horsemen, were in general associated with the border areas of the north and west.[102] It is a striking fact that the grooms and handlers of horses appearing in Chinese art seem almost always to be depicted as non-Chinese.[103] The Chinese knew that they had to have horses, and they addressed themselves with great seriousness to the problem. They built up a huge bureaucratic apparatus for dealing with it, but there is little to indicate that they brought real zest and zeal to the task. The very impersonality of their approach may have helped to defeat their end. Anyone with even a modicum of experience with horses knows that a spirited mount will not perform at its best unless there is a great deal of rapport between horse and rider. And it is doubtful that the great mass of Chinese cavalrymen could compare, in establishing such rapport, with the nomads who rode from infancy and lived with and on their horses.[104] The Mongols, it appears, had no bureaucratic structure for the management of their horses until after they conquered China; after they established the Yüan dynasty they copied and elaborated the Chinese system.[105] But it is significant that, before doing so, they conquered China.

100. His proposed remedy was not for the Chinese to become better cavalrymen, but rather to enlist barbarians to fight barbarians. (*Han-shu*, 49.10b–12a.)

101. Sung, *Ching-wen Chi*, 366.

102. *Yüan-shih*, 100.1a; Hsieh, *Yang-ma Shih*, 25; Eberhard, *Lokalkulturen*, I, 15.

103. See Jane Gaston Mahler, *The Westerners among the Figurines of the T'ang Dynasty of China* (Rome, 1959), plates XIIc, XVIIIa–b, XXa, XXIIIa–d, XXIVa–b. My colleague, Father Harrie A. Vanderstappen of the department of art of the University of Chicago, tells me that he has paid particular attention to the attendants of horses depicted in Chinese paintings and that it is his impression that they are without exception shown as being non-Chinese. (Verbal communication of Mar. 9, 1964.)

104. *Shih-chi*, 110.3; Watson, *Records*, II, 155.

105. Wang Yün 王惲, *Ch'iu-hsien Hsien-sheng Ta-ch'üan Chi* 秋澗先生大全集 (*Ssu-pu Pei-yao* ed.), 91.3b; Hsieh, *Yang-ma Shih*, 184.

Judiciously to evaluate the role of the horse in Chinese history is not easy. From an early time it was prized for pulling the vehicles in which men of rank were transported and the chariots from which noble warriors fought. An entirely new phase was introduced, at some time not long before 300 B. C., when the technique of cavalry warfare, which had been diffused across Central Asia, reached the borders of China. The "barbarians" of the north and west suddenly became a much greater menace than before. The Chinese were compelled to bribe them, court them, and fight them. To fight them effectively the Chinese had to convert some of their soldiers into cavalry, and to have large numbers of horses with the qualities needed in a cavalry mount. Chinese attempts to breed such horses were seldom more than partially successful; thus it was commonly necessary to import large numbers of horses. In order both to obtain superior horses and to outflank their nomadic enemies, the Chinese expended great efforts, including some huge military campaigns, to establish and maintain political and commercial relations with a number of the peoples of Central Asia. At some periods this carried Chinese suzerainty far to the west and provided the conditions for China's early overland contacts with the Near East and with the Mediterranean world.

Not only foreign relations but China's internal history as well was affected by the problem of the cavalry horse. It gave an importance to the northern and western borders that produced phenomena having some intriguing parallels with those associated with "the frontier" in American history. The continuing need for buying horses, often from their enemies, had a deleterious effect upon China's economy. Yet in spite of great expenditures and strenuous efforts, the Chinese never became the equals of the nomads in the employment of the cavalry horse in war, and this is an important part of the reason why China was repeatedly conquered by nomadic horsemen. It seems entirely probable that the course of history would have run differently, in some significant respects, if the Chinese had never had to deal with the cavalry horse, or if they had been able to deal with it more effectively.

INDEX